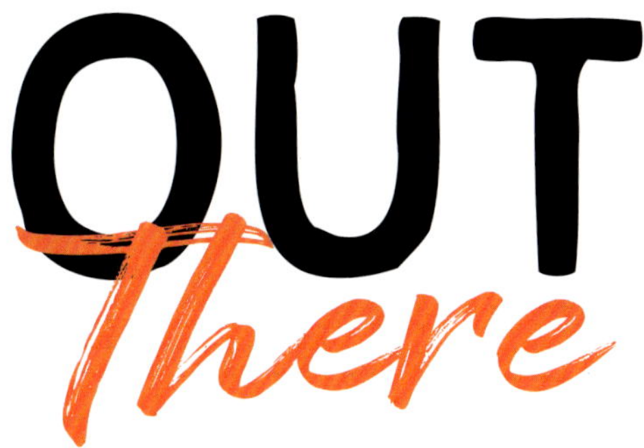

An Uncomplicated Field Guide to
Outdoor Photography

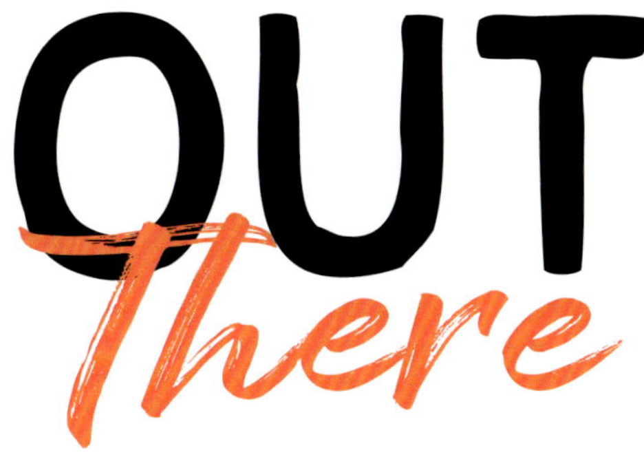

Out There

An Uncomplicated Field Guide to Outdoor Photography

CHRIS BURKARD

with Michael H. Kew

CHRONICLE BOOKS

SAN FRANCISCO

For those who were kind . . . patient . . . and took a chance
on a young kid eager to learn about photography.
I owe you my career and my life for helping to show me
a world much bigger than I ever thought existed.

Library of Congress Cataloging-in-Publication Data available.

ISBN 978-1-7972-3905-7

Manufactured in China.

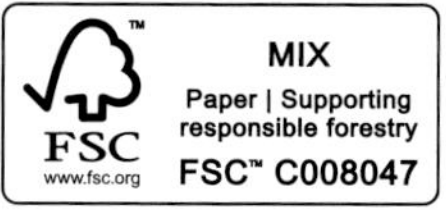

Design by Barbara Bersche.
Illustrations by Brendan Leonard.

10 9 8 7 6 5 4 3 2 1

Chronicle books and gifts are available at special quantity discounts to corporations, professional associations, literacy programs, and other organizations. For details and discount information, please contact our premiums department at corporatesales@chroniclebooks.com or at 1-800-759-0190.

Chronicle Books LLC
680 Second Street
San Francisco, California 94107
chroniclebooks.com

CONTENTS

INTRODUCTION

Back in the day, photography wasn't a creative, artful pursuit for me. It wasn't about trying to be the next Ansel Adams. It wasn't even about being in nature.

It was about *traveling*.

At the time, I was running up and down the California coast with my friends, surfing, and shooting with expired film. That was fun. But eventually I started to see the camera as a tool that could help me to escape and explore the world beyond my small town. To visit sites that really interested me. To share those places. To elicit inspiration and joy in others and to draw awareness to special nooks and crannies around the world.

But first, I sought answers: What would this career mean? How would I connect with potential clients? Could I make money, and how much? Would I be able to support my family? What would happen if I failed?

I contacted every surf photographer I knew of. I sent dozens of emails inquiring about internships and opportunities, and I asked whether the photographers would let me shadow them. Everyone blew me off. People were busy. It was a different era. Photographers kept their trade secrets close.

I never liked that approach.

I told myself that if I ever succeeded in this business, I would be a resource for other photographers. I would be an open book (no pun intended). And this is why, over the years, I've poured my heart and soul into doing workshops all over the world, creating online resources, writing blog articles, giving presentations—you name it, I've done it.

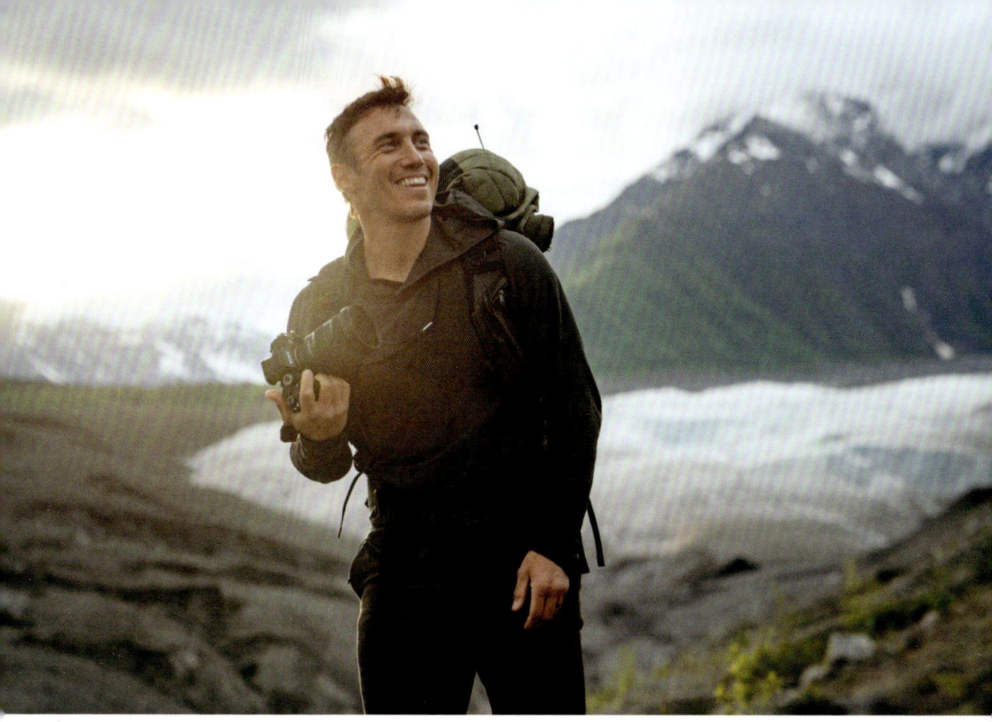

I want to help people learn photography in a way that is less robotic, less formulaic, and more realistic. More *human*. This book was born out of the idea that maybe I could help the younger me. It was the classic "if I only knew then what I know now" type of thing.

So, what's my reasoning—my "why" for getting into photography? Over the years, it has changed. In the beginning, a big part of it, of course, was to get outa town. Then, the more I started to pursue it, the more I began to see photography as a beautiful, creative passion. And with that came the strong desire to learn and grow and share with people the beauty I was seeing.

For several years, that was my "why" before it evolved more into contemplating these wild places and realizing I felt a sense of responsibility to protect them. So while my "why" has always morphed and rearranged itself, each iteration has served its purpose in its own time and place.

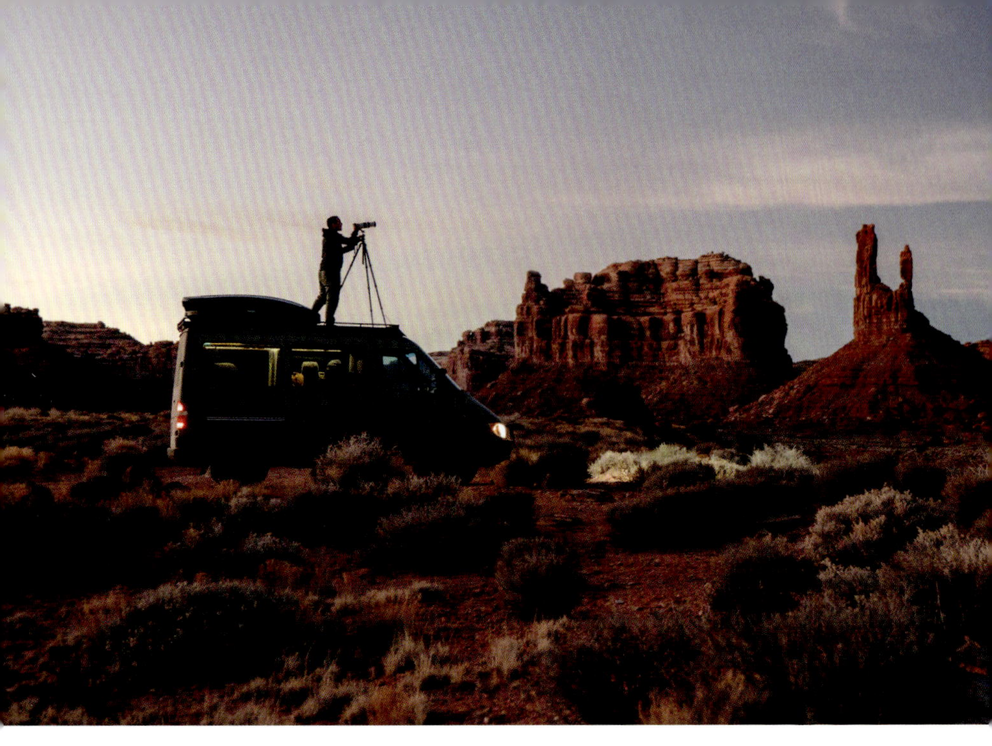

Far too much jargon has overcomplicated the basic process of being creative and using a camera. My hope is that this book will shed light on the simplicity and the beauty of what it means to be out in the field shooting and documenting something unique: telling a story and learning how to prepare yourself for an experience that may be outside your comfort zone. When you're in that moment, it doesn't really matter what camera you're using and what settings you've selected. What it really boils down to is this: knowing how to create a good, simple composition, learning how to apply and practice this. At its core, that's what good photography is all about: practice.

Your camera is not only a tool but also an incredible teaching device, something that will enlighten you about yourself. The photographers I look up to the most aren't hiding behind their images. They're the folks who can articulate their experiences and their emotions and be vulnerable.

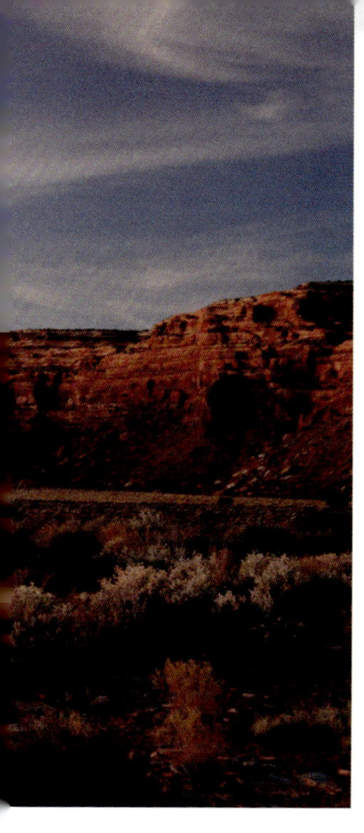

As you go along your journey, creating beautiful images and lasting memories and all those things you've read about in other books or magazines or online, I hope that you will learn something about yourself. I hope you will see how you can connect with places and with people, and then learn how to express to others what you discovered and what you felt in those experiences. To me, no photograph is ever "worth a thousand words"—though people say this all the time. That's nonsense. No photograph is ever going to compensate for you not being able to express what you felt in the moment. *That* is what matters.

So let's do this!

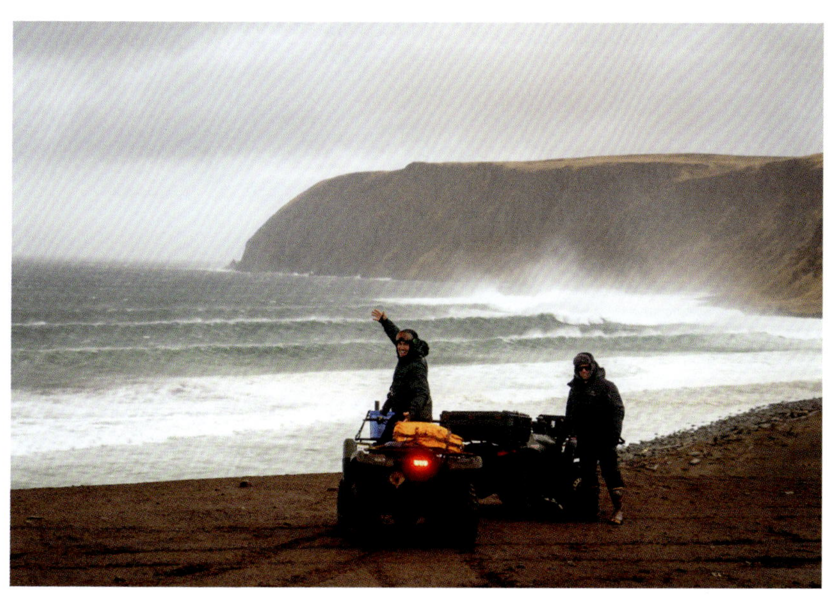

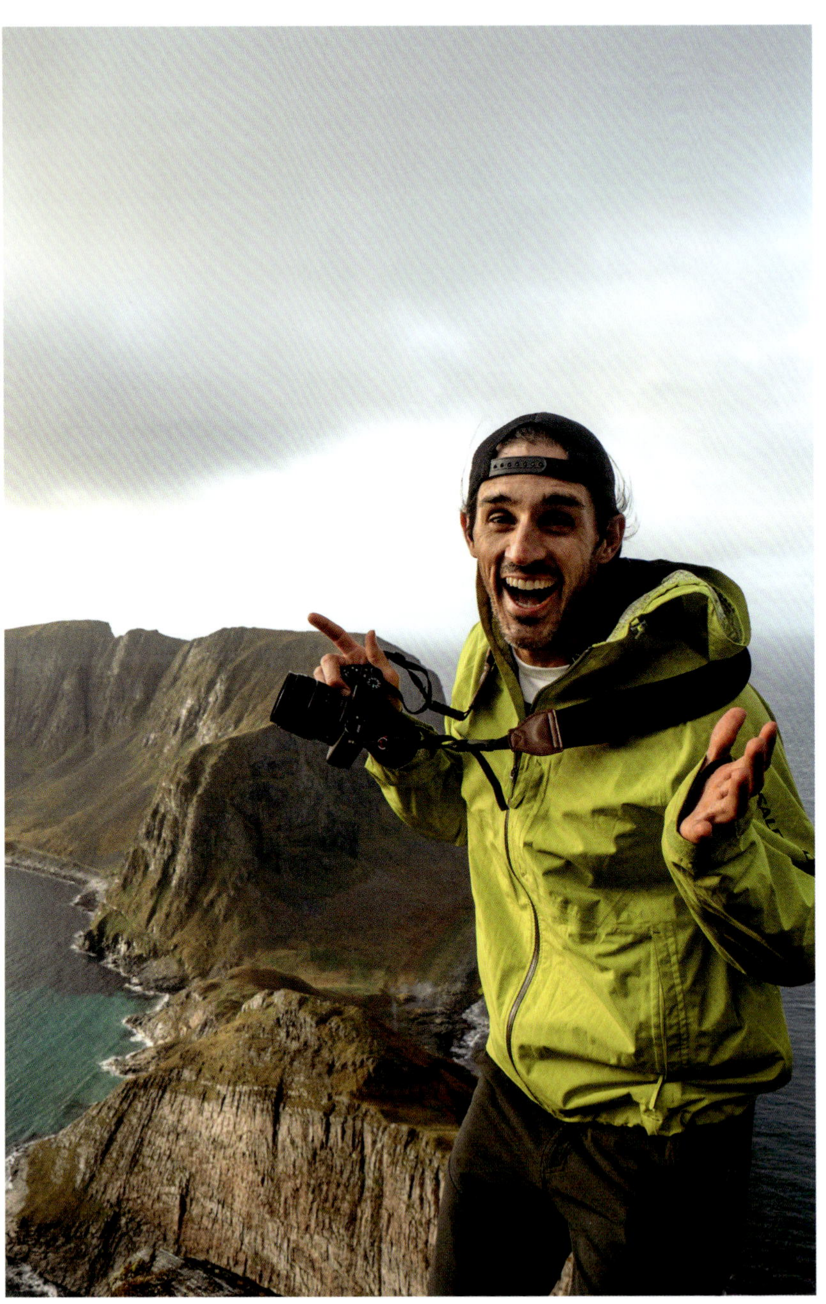

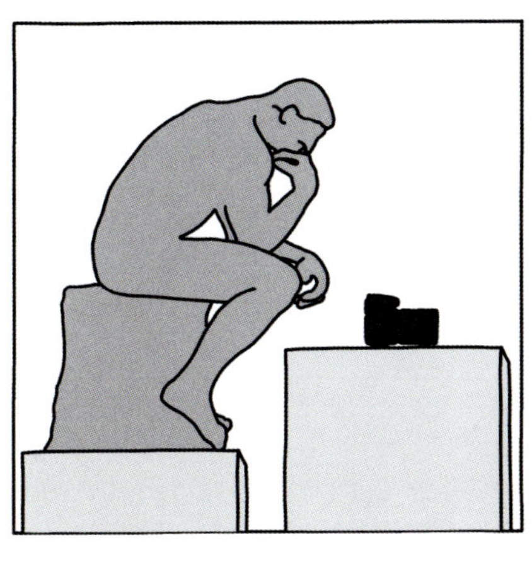

CHAPTER 1
What's Your "Why"?

Look in to look out

Over the years, I've reflected deeply on my mistakes and studied what I've learned from them. When it comes two analyzing yourself, you must decide: *What is my goal with this camera?* If there's no goal in mind, ask yourself: *What do I want to shoot? Where do I want to go? Why am I doing this in the first place?*

Perhaps you want to make more friends on Instagram, or gain popularity, or inspire somebody, or shoot photographs for someone back home, or make timeless pictures of your kids. You may have many reasons for taking photos, and each one is quite different. And that's actually incredibly beneficial because the more we identify the different ways of using a camera, the more you can home in on *why* you want to use it.

There are those of us who want to use a camera for a career path. There are those who want to use it to document far-flung travels. There are those who want to use it to inspire. There are those who want to use it to explore the environment. There are those who want to use it to help change the world. And so on.

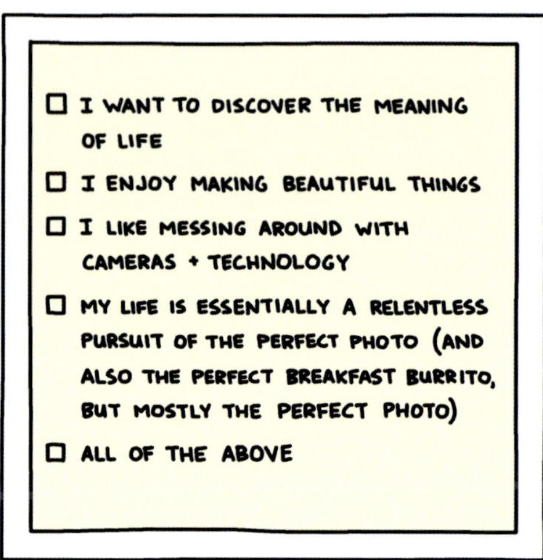

Maybe you've circled all of the above. Your goal now should be deciding where to start. What is the simplest plan of action? What are the emotions you want to raise in someone, or the feelings you want to create, or the actions you want a person to take when they see your photos? These are usually the questions I ask myself when I'm redefining my "why." Even as a professional who has done this for almost two decades, I still have to regularly redefine my "why."

The need for understanding your "why" is not to figure it out and then never change it, to never introspect or look back at it. Realize that you need a purpose in this time and place. Establishing that purpose will help you because it really reflects back into your own life.

Looking back at my life, I've realized that a big part of my purpose growing up was that I wanted to please other people. I've had examples in my life, including my mom, who sacrificed a lot for me and worked really hard. When I started using a camera, I realized that part of my purpose was to demonstrate to my loved ones that I was hardworking and that, if I put my mind to it, I could be good at what I was doing.

So what's the *purpose* of all this, anyway?

Purpose—such a broad word! It feels all-encompassing, right? Purpose—like, purpose for what? For living? For existing? For taking photographs? As you whittle it down, try to identify your purpose: why you want to shoot photos. These analyses should build upon each other. You'll realize that these things all go one layer deeper into the onion that is your creative life.

Maybe what you're left with is this: "Wow, photography for me is a very emotional experience and a very vulnerable experience. I use a camera, most of all, to create a narrative that pulls me out of my comfort zone and allows me to understand my place in the world."

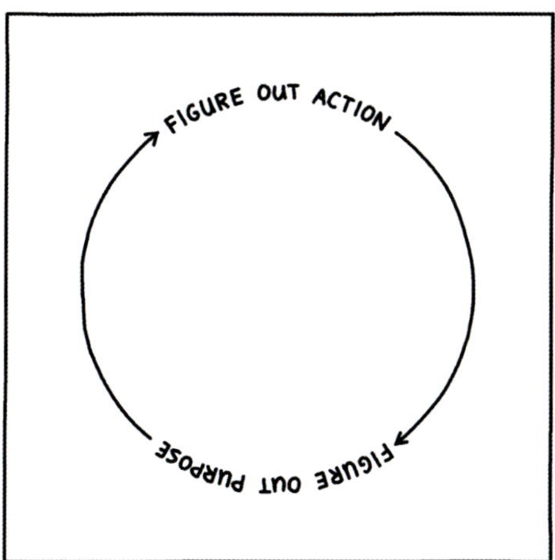

So to identify your purpose, do this analysis. That's your first step. Seek to understand not why you are using a camera, or what you hope to achieve with your photos, but what your purpose is for being alive:

What drives you? What pushes you forward? What motivates you? And if you take the time to do this, you'll realize that photography as a creative outlet is an absolute manifestation of that.

Inspire your desire

Don't worry if your inspiration comes and goes. It doesn't have to be linear. (Is it ever?) You don't always need to grab a camera.

I need to oscillate between different creative outlets. Sometimes it's speaking, sometimes it's directing a film, sometimes it's photography, sometimes it's drawing, sometimes it's making a book. Having multiple creative outlets gives you variety. Spice of life, right?

Figuratively speaking, it's critical that you do not limit yourself to one ice cream flavor that you have to eat daily. How boring would it be to go into an ice cream shop that sells only vanilla? That's what it's like when photography is your only outlet.

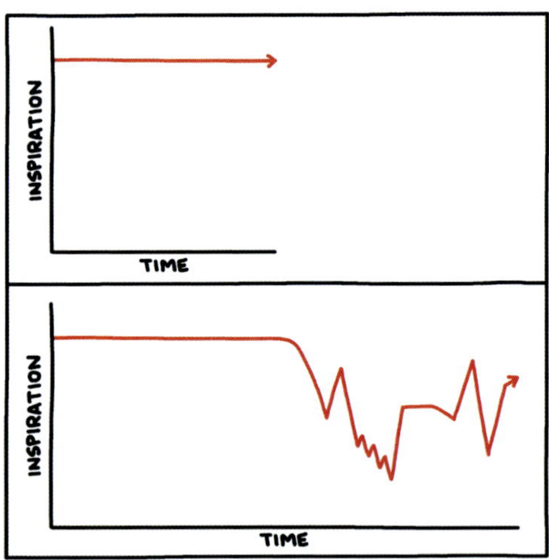

Remaining inspired can look like a lot of things to different people. For some, it's about keeping up with those who inspire and motivate you, whether that's on social media, through books, or whatever. I'm

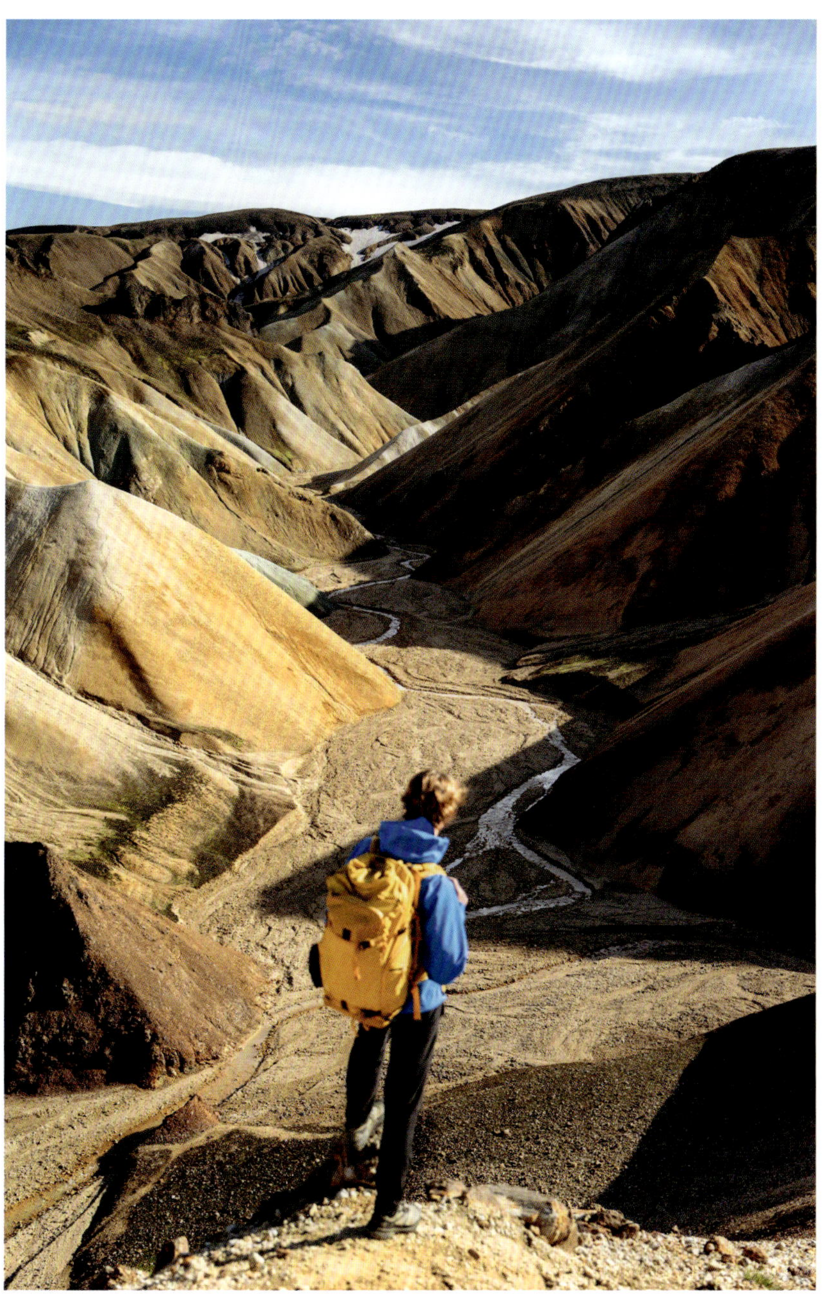

a big advocate of reading books and trying to understand subject matter that's outside my norm.

Commitment is cool

When you outline the stories you want to tell, you'll realize it becomes so much easier to be passionate after you've committed yourself. You need to invest in your work. Find a story you care about. This will keep you inspired. For me, that can be telling a story about friends or about people whose voices are not elevated or about special places in nature.

Ultimately, it's the stories that make you willing to get out of your tent when it's freezing cold outside. It's the stories that make you willing to shoot while your fingers are cracked and bleeding. It's the stories that will keep you up all night, racking your brain about how to shoot a better image. That's what you want. You want to feel the obsession. You want to feel almost like you're being fed by this experience, and that's a great sign.

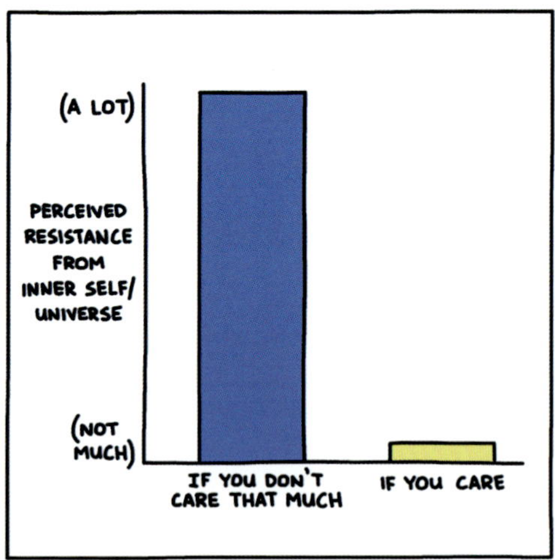

Pick stories you feel personally connected to and motivated by. It's sometimes challenging for professionals to tell stories that they don't really know or care about, because they're just doing it to get a paycheck. That's perfectly normal. But if you really want to stay inspired, then make sure you're also working on assignments that you care about or shooting in places that motivate you.

But you can't force it! If you need to, set the camera down. You need visual, verbal, and mental cues to make sure you're still being inspired. Just because you're going on a trip somewhere with your family or friends doesn't mean you *must* shoot photos. If you don't feel moved, don't shoot. That's OK.

"I'll take 'Appendage' for 10,000, Alex"

Shoot everything! Which is funny because that contradicts what I just said, right? Well, if you're a beginner, you should work toward shooting ten thousand images. That's an arbitrary number, sure, even if it really was featured in an old episode of *Jeopardy*.

Anyway, you really do need to shoot *everything*. Mainly because you will eventually get to the point where it feels like the camera is an appendage of your body. It's no longer a complex tool; you know how shutter speed works, how to set it up for a low-light shot, how to use the burst mode, and so forth. Maybe you're confused now—but that's OK! You'll work through it.

Eventually the camera becomes an extension of you. You'll know what your shutter speed should be just by looking at the ambient light. Or you'll be shooting in manual and be totally comfortable and nailing shots because you've already spent so much time shooting in manual.

If you truly want to excel in photography, there is no book, there is no advice, there is no self-help guide that can take the place of just depressing that shutter button thousands and thousands of times. This doesn't mean picking up the camera on a Monday and setting it aside until Friday, or giving it an hour on the weekend. It means waking up,

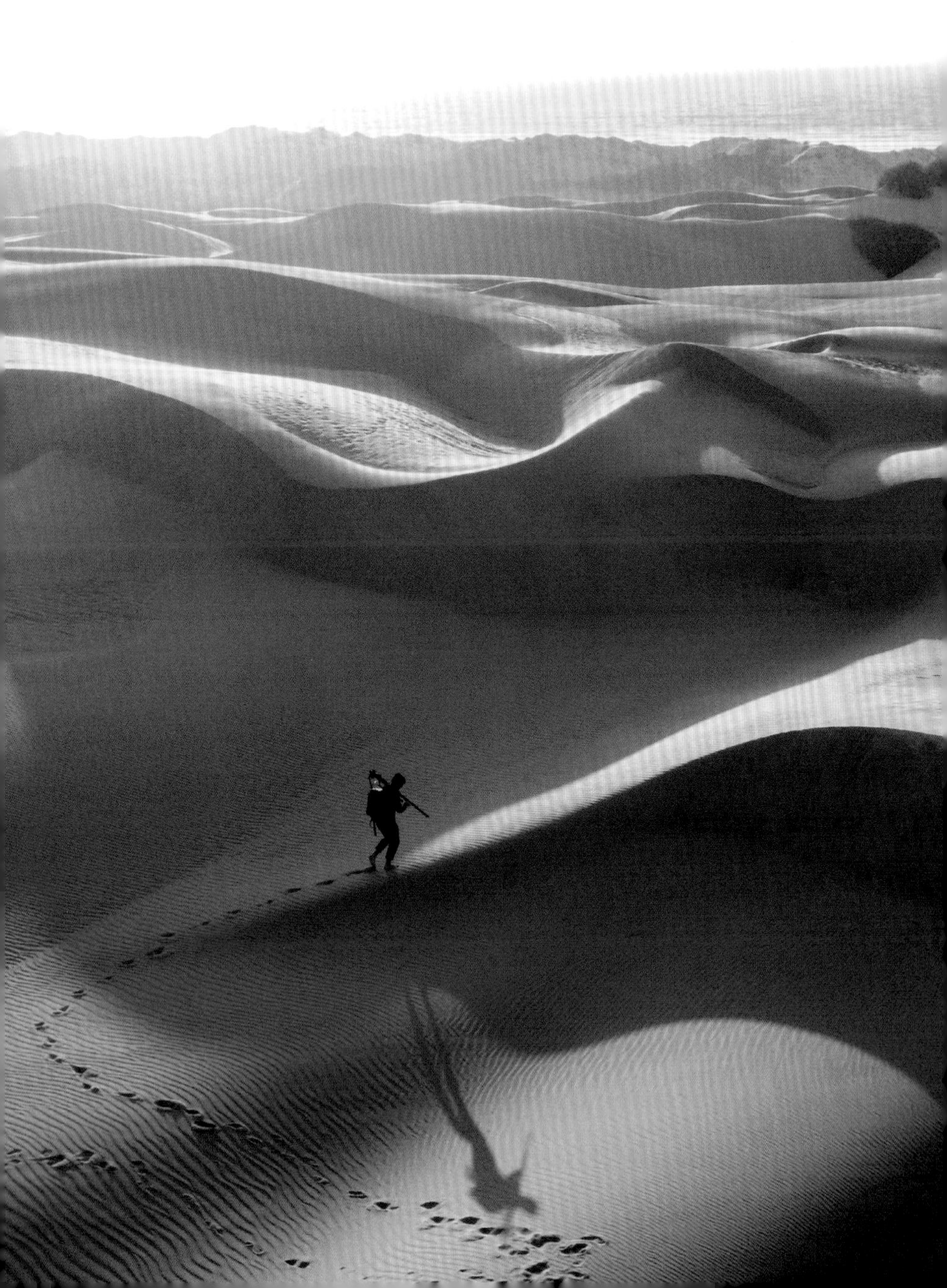

going to sleep, living, and breathing with the camera every single day to get that solid connection.

What if the first thing you did in the morning and the last thing you did at night was take a photo? I strongly suggest that you explore being connected with the camera in a way that makes it become your voice. As you shoot everything, you will become so comfortable with the camera as a tool that it will become an appendage—an extension—of your body.

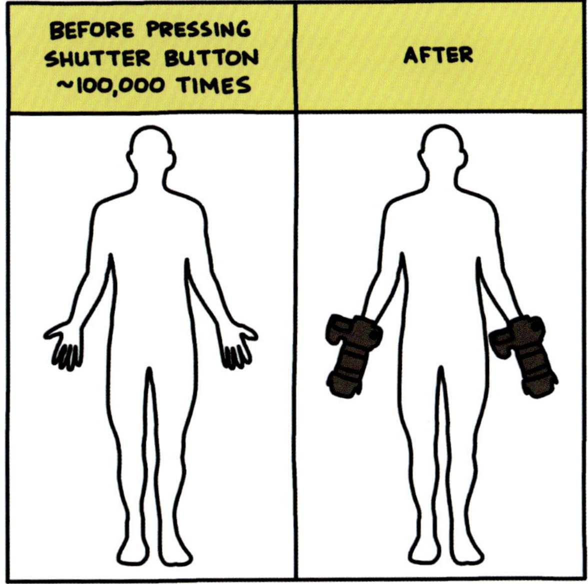

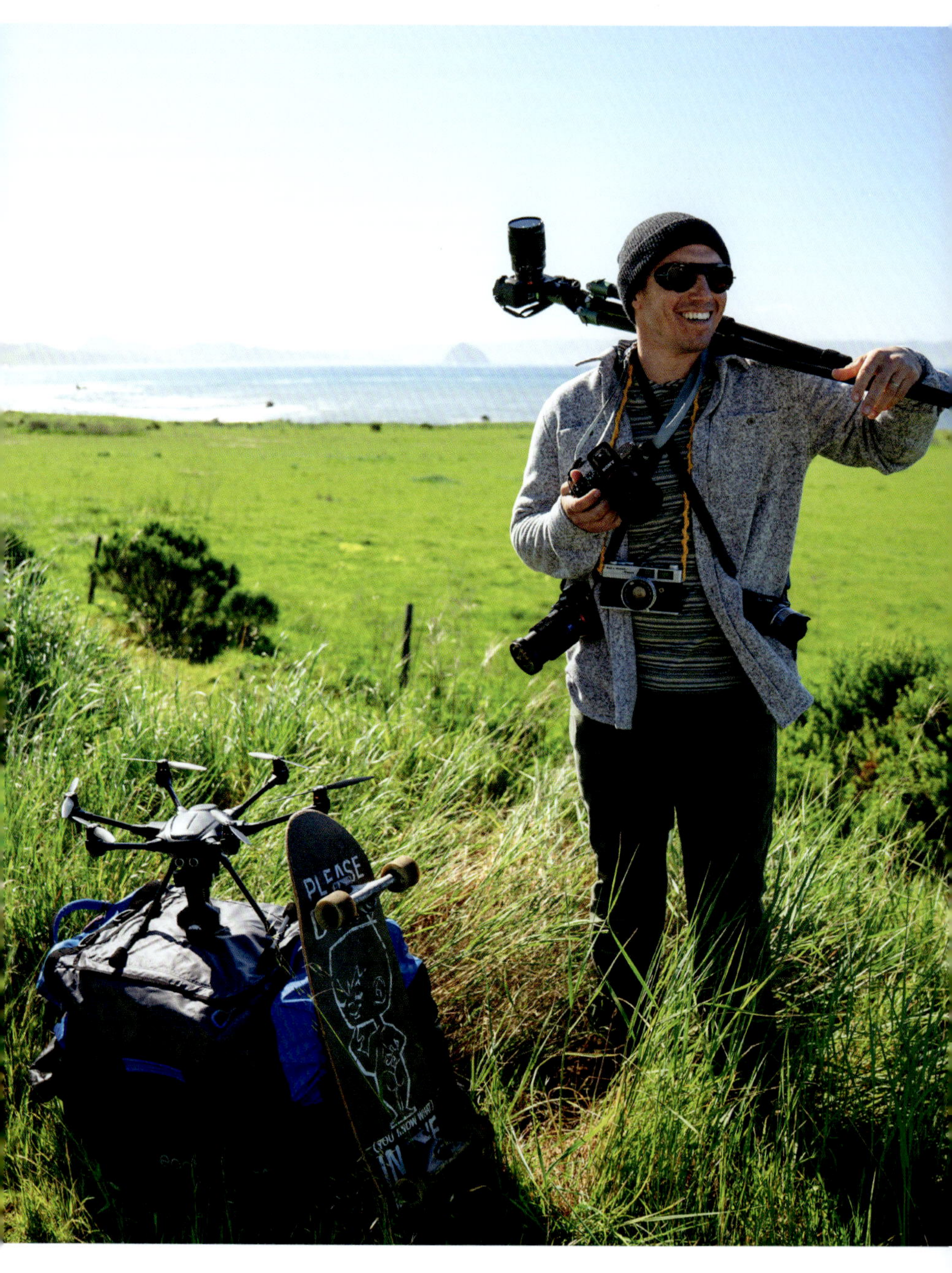
PLEASE
(YOU KNOW WHAT)

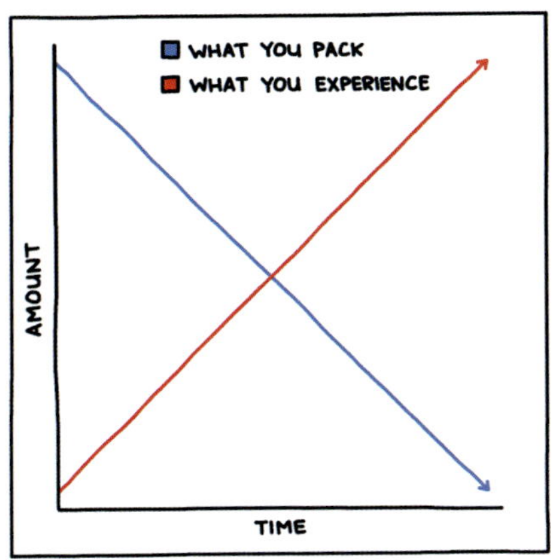

CHAPTER 2

A Good Photographer Is a Prepared Photographer

Preplanning for a successful trip is just as important as the preparation itself. I like to study a destination to educate myself about its nuances and to be ready for all sorts of sneaky surprises (good or bad). I don't do this because I want to remove mystery from the experiential equation. In fact, I love mystery—you could call me Sherlock Burkard.

Preparation doesn't just mean you've brought your memory cards and chargers and all the basics. It also means you've prepped mentally and emotionally. I research so I can be as open as possible to experiencing new places but without getting wrenches thrown into my plans: "I didn't see *this* coming" or "Wow, I sure didn't plan for *this*!"

So, let's talk about what preparation means from a practical point of view.

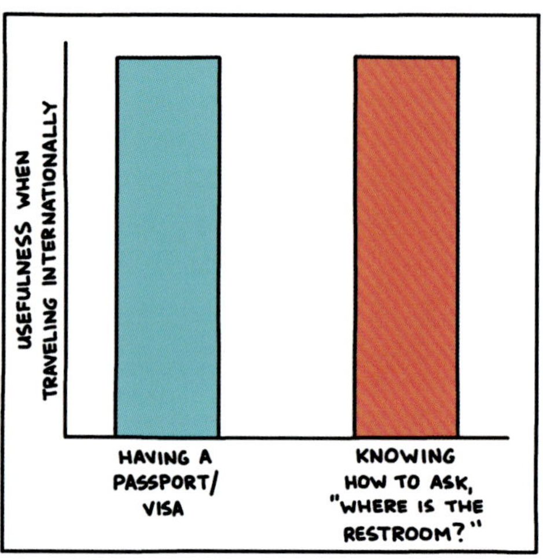

SOME INTERNATIONAL TRAVEL DOS AND DON'TS	
DO:	DON'T:
• LEARN SOME BASIC WORDS + PHRASES IN THE LOCAL LANGUAGE • BRING ADAPTERS FOR ELECTRICAL OUTLETS • KEEP YOUR PASSPORT IN A SAFE PLACE	• DO ANYTHING THAT COULD LAND YOU IN A FOREIGN PRISON FOR >5 YEARS • OR HECK, FOR ANY AMOUNT OF TIME, REALLY

Turn a phrase.

If you're visiting a foreign country, learn some bits of the language. Know how to say "Thank you" and how to ask "Where's the restroom?" and "Do you have any Grey Poupon?," yada yada, (though I'm not sure what language the latter is—Seinfeldese?).

Grok some no-no's.

Before Cuba was reopened to Americans, I was detained by Cuban customs because I had brought a few walkie-talkies. I quickly learned that walkie-talkies were prohibited in Cuba. Knowing such details can save you from a lot of stress and possible duress.

Be weather aware.

Before I pack, I imagine what it's going to be like on location. If there's one thing that hinders creativity, it's feeling like you didn't bring the right jacket, or realizing you forgot your sunglasses in the blinding snow. D'oh!

Less truly is more.

A cliché is a cliché for a reason, right? The idea here is that the less you bring, the more you can experience. We've all seen those folks loaded down with clothing—multiple pairs of socks and multiple jackets and different styles for different outings. And that's great if you're on vacation. But if you're trying to go and simply shoot, the less burdened you are with things, the easier you can move around and focus purely on photography.

I can't tell you how many times I've been on a trip and brought twenty outfits I never wore. Instead I wore the same thing every day because it was easy—my focus was just on shooting. Eventually, you'll start to care less about what you look like or which accessories you're going to wear. You just want to wear what's casual and comfortable and what works.

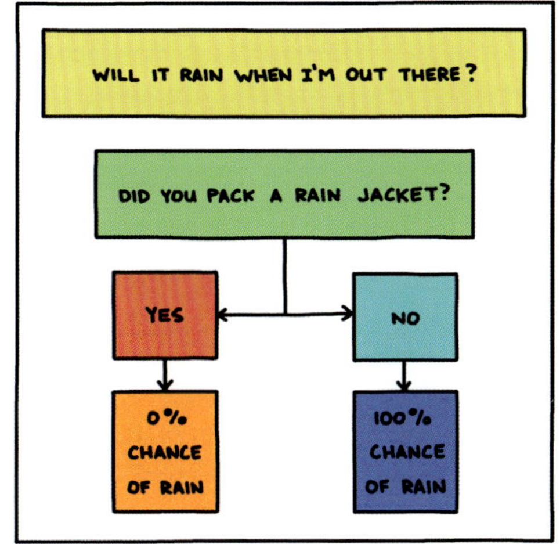

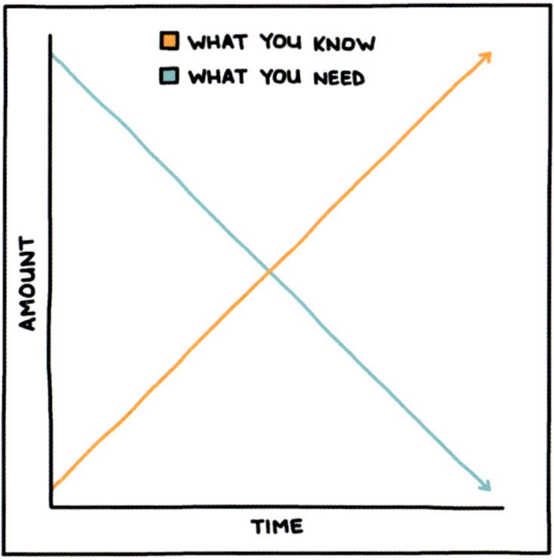

Choose wisely.

I like to bring my camera gear onto the airplane with me. It's helpful to keep it all in a backpack with an AirTag so my gear has its own tracking device. I ensure my pack isn't a heavily branded thing that screams, "Hey, I'm a photographer!" Oftentimes I've traveled with camera gear inside of a backpack that looks like a normal climbing pack because I didn't want to be an obvious target for theft or other negativities our fellow loving humans are so capable of.

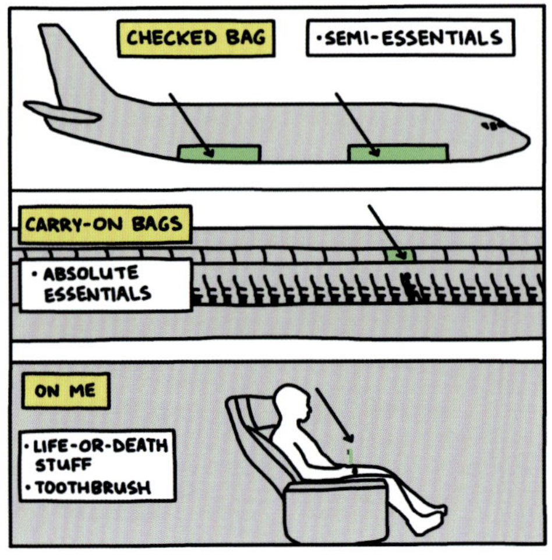

The only items I'll throw in a checked bag are typically things I wouldn't mind losing for a couple of days. When I'm heading to a place where I'll need certain things immediately, I'll get on the plane wearing, say, my down jacket and my winter boots. Certain stuff you just can't afford to lose, especially when you're going somewhere freezing!

The same thing with my camera gear. I try to carry it all, but sometimes I simply have to check a few items. So I separate my gear into essentials and everything else. The essentials are what always end up on the plane with me. In addition to the necessary camera gear, I carry on a toothbrush, a small portable charger, my laptop—the things that will enable me to do the assignment and get the shot. And have clean teeth!

Relax and get (un)comfortable

Traveling is a bit of an art form. I don't need to bring all my conditioners and soaps and shampoos and all the niceties from home, because that makes traveling feel like you're *at* home. When I'm thinking about what to bring, I really want to strip down the experience and practice minimalism. As a photographer, I'd love to exist in a carry-on world—just living in and among my most essential items.

You've got to be comfortable living in uncomfortable situations, and that includes living in dirty clothes. I'm not saying that's what you *must* do, but you want to make sure your kit feels dialed down.

If you're going somewhere you've never visited and you have

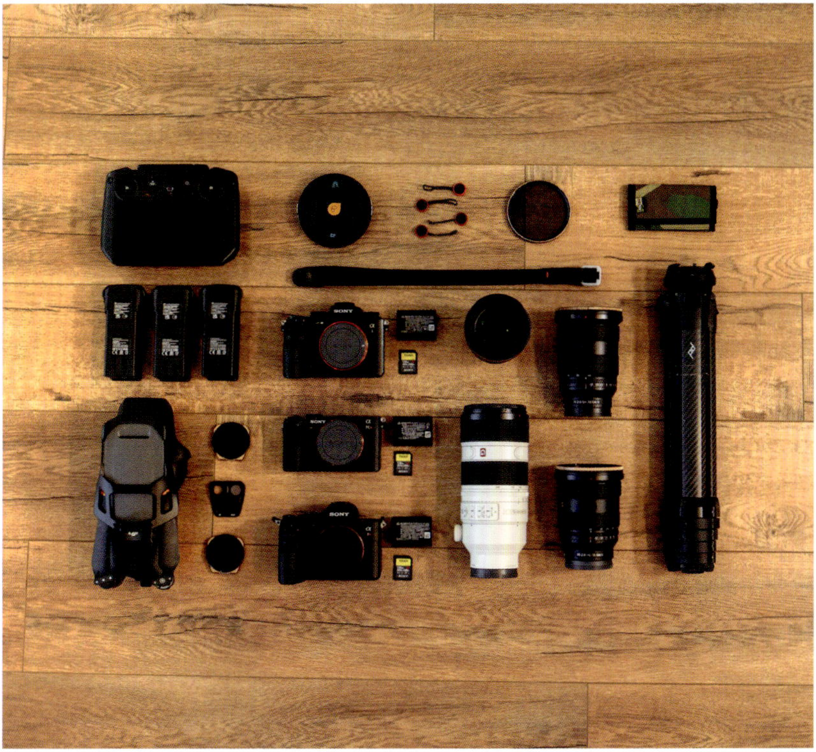

clothes you've never worn or things you've never tried, this will only add to your discomfort. Instead, I would highly suggest trying everything out before you leave! There's this old saying I love: If you don't do it in practice, you won't do it in a race. It's the same thing with photography.

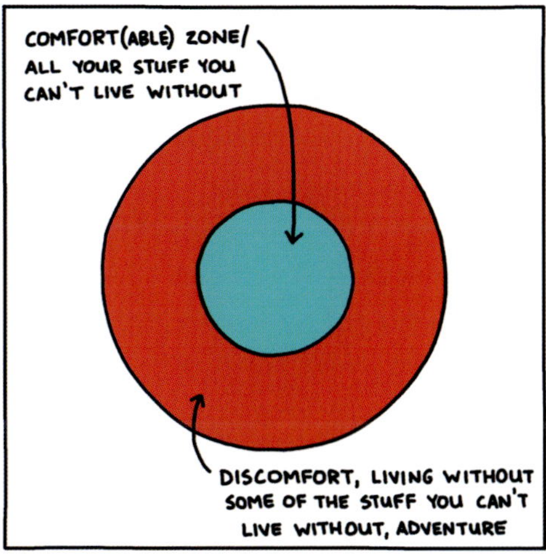

If you can live in that puffy jacket and in that rain shell and in that long-sleeved merino wool layer, go for it. That's what I tend to pack. I always have my layers and make sure that my next-to-skin layers are a natural wicking fabric that is *not* cotton, because there's nothing worse than sweating balls in cotton for days on end. That's gonna be gross, right?

My "everywhere" gear

Regardless of when or where I'm going, certain things always come with me:

- Noise-canceling headphones or earbuds because they allow me to get into my thoughts while on an airplane.
- A Buff (neck gaiter) so I can cover my eyes if I need to sleep or cover my ears. If it's windy, I can cover my neck and stay warm.
- A rain shell, no matter where I'm going. In fact, some of the coldest days I've experienced were in the tropics. It was super windy and hot during the day, and then at night it cooled way down and the wind was freezing. I got sunburn and then windburn and realized I didn't bring anything. After those experiences, I always bring a rain shell! I'm not a big fan of the lightweight windbreakers, because what's the point? A rain shell will keep you warmer and, if needed, it will keep your camera gear dry. In fact, I've used my rain shell as a camera cover so often that it's one of the hacks I really like people to consider—how certain things can double as a way to protect your gear or you (or both!) in unforeseen circumstances.
- At least one pair of waterproof socks because there are times when your feet get wet and cold in normal socks. Waterproof socks have lots of uses. They can be used as booties in a pinch, or

as an extra layer under your booties if your feet are freezing. They can be used to help you cross a river and provide some traction on your feet.

- Polarized sunglasses. Don't bring some cheap pair, but something that really does protect your eyes, because as a photographer, your eyes are everything.

- A good do-it-all salve for your skin.

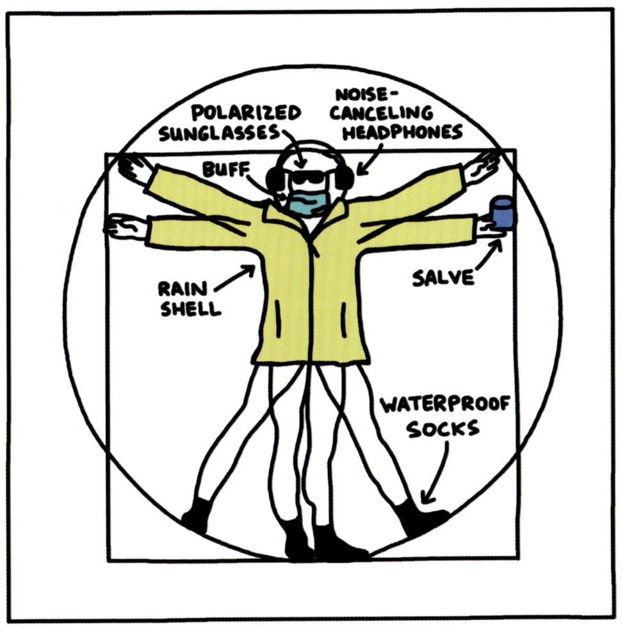

Scout about!

Scouting is a crucial part of your preplanning, and it can take different forms. It can be browsing location photos online or on Instagram so that you're visualizing the place(s) you're going to see. On a bigger-budget project, scouting can mean sending somebody out to go get actual photos of the locations you want to shoot.

Scouting can also be going on a trip by yourself to get some reference images. Then when the time is right and you want to come back and shoot the Milky Way in this place, or shoot the aurora borealis, you'll know where to post up.

A lot of times, if I have a big shot in mind (like a crazy Milky Way image), I might go to a location once and just put my camera up and get the composition nailed so that when I go back there, I'm not doing it in the dark for the first time.

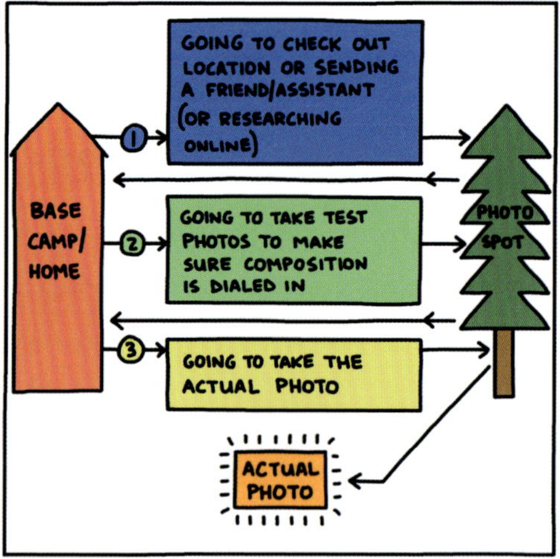

A lot of professionals scout locations, and obviously it's better to go there yourself so you can get a feel for the lens you need, the gear you need, the weather, where to be, what time of day. That's the sort of information you hope to glean.

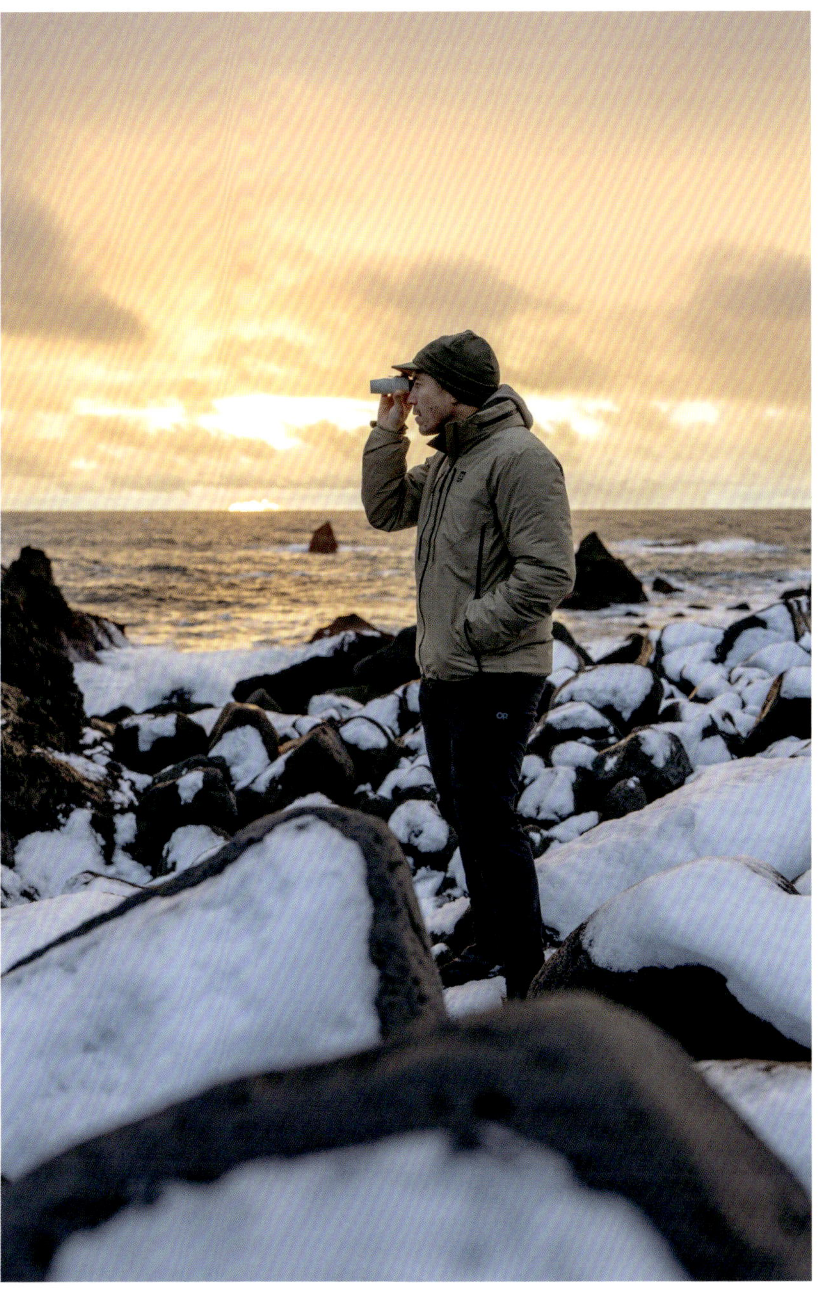
OR

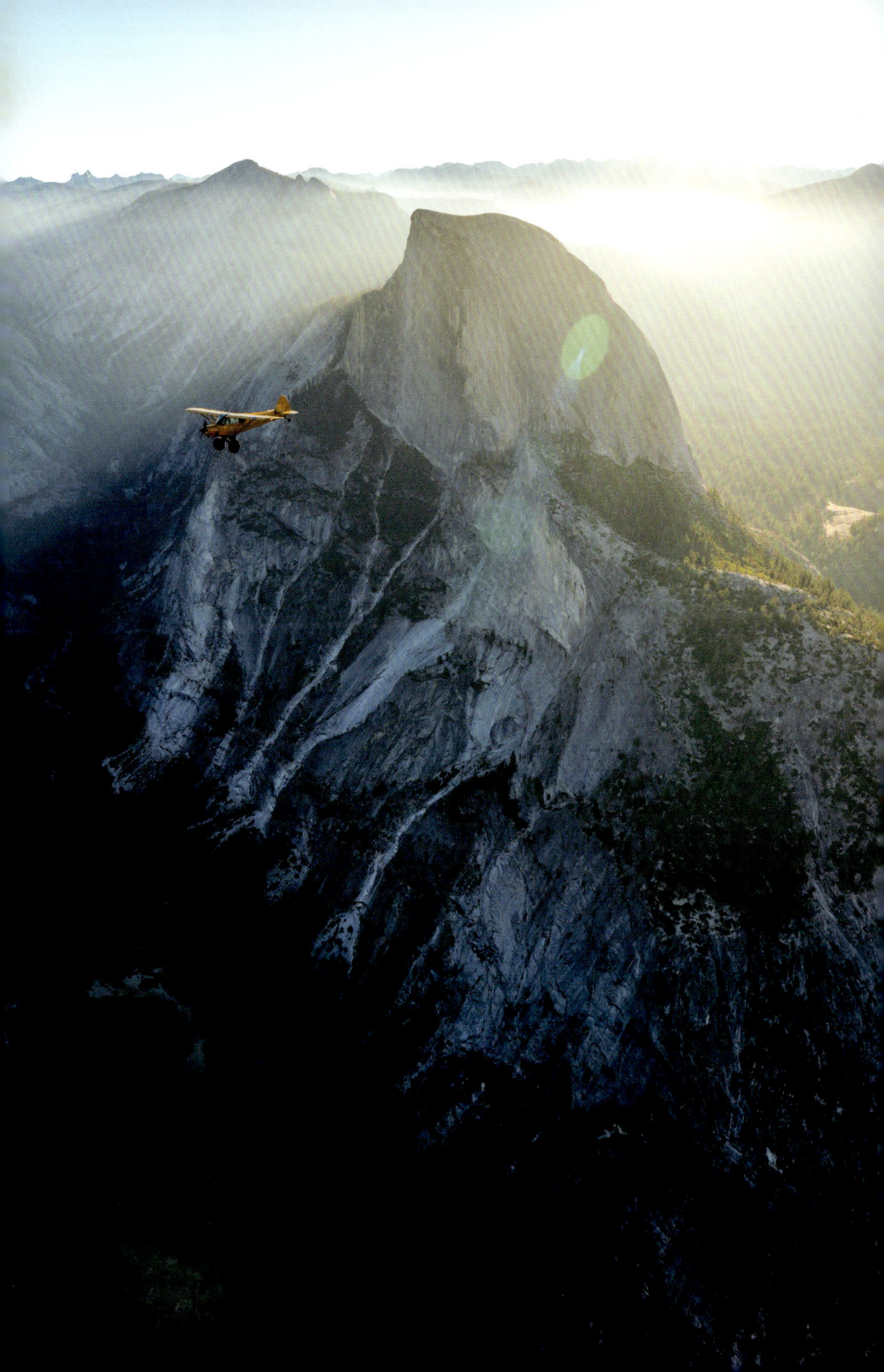

Be like Ansel

This is getting into the more ethereal part of photography. Say you go somewhere like Yosemite for the first time and you're wondering, *What is the image I want to create? Something with big puffy clouds and a rainbow and this going-over-tunnel view?*

You have to think, *OK, if I'm visualizing this image, how do I execute it?* You'd need to visit Yosemite in the springtime when there are colorful clearing storms happening or in late summer when there are exciting thunderstorms. This kind of visualization or imagination—imagination being a form of visualization—can inform you about the where, when, and why for shooting this image.

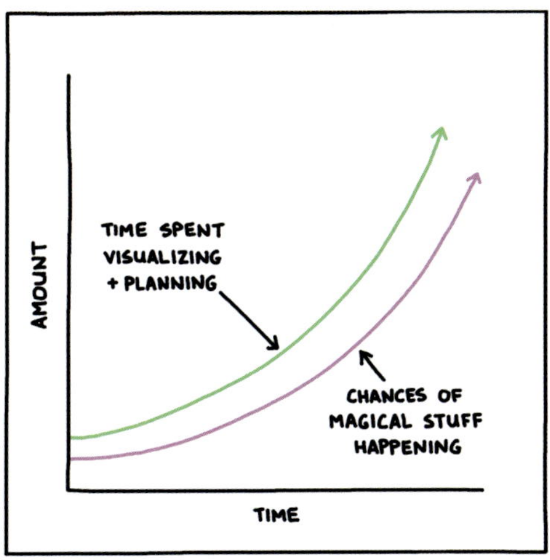

Ansel Adams was a huge advocate of visualization. It was his magic potion. He always visualized the image before he went to the location, hoping that his visualization would match his experience.

Going somewhere with no plan and no idea is almost like standing outside hoping for rain or a thunderstorm. It's not gonna happen. So be like Ansel—visualize!

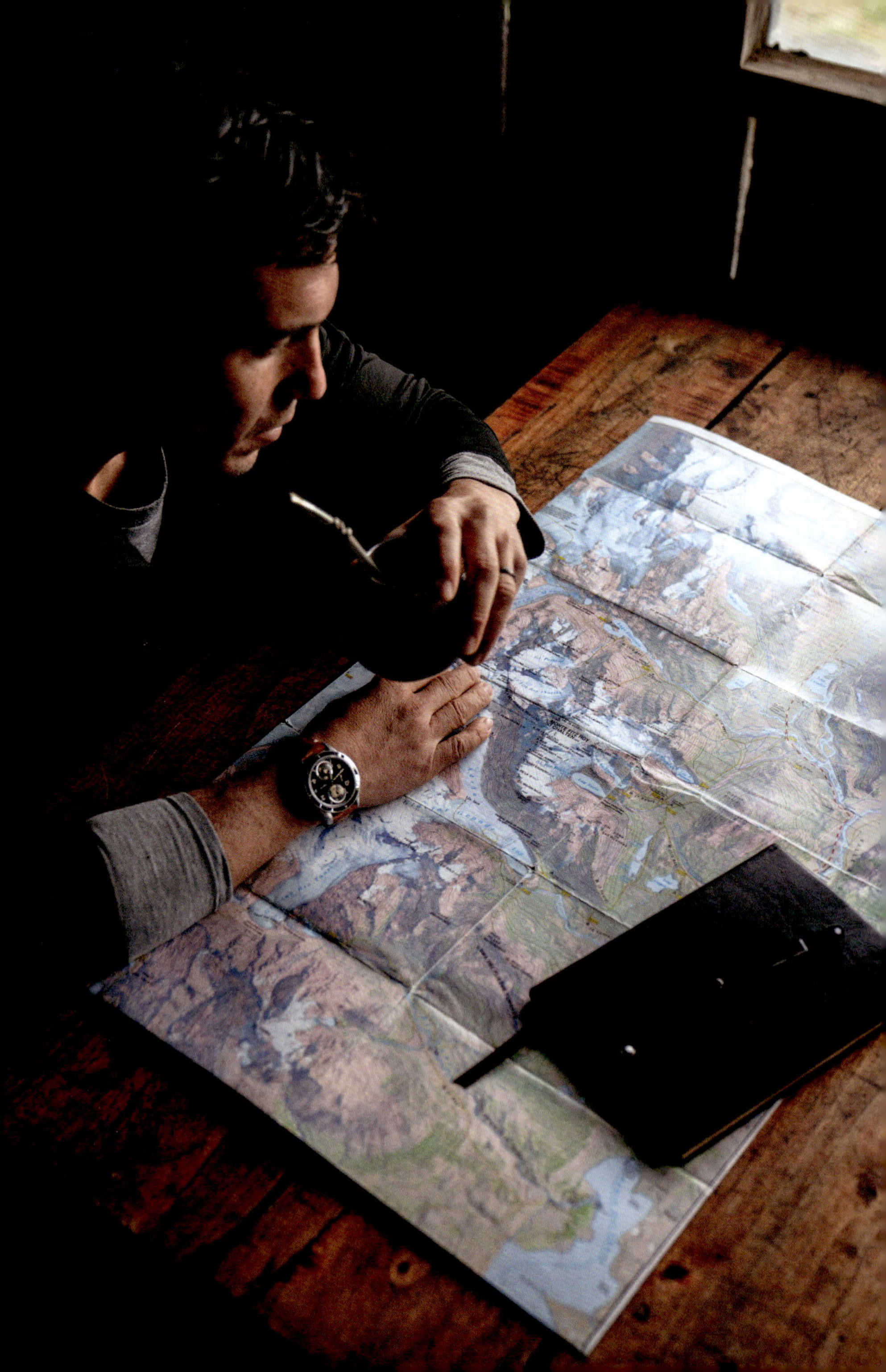

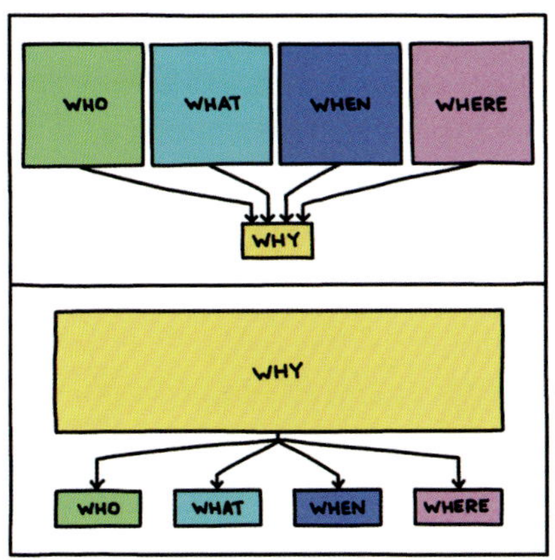

CHAPTER 3

Researching Your Trip

First, ask yourself: *Why do I want to go there?*

Why is X or Y or Z a place that calls to you? Is it because you've seen photos of it by people who inspire you? Is it because you want to go shoot a particular location?

Hmm.

By defining your desire, you can start working backward. In most of what I do—most of the decisions I make pertaining to jobs and projects and assignments—I try to work backward from the end goal, the end goal being that I want to shoot X, Y, or Z or I want to have a specific experience.

What are you hoping to walk away with? Is it simply photos of a particular place? Or is it an experience? If it's the latter, "researching" your trip is really just another word for planning your trip, and in planning your trip, you're orchestrating the experience you want to have. To do that, here are some tips and tricks that can go a long way.

What do you see?

Start with visualization. Let's say you're planning a trip to Iceland. What are you hoping to experience? Do you want to get misted by waterfalls? Be wowed by glaciers? See big black-sand beaches or crazy surf? As Ansel Adams said, it's important to premeditate or previsualize what you're hoping to shoot or experience. If you just say, "I want to see it all!"—well, that's great, but as you know, you need to home in on your goals, because seeing everything is usually unrealistic. It's better to start with a couple of key objectives and expand from those.

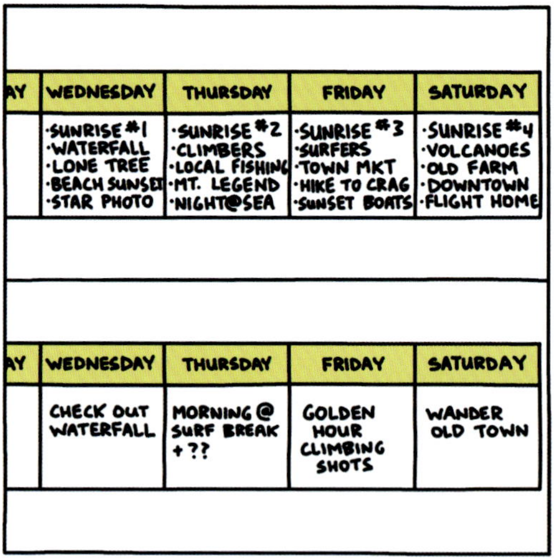

AY	WEDNESDAY	THURSDAY	FRIDAY	SATURDAY
	·SUNRISE #1 ·WATERFALL ·LONE TREE ·BEACH SUNSET ·STAR PHOTO	·SUNRISE #2 ·CLIMBERS ·LOCAL FISHING ·MT. LEGEND ·NIGHT@SEA	·SUNRISE #3 ·SURFERS ·TOWN MKT ·HIKE TO CRAG ·SUNSET BOATS	·SUNRISE #4 ·VOLCANOES ·OLD FARM ·DOWNTOWN ·FLIGHT HOME

AY	WEDNESDAY	THURSDAY	FRIDAY	SATURDAY
	CHECK OUT WATERFALL	MORNING @ SURF BREAK + ??	GOLDEN HOUR CLIMBING SHOTS	WANDER OLD TOWN

Visually, I often take my cue from photographs I've seen online or in magazines—this is usually what entices me first. I mean, most of us are not going to travel somewhere we haven't seen a photograph of. Therefore, other people's photos are a kind of visual cue. You see a picture of a place and you're inspired. You're hoping to create an experience, and you book your ticket.

Greetings, Google Earthling.

If you're intrigued by an area and don't know much about it, Google Earth is an *incredible* tool. When I was searching for waves, for years we would use Google Earth to figure out where the point breaks and beach breaks would be. We'd simply look at Google Earth and find little points of white water that might tell us where the waves were. It was so easy.

You can also take a three-dimensional view and, for example, see if the mountains are steep, if you're looking for a dramatic landscape, or where a glacier might line up. Google Earth makes it easy for you to understand the terrain. If you're looking at a flat map and see that a waterfall you want to get to is only one mile from a trailhead, you might not realize that the route is some crazy steep bushwhack trail. *Baa!* (Your inner goat.)

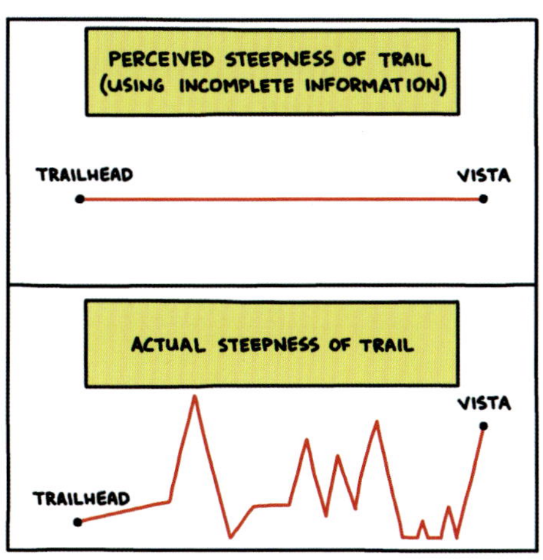

Out like a light.

OK, so you've homed in on the thing you want to shoot or the place you want to go—this waterfall, that beach—and maybe you've seen some images, but the images kind of suck or you still don't know much about the place. It's crucial to understand how the light will interact with that location. Usually, you can go on Google Earth and determine how the sunlight interacts at that spot—where does the sun

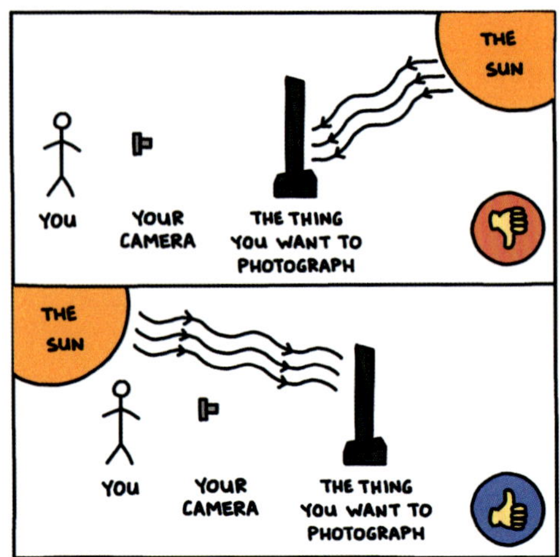

rise, where does it set? If you're there at the end of a clear day, you might be able to get the sun *here*. Or if it's backlit in the morning, you'll find the sun *there*. Think along those lines. Try to understand and almost create in your mind a three-dimensional map of what you're going to see and experience.

I often take notes. This is why it's important, to get back to my earlier point, to pick the key places you want to go—because if you try to do this with every spot, it's impossible. It's good to focus on maybe a half dozen places that you really like, map them out mentally, and take notes, and then be open to everything else you're experiencing along the way.

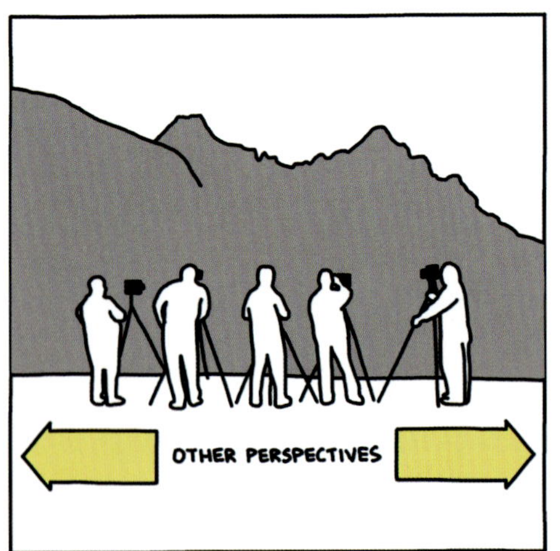

Angles away!

Angles are another thing to look for in other people's images of a particular place. A lot of times I'll study photos I see online to figure out what angles have been shot and try to figure out how I could bring a different perspective to the place.

Pass in review.

Reading quick online reviews of a place can be kind of funny because you don't know who's leaving them or what their perspectives or motives or biases are. To get

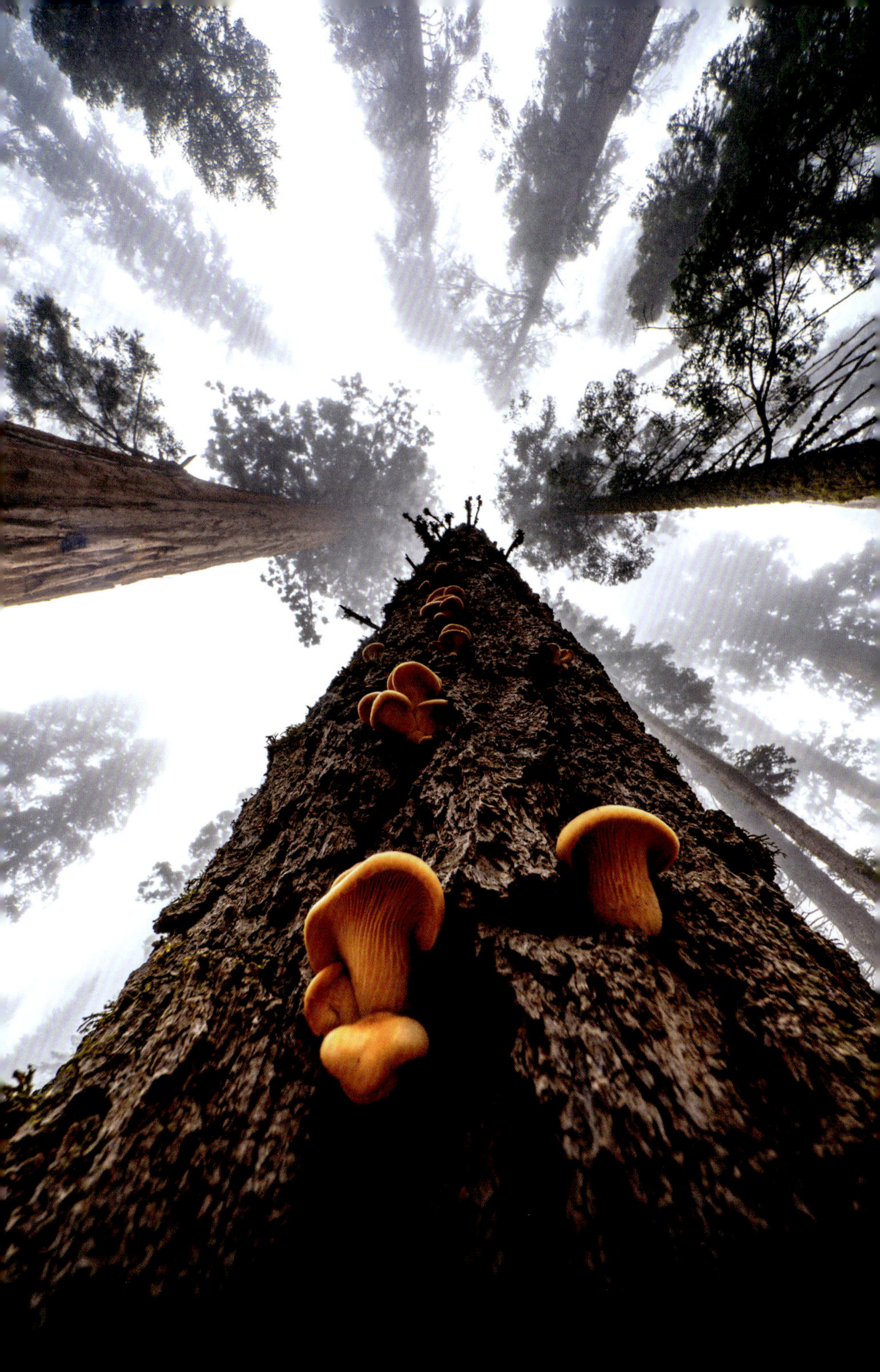

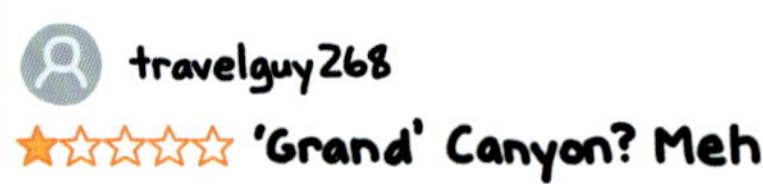

Got there after sunset and couldn't see anything. Why are there no lights in the canyon? I would like to speak to a manager.

real intel, in-depth blog posts or magazine articles that actually delve into a location can be really helpful. I find that a lot of heartache and headache can be avoided by reading somebody else's review. They might say, "Oh man, we parked here but we should have parked there!" Or "We went there in the middle of the day, and it was terrible. We should have gone in the middle of the night!"

Swagtime.

People message me and ask, "Should I bring this big lens? What else should I bring?" This is tricky. You don't really want to go to a place and bring a bunch of lenses and other equipment you've never used. It might be kind of complicated to figure out when to pull it out, how to use it, all those things. If you have new equipment or other gear that you must use, work with it before your trip. To repeat that old saying I love: What you do in practice, you'll do in a race. If you use a particular piece of gear a lot, you'll probably use it on this assignment or trip.

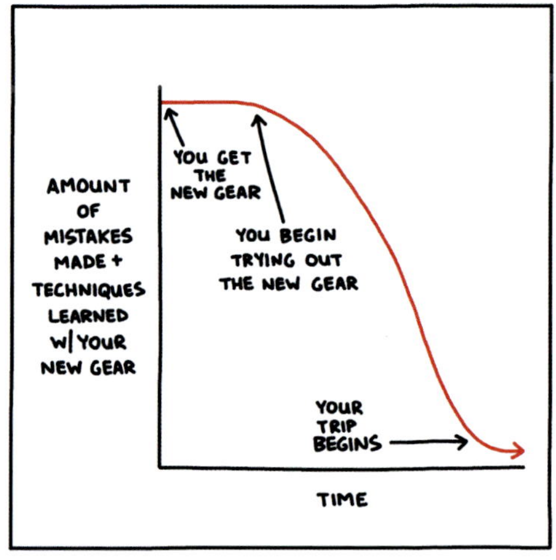

Don't break the bank and buy a whole new camera kit. Try to work with what you have and what you know. Consider if there is a specific shot you want. If you're shooting wildlife off a boat in Svalbard or

Alaska, then yeah, a long lens is helpful, and maybe that's a worthwhile purchase.

"Maybe I'll use a drone!" Well, if you've never launched a drone off a boat, this might not be the best opportunity to try it. Take the time before your trip to use new equipment and feel comfortable with it. Don't just bring it to a foreign environment and throw it up there.

Don't worry, be appy.

Apps are your friend. One I use is PhotoPills, which allows you to hold your phone up to the sky and determine where exactly the sun is going to be that day. It also allows you to see where nighttime stuff like the Milky Way will be later on.

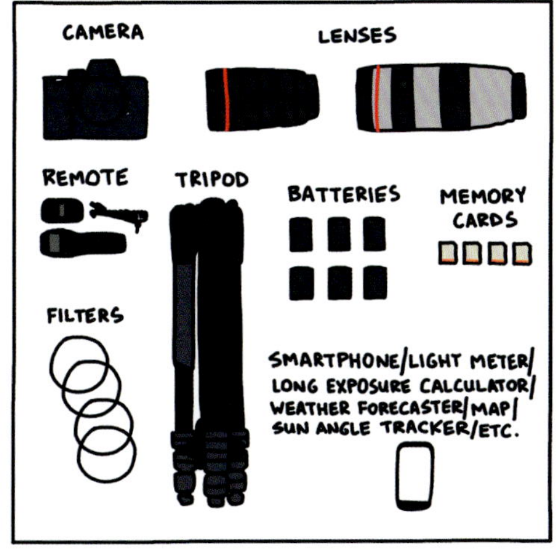

This is an incredible tool, and one that I use anytime I am trying to understand how the sun, stars, and moon will correspond to my scene despite the time of day. Tools like PhotoPills and other augmented reality apps allow us to view the correlation of these celestial bodies within our landscape or chosen "frame" through the phone camera. I'm a big advocate for scouting a place and actually setting up your tripod, even during the wrong time of day, to compose an angle that you might go back and shoot. If you plan for a shot, you're always going to have more success. The worst thing you can do is go to a new place in the middle of the night and try to set up a tripod. Trying to do that and having no idea what you're doing, maybe out on a wet, mossy cliff edge—not a good recipe.

Seek guidance.

Guidebooks are great, and there are lots of them out there. Bradt Guides, Rough Guides, and Lonely Planet books are classic. In some cases, it can be important to have an actual human guide with you on location. For example, if the ice cave you want to go to isn't a place you can drive to in your tiny rental car because you'll need to cross big rivers in a specialized jeep, then you should hire a guide.

NOTABLE HEROES + GUIDES	
HERO	GUIDE
LUKE SKYWALKER	OBI-WAN KENOBI YODA
REY	LUKE SKYWALKER
ROCKY BALBOA	MICKEY GOLDMILL APOLLO CREED
KATNISS EVERDEEN	HAYMITCH ABERNATHY
HARRY POTTER	DUMBLEDORE
YOU	GUIDEBOOKS TOUR SERVICE LOCAL FRIEND/FIXER

Will you need a tour service? A tour can make your life much easier and your trip more productive. Conversely, sometimes you might book a tour and then learn that you could have easily reached the location by yourself. That can suck because then you're stuck with all these other random tourists on a tour bus that has a completely different vibe from what you wanted for your trip.

Let's take a second to summarize

When it comes to researching your trip, the goal is to figure out your objectives and work backward. If it's a remote place in a super wild environment, sometimes researching can take six months to a year—or longer! Research can be difficult but can often hatch the best trips—the ones you really pour yourself into. So don't be afraid to spend that extra time, effort, and energy.

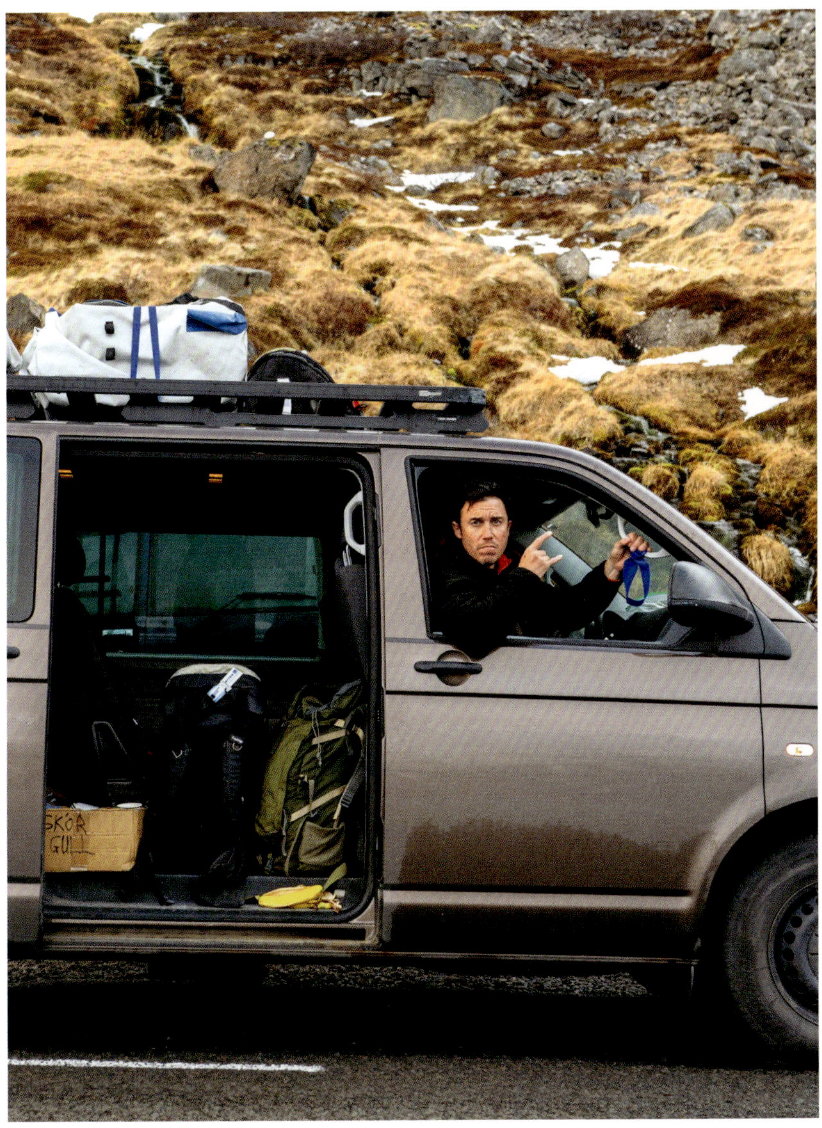
SKÓR
GULL

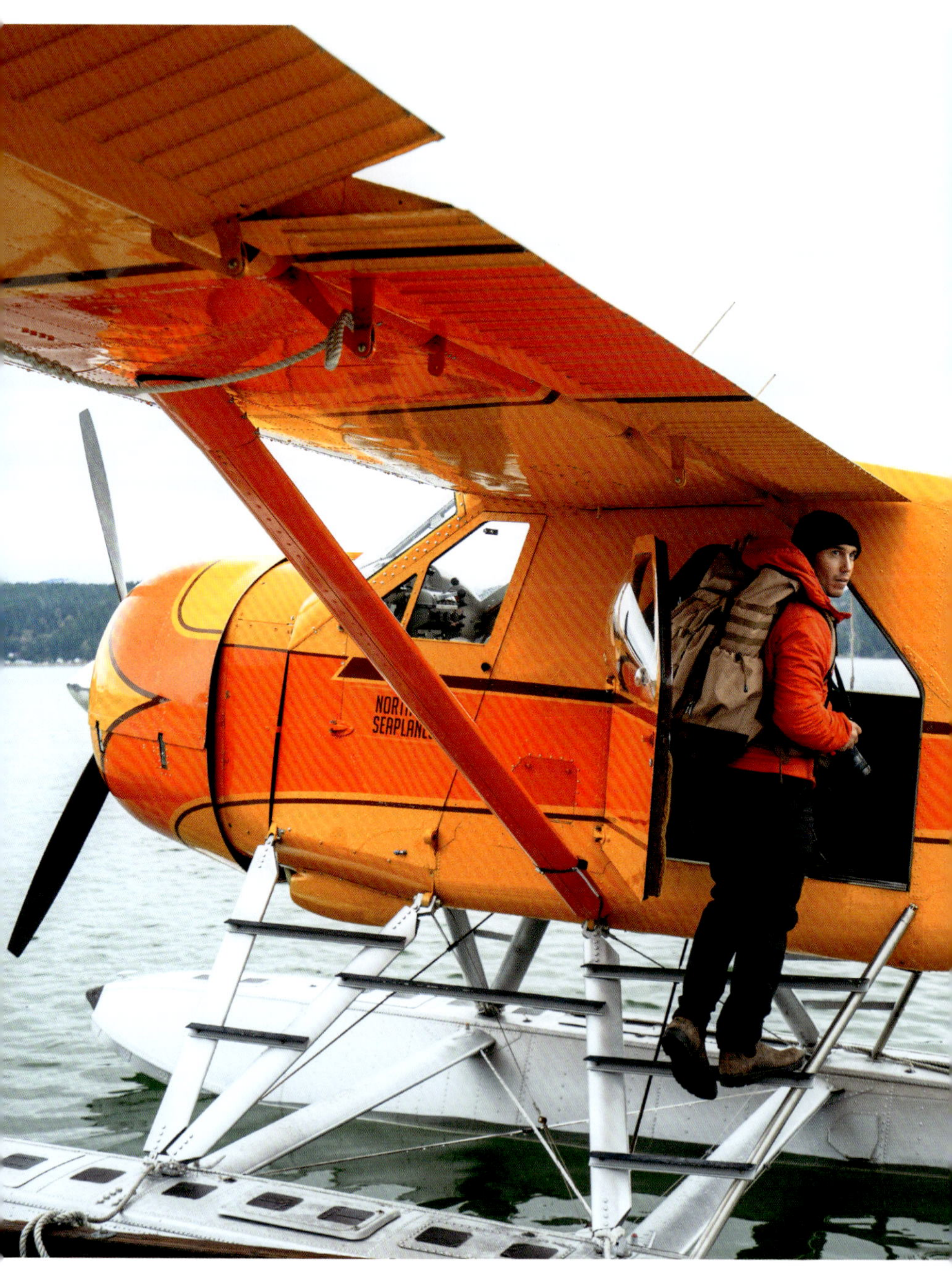

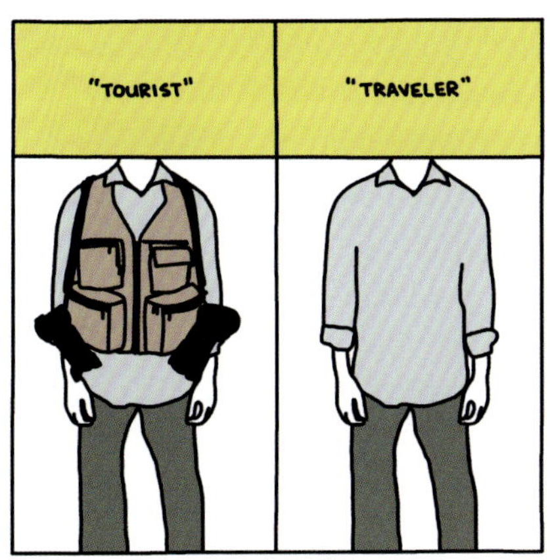

CHAPTER 4

Traveling with a Camera

Guess what? Journeying with your camera is a *lot* more than simply tossing one into your bag and going somewhere.

Be a *traveler*—not a *tourist*. Cliché, right? Sure. But a huge part of being a photographer is learning when to set your camera down and just be present. In certain situations, your fancy Sony camera body with a Sony shoulder strap (plus your snazzy lenses) might seem a bit threatening to some folks.

Years ago in Cuba, I was walking the streets with my big professional camera, and every time I'd hoist it up to shoot photos of kids along the road, they would ask me for money. All over the island, people shied away because they were sick and tired of foreigners coming to Cuba and shooting endless photos of the local people.

I wanted a more honest experience. So, the next day, I shot everything with my little point-and-shoot. I removed the Sony strap and used a shoestring instead—overall a much more intimate scenario. My gear wasn't threatening to those I was shooting.

So, what kind of experience do you want to have? And do you *really* need all that gear?

Keep these tips in mind as you prepare for your next adventure:

- **Don't scream "I'm a tourist!"** Try to blend in. This could entail using your beat-up backpack or wearing some older clothes. By assimilating into the local scene, you'll have the magic ability to document everyday life experiences and not stand out like a sore thumb. Unless that's what you want!

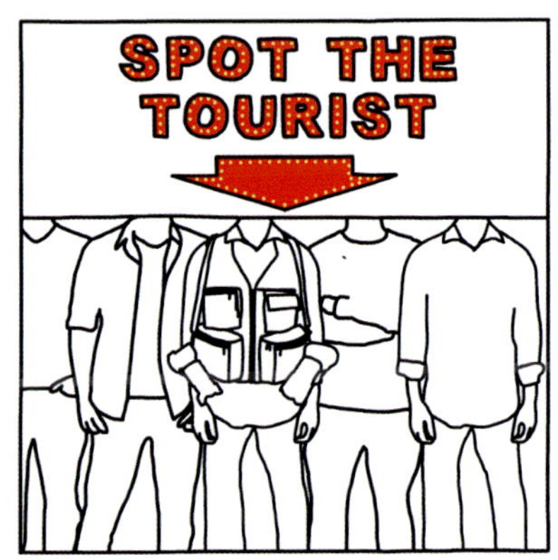

- **Keep 'em close.** Bring your most important gear onto the plane with you. Never let your equipment out of your sight. In fact, never let it out of your hands. I've lost gear that was checked in. I've had water housings broken. I've had big 600mm lenses stolen from me while flying to Hawaii. At all costs, if you can manage it, do not check camera gear.

  Having said that, not checking stuff can be difficult or outright impossible when you're flying in a small plane. I always make sure that inside my bag I have a packing cube containing my most precious camera gear. So if they tell you, "You can't bring this whole thing on the plane," I can say, "OK, let me just pull out this cube." Then, no matter what, I'll have my core essential gear. And I always throw an Apple AirTag into each bag—checked or not.

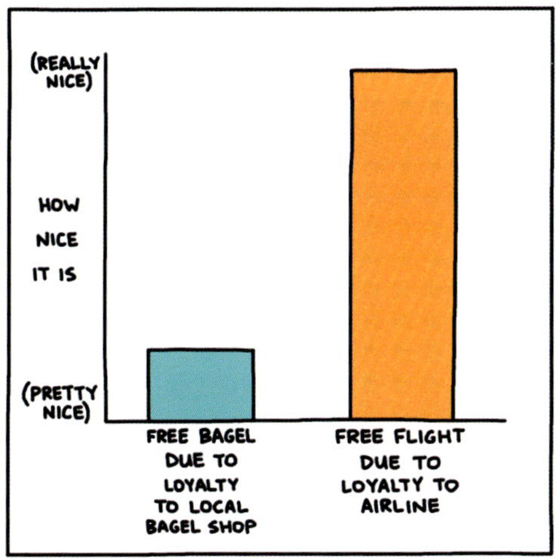

- **Stay on point(s).**

Always try to gain airline points. Join those mileage plans and airline clubs. It definitely helps to have some kind of preferential service—and free flights when you earn enough points!

- **Be the early bird and get the overhead bin space.**

It's super uncool to board the plane first, right? Do it anyway! So many times I've seen people wait and wait, get on the plane at the very end of the boarding process, and say, "I didn't want to be stuck in this metal tube for any longer than I had to." But guess what? They find there's no space for their bags. I'd rather get on first, find a good spot for my bags, and relax.

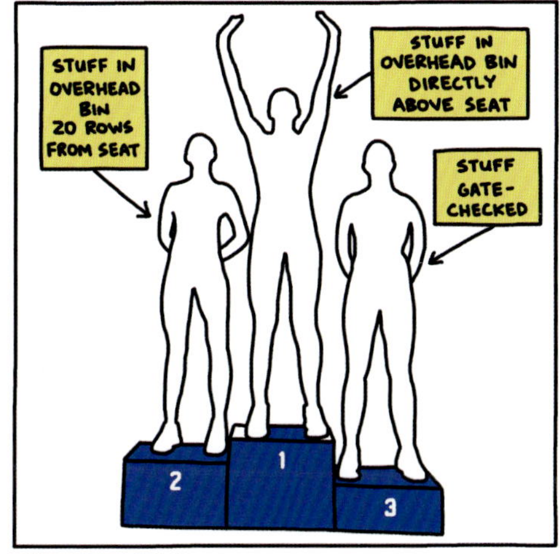

What's in your base kit?

NUMBER OF LENSES I WOULD BRING IN A PERFECT WORLD	NUMBER OF LENSES I WILL CARRY IN A BACKPACK IN THE REAL WORLD
∞	3

It's tempting to bring all the camera gear you own. But if I'm going to Majorca to shoot climbing, and I know that the best shots are going to come from wide angles while I'm hanging on the wall, or if I'm planning to shoot wide landscapes, then maybe I'll leave the 70–200mm at home.

However, a 24–70mm and 70–200mm are my go-to lenses—my base kit. Often, if I can minimize my kit by bringing, say, a 70–200mm and a doubler or a 1.4x converter, I'll do that rather than bring a 400mm or 600mm. I'm after a simpler kit that can fit in a shoulder bag or backpack.

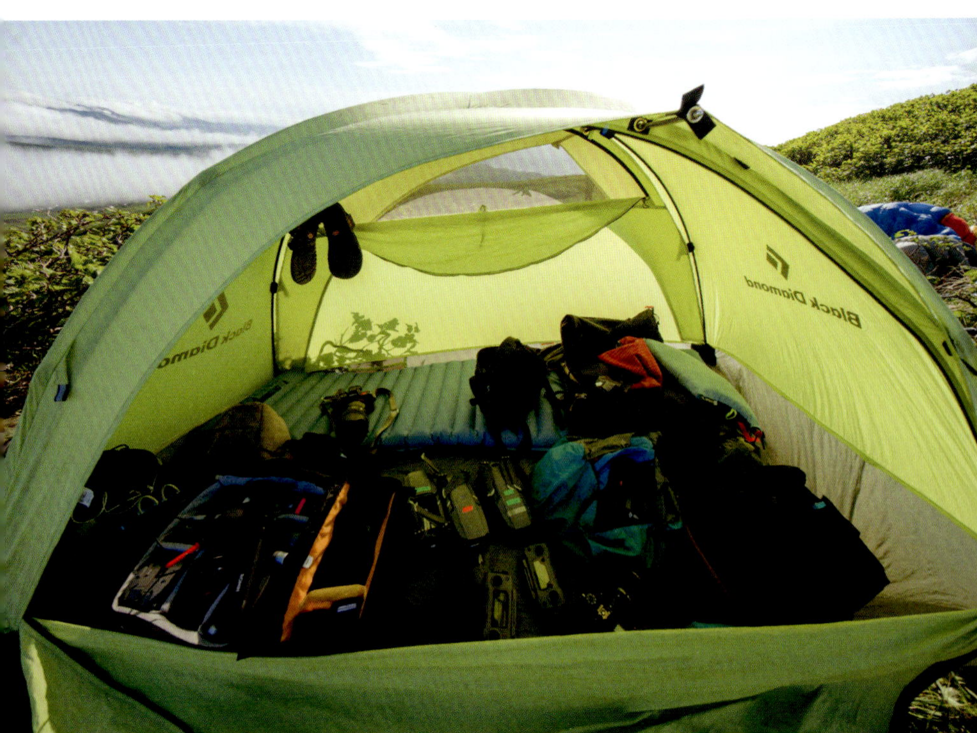

By having a more minimal kit, you allow yourself to really use those lenses to their fullest extent. I prefer to shoot on f/2.8 glass if possible, but if you want to save space, you can explore f/4 glass. It's lighter and not as bulky.

The 16–35mm is always on my camera at the beginning of the day. I love this lens format. It's just how I see the world—how I picture things. When I want to extend or expand, I will use the 24–70mm. Beyond that, I'll ask myself: *Am I shooting anything that needs to be telephoto? Should I bring a 70–200mm, a 300mm or 400mm, or something even bigger? Am I shooting animals? What is my subject? Is it far away? Do I need to compress? What is the perspective, the angle? Am I shooting a wide-angle landscape? Am I shooting a compressed animal photo? Am I shooting night photography?* If so, I need to bring a dedicated night lens—a 14mm or 20mm with a wide-open aperture.

So, nailing your base kit and knowing where to start is *really* helpful.

Make a clean getaway

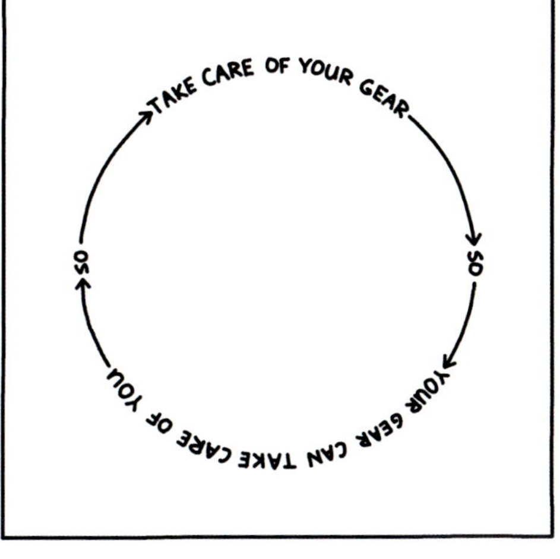

Bring at least one proper lens-cleaner cloth. I always have one at the bottom of my bag. I also carry a tiny blower and, just in case, a sensor swab. These are all critical parts of your base kit.

When you're shooting in wet weather, how do you keep your gear clean and dry? Here's a hack I love: I bought one of those big microfiber cloth blankets from REI and cut it in half. But it's still massive, right? I can wrap my whole camera inside it. I put that blanket at the bottom of my backpack, and if it's raining and I need to dry off my camera constantly, that's what I'll use. There's nothing worse than putting away wet camera gear or getting water on a lens. That's what really starts to create some issues for your glass.

At the end of the day, I always wipe down my gear, especially if I've been shooting by the ocean. Salt spray is brutal on lenses. I wipe my camera down with a wet cloth to clear off any debris—any black sand or lava, things like that. I take off the filters, unscrew them, blow out everything, and then lay it all out to dry. I make a conscious effort to do this each night.

An anonymous tip

A BAD PLAN	A BETTER PLAN
① SHOW UP + TRY TO TAKE PHOTOS	① HAVE SOME FUN/ BUILD A LITTLE RAPPORT/ BLEND IN/ MAKE SOME FRIENDS ② TRY TO TAKE PHOTOS

Blend in! That's key. One day while I was in Cuba, I noticed that a bunch of kids were jumping off a seawall. Instead of going there and just shooting photos of them, I stripped down to my board shorts and jumped in. I swam around and hung out. Lots of laughs! It was my opportunity to be anonymous, to be a part of that group. Within a half hour, I'd gained their trust and I was capturing images of them leaping and swimming and enjoying the simple innocent fun that kids can have.

Stay locked in

Always bring a little U-shaped travel lock—but not one that needs a key. Use a combo lock for the win. And *never* leave your camera gear anywhere in plain sight!

If I'm leaving a backpack or Pelican case in a car, I always try to lock it to some metal part of a seat frame. It takes me an extra 10 seconds but would take a thief an extra 10 minutes to try to undo or cut the lock. Now, this is not going to solve all the problems. But it is an opportunity to deter or slow a thief down. They might see the lock and think, *Oh, shit—this person is serious! I'm not going to try to break in and steal this thing.* And of course I always have an AirTag in that bag.

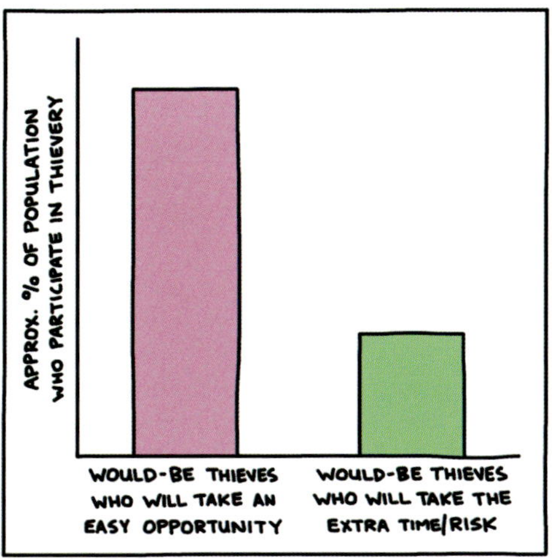

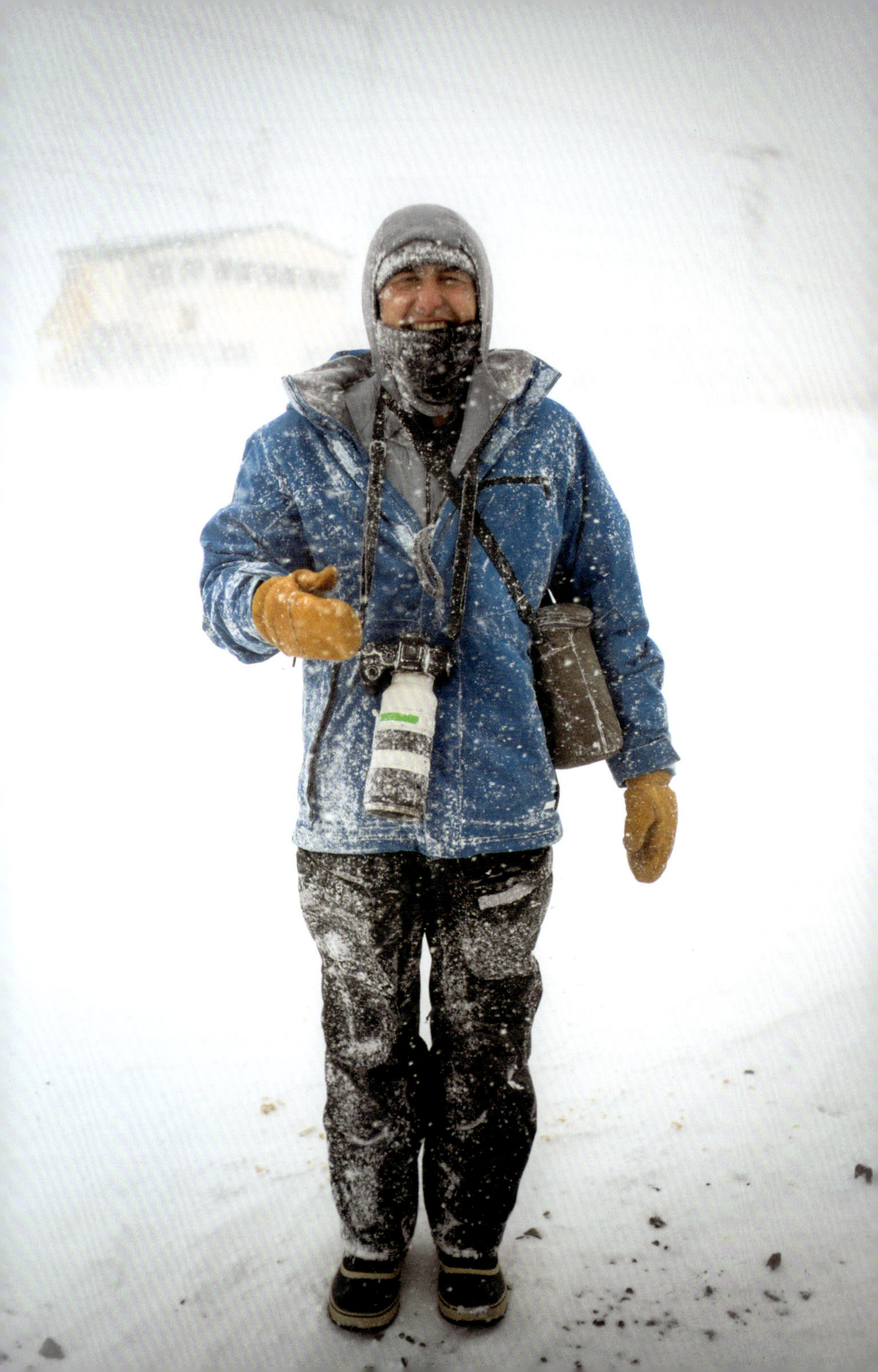

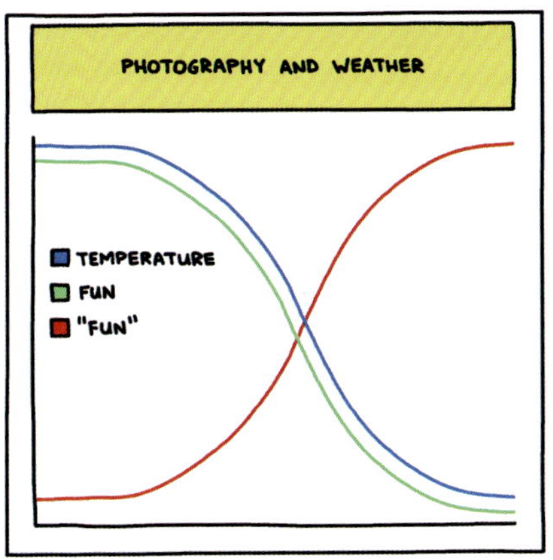

CHAPTER 5

Embracing Extremes

First, we should probably define *extreme* . . .

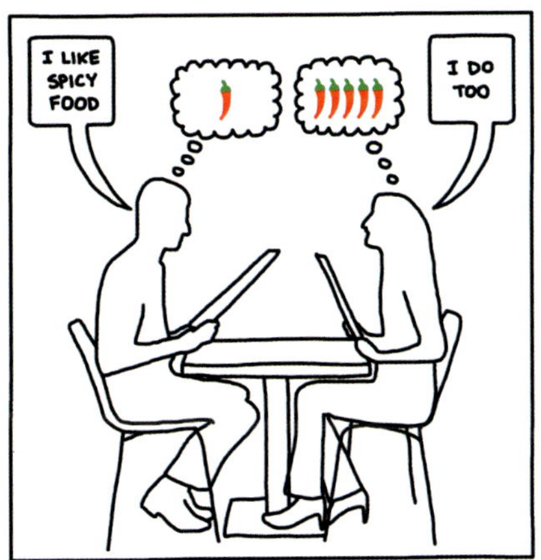

It's many things to many people. For some, *extreme* might mean being a camera-toting daredevil skiing down K2. For others, it could simply involve a first trip to a climate that's harsher than, say, San Diego's.

Inclement weather often helps you take the coolest (pun unintended) photos. There's always a moment after a rainstorm when things mellow out, and you can get crazy light, rainbows, and all that stuff. Extreme weather usually yields great contrast and interesting images. In alpine or desert environments, you can often create your most unique work.

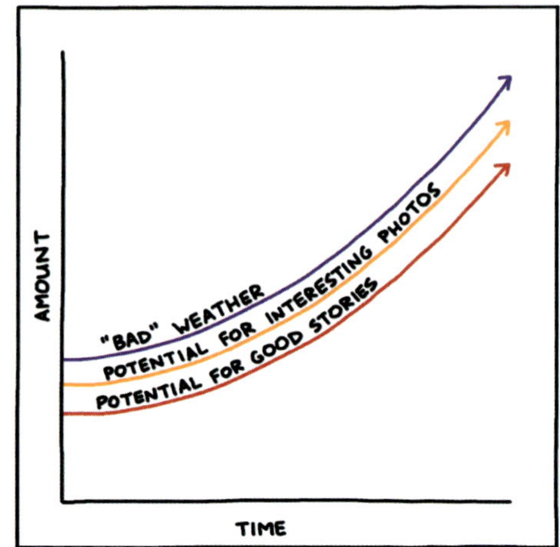

But what can you handle? Earlier in my career, I never would have considered making my film *Under an Arctic Sky* (2017), because the weather was hellacious and it was outright terrifying driving through those crazy storms. But having been to Iceland thirty or forty times by that point in my career, I felt comfortable.

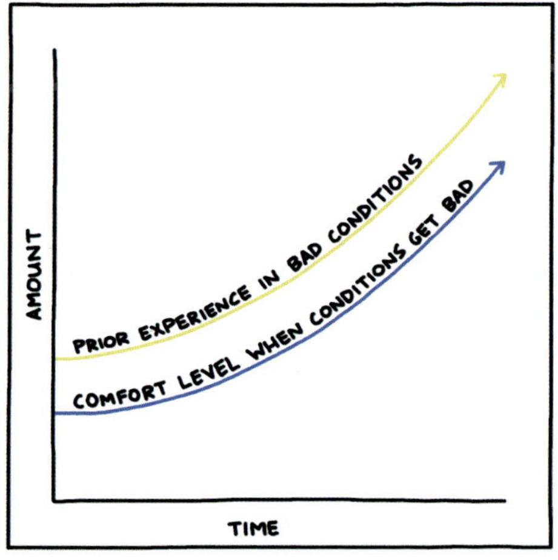

This level of extreme comes with some risk. You need to ensure you can handle it and that you feel safe—that these are places where you are ready to accept whatever comes your way. This means having the right equipment, the right clothing, and the right mindset.

Here again, the old adage comes into play—what you do in practice, you'll do in a race. You don't want to arrive somewhere new thinking, *This is the first time I've ever been in freezing temperatures.* Prep yourself for those temps before you bring your camera into them.

If possible, practice and experiment in similar environments close to your home before you end up in a blizzard in the middle of nowhere halfway across the planet.

Always be prepared!

But don't rush it. Deciding what you can handle is something that only comes with time. This is a lifelong experience. Slowly define what you can process.

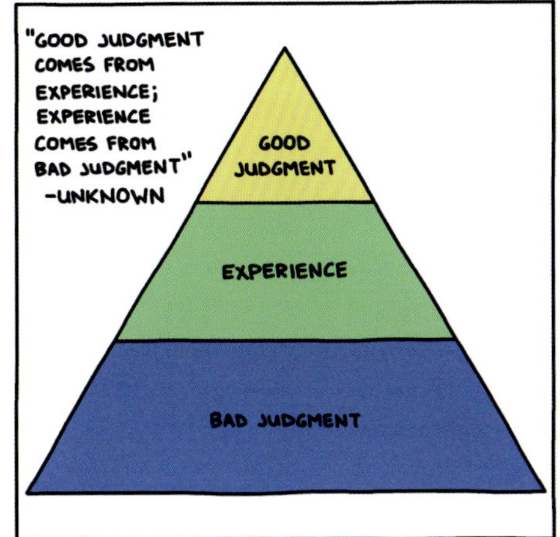

Take cold comfort

The traveler with the most experience carries the least amount of stuff, right? The more clothing you wear, the more effort is required to access your camera. If you're in a ginormous puffy jacket, looking like the Stay Puft Marshmallow Man, it can be challenging just to get your backpack off.

So, how can you have clothing that's not only warm but also minimal? There are two types of insulation. One is "active." When you're moving and you're going to be sweating, you need clothing with breathability. You need functionality too, so that water or sweat can release. Merino wool and vented mesh material offer active insulation. These fabrics are still insulating and warming, but they're meant to actually

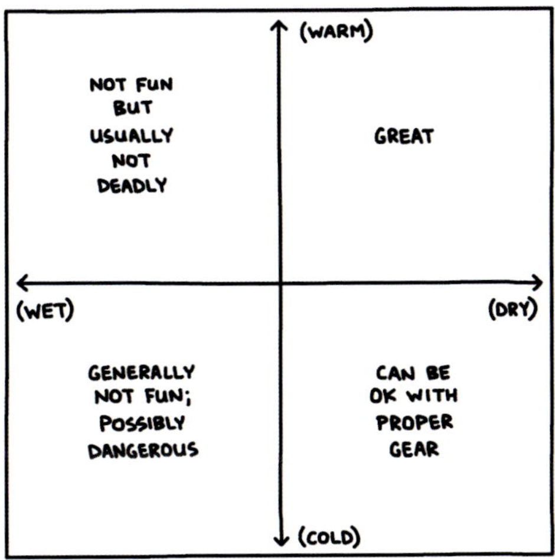

breathe and wick moisture away from your body. Being sweaty and cold is a dangerous combination.

The other insulation type is "inactive." Say you're sitting on a boat in Antarctica shooting penguins and you're not really moving. You don't want to wear anything that breathes. You want to have an absolutely impermeable layer protecting against wind, snow, and rain.

Another thing to keep in mind is that cold is not wet. Cold is cold. Freezing temps are actually a lot easier to deal with than rain because freezing temps won't affect your cameras much. You can usually brush or blow off snow if it's the dry, fluffy stuff.

Consider the local climate you're visiting and ask yourself: *Will I be active or will I be stationary?* If you're ski touring and shooting, you'll want active insulation. You can wear four layers and add or remove some depending on the temperature.

If you're going to be on a boat shooting polar bears or just chilling outside your Norwegian cabin tripping on the aurora borealis, you don't need active insulation, because you're not building up a sweat. Instead you'll need thicker materials that don't really let air in: canvas, for example. And yes! You're going to want that big, thick Marshmallow Man jacket.

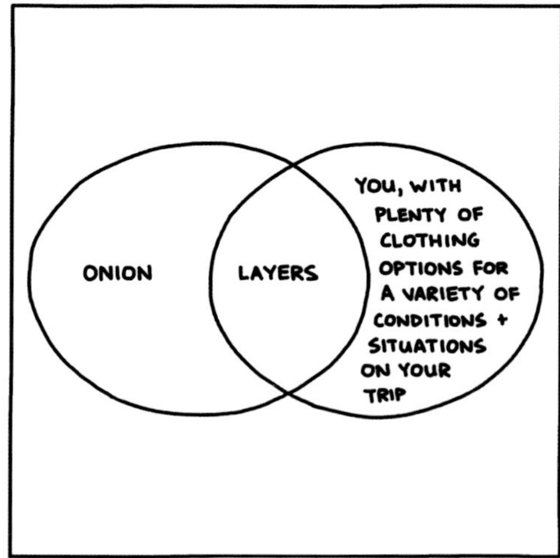

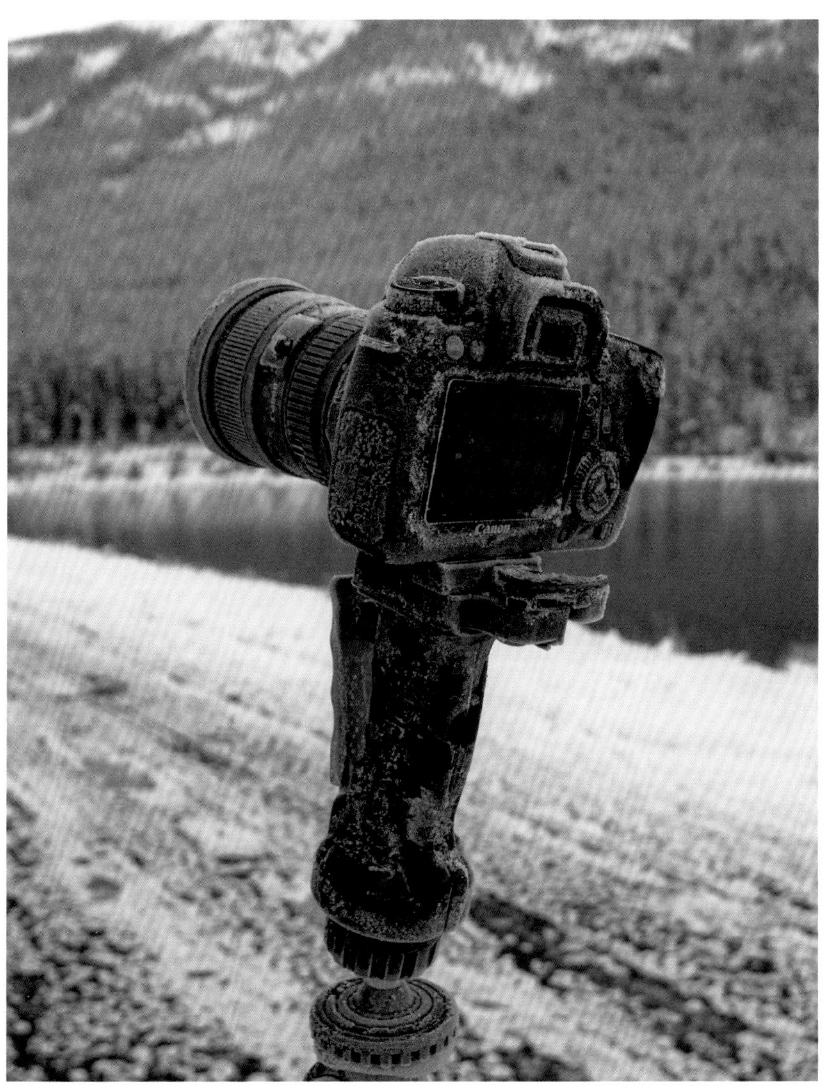
Canon

Avoid wearing a bunch of hooded layers. I don't like to have six layers with hoods because they just get in the way every time I put my camera strap over my back. It's annoying. So, I opt for non-hooded layers underneath. I would rather insulate my neck with a Gator or a Buff. I always carry one or two with me. I can cover my ears and my eyes and sleep with it at night.

A handy tip

Gloves are crucial, and a good pair can be hard to find.

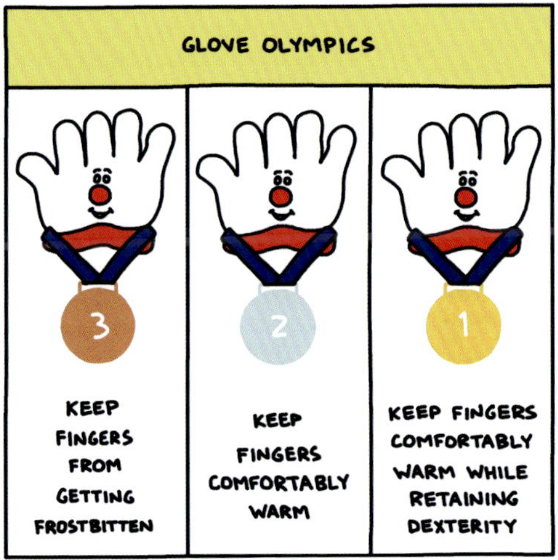

- You want gloves that allow you to use your camera easily as well as potentially expose a finger or fingers, like if you need to yank half a glove down to operate a drone.

- Consider the thickness of the gloves you choose. I tend to have a box full of gloves so I can pick the right ones for a particular situation.

- Glove liners are really helpful if you need to access your camera without the outer gloves. Having your hands fully exposed in snowy conditions is brutal.

Don't get mugged

Humidity is tricky because it can create a whole slew of issues within the camera. One of the worst is when you step from a steamy outdoor environment into an air-conditioned room. For example, if you're shooting in Costa Rica and the humidity is 99 percent, and then you take your gear back into your air-conditioned hotel, that can ruin your camera and create a fog in your lens. Be very careful when you move your camera in and out of such environments.

If I'm in a hotel somewhere tropical, I might remove the batteries and leave my camera outside so it will be acclimated at all times. Or I'll put my camera bag in the bathroom with the window open and switch off any AC in there. Then I'll wedge a towel beneath the door so no cold air can sneak in. Essentially, I try to keep my camera gear in a state of equilibrium.

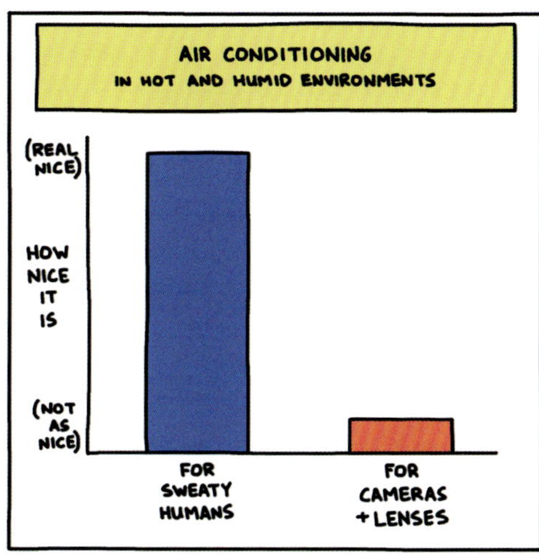

The same goes for the car. In cold destinations, don't put your camera down by your feet where the car heater is probably blasting from a vent. Swinging temperature extremes are bad for your camera.

While we're on such a hot topic . . .

What about clothes? Pack stuff that allows ventilation. In the tropics I lean toward wearing a long-sleeve shirt with a hood. Although that might seem counterproductive in terms of keeping you cool, it's much better for you to *not* get sunburn and *not* get heatstroke. I prefer wearing tactical products like Patagonia's Tropic Comfort 40+ UPF

HOW MANY TIMES YOU SHOULD RE-APPLY IT IN A 10-HOUR PERIOD, ACCORDING TO EXPERTS	
SPF 45 SUNSCREEN	UPF 40 SUN SHIRT/HOODY
𝍸	

hoodie rather than lathering sunscreen all over myself. And if I need to wipe the sweat off my face, I've got the shirt sleeves for that.

Sunscreen is messy and greasy, and it doesn't really allow your skin to breathe. Plus, all those weird ingredients soak into your pores! When you smash your face up against your viewfinder and camera back, you're going to get sunscreen on your camera. Don't do it!

For footwear, I always have a pair of sandals, maybe some Bedrocks, that I can get around in. Obviously, it's great to bring shoes if you're in a hot desert environment where you're dealing with stickers and thorns, rattlesnakes and scorpions, and so forth.

Go electro

Remember to stay hydrated in hot environments. Drink water with electrolytes. If you're drinking water without electrolytes, you're basically not even absorbing your water. And bring more water than you think you will need.

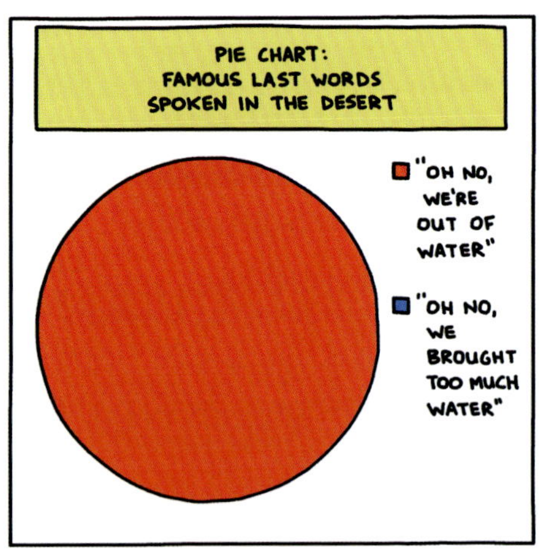

Wet is tricky too

Folks get hypothermia when they underestimate the combination of cold and wet conditions, thinking *It's only 45°F (7°C). I'll be fine.* But then they get soaked and they start shivering. If you're wet and your gear is wet? Not good!

Investing in quality rain gear will make all the difference. I'll pay extra for something good that works rather than, say, a rain shell that looks cool and is a great fit for the one day it rains in San Diego. If you buy something inexpensive, you'll know it immediately.

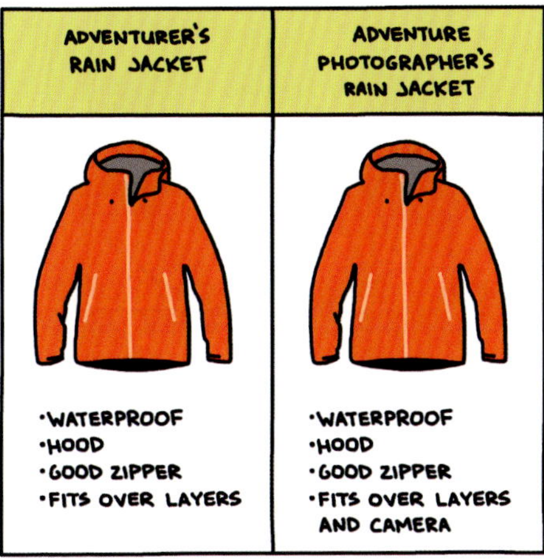

Here are some tips for shooting in wet environments:

- Avoid clothing with down insulation. When down gets wet, it doesn't insulate, so you'll get cold and miserable very fast. My go-to is a synthetic insulation layer beneath a rain shell.
- Sport multiple layers instead of trying to wear one layer that does it all. If you are in and out of a place, the worst thing you can do is have just one big jacket that's drenched. It's nice to take off a rain shell and shake it out.
- Buy a rain shell one size larger than you normally wear. I like to be able to strap my camera around my neck, put it down on my chest, and cover it with my rain shell. When I'm in Canada, if it's raining, and I'm in the field shooting or on a boat, I want to be able to have my camera on my chest, zip the shell open, take a photo—*snap!*—and slip the camera right back under my shell.

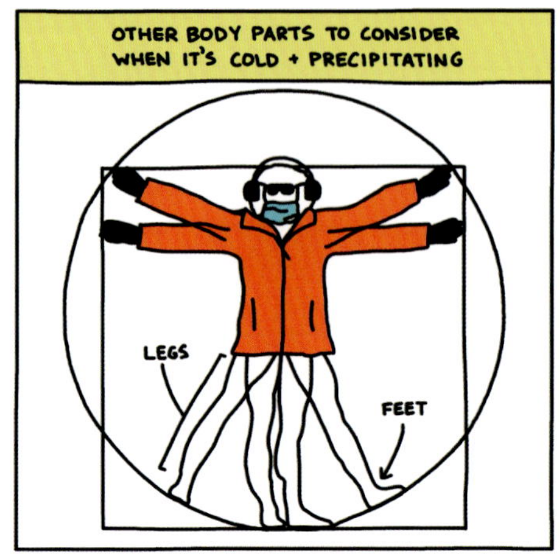

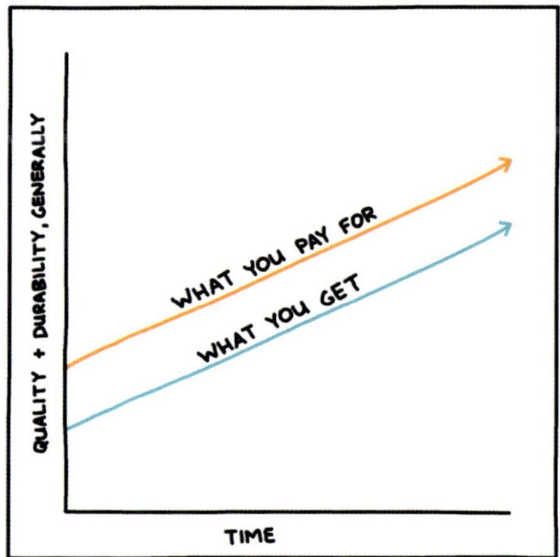

- Keep your legs and feet dry with rain pants, waterproof socks (Sealskinz), and mid- or quarter-length rain boots (Grundéns or XTRATUF).

- Bring a microfiber cloth towel. I keep a cut-down REI towel somewhere in my rain shell so I can clean my camera off if needed.

- Consider whether you actually need camera covers, plastic bags, or other protectants. Peak Design makes some great stuff, but I tend to not use such items much because if I'm putting a camera in my jacket, then it's already protected. I usually find that those pieces of kit are cumbersome, and if it's raining that much, are you actually out shooting? Rain is one weather condition wherein you really can't shoot. Same with dense fog.

Don't get left in the dust!

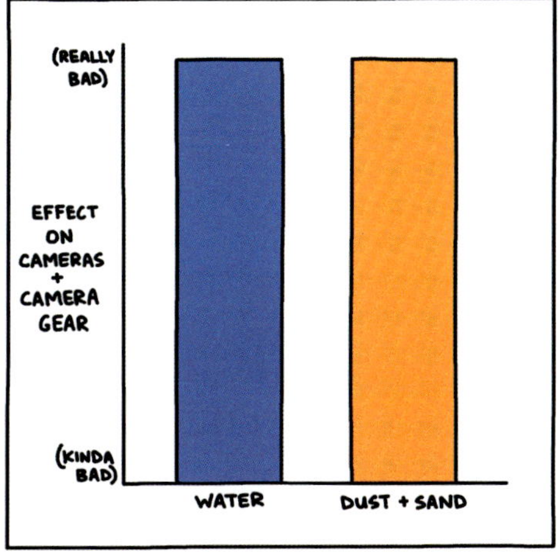

The worst thing you can do after a long, gnarly, dusty shoot is just put your camera things aside without cleaning them. For dry, dusty environments, I have a little cleaning kit that I bring with me. It usually contains a blower, a sensor cleaner, and a microfiber cloth or two. It's got everything I need for cleaning my cameras and lenses, and I'll do that diligently at the end of each day. I'll clean the camera's image sensor, the lens mount and its contacts, the viewfinder, and the LCD display so I can actually see it, especially on a really bright, sunny day. I don't use UV filters, but I do use polarizing filters, and those will typically shield the lens from dust.

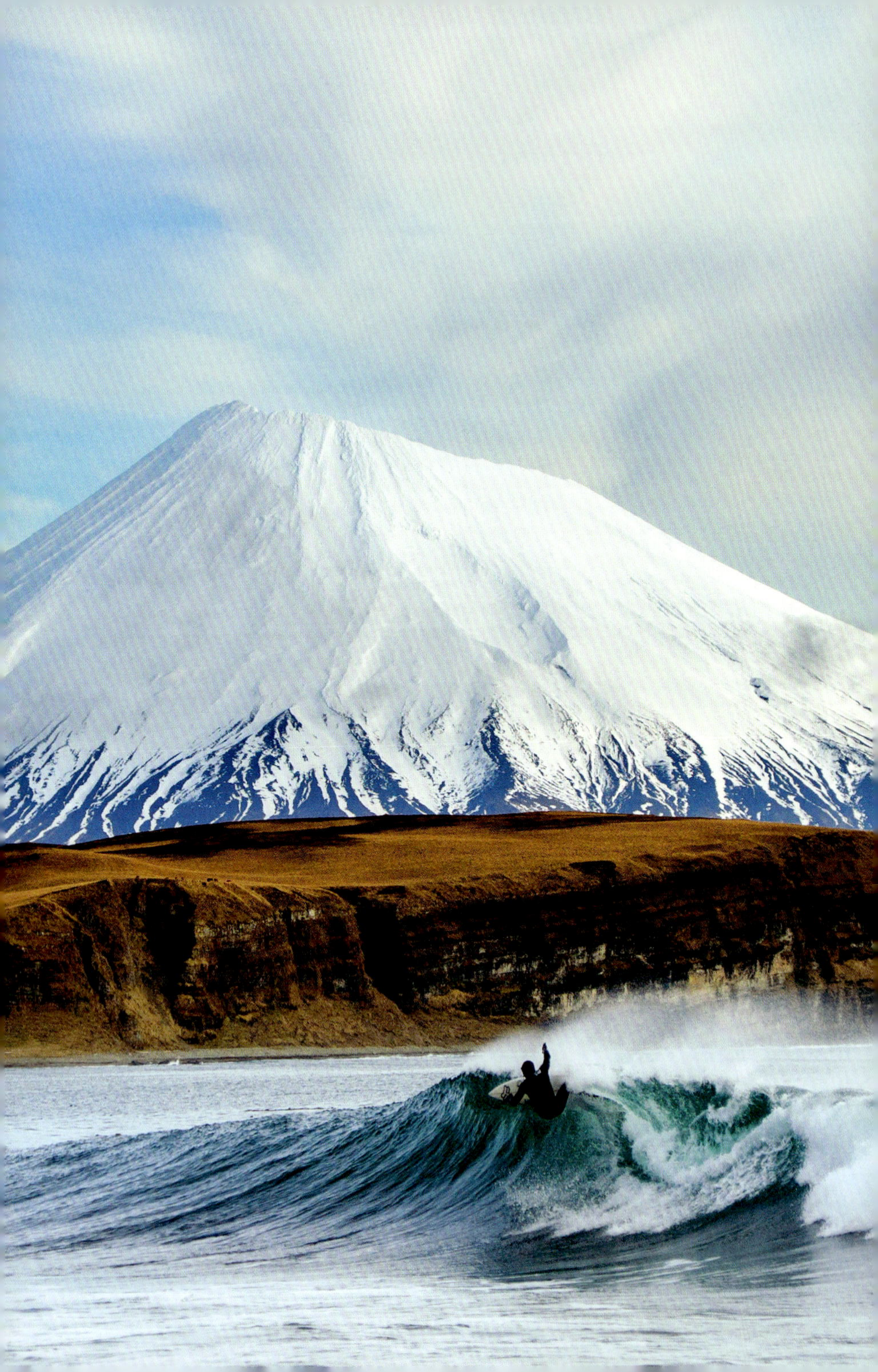

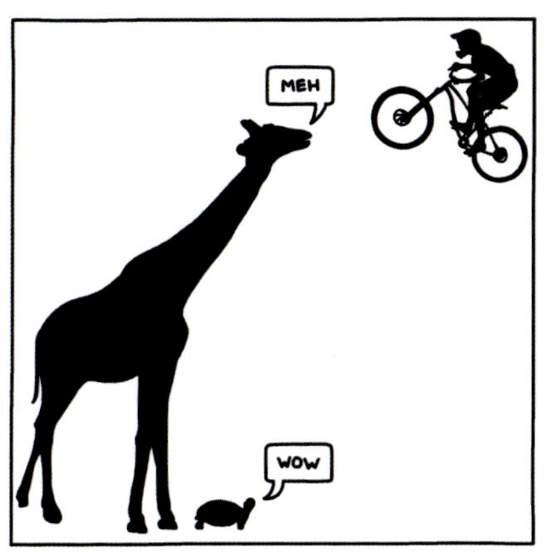

CHAPTER 6

Composition Basics

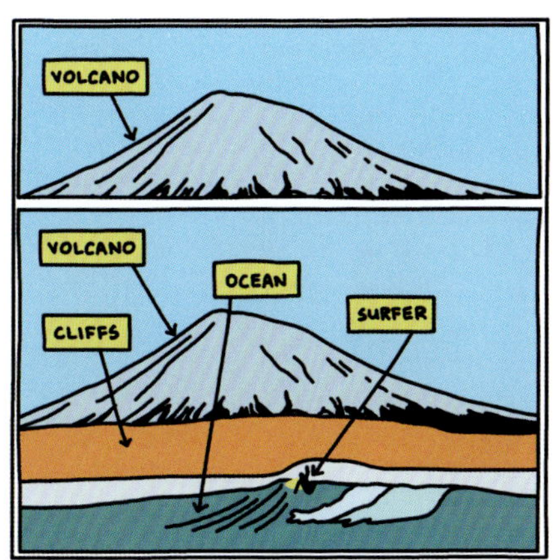

What is composition? Simply put, it's how we choose to frame our image. It is the idea of taking something that is one-dimensional and making it three-dimensional. Something I loved that I heard long ago was that painters consider a blank white canvas to be pure inspiration. An artist has this two-dimensional thing and they have to add everything to create depth and make something come alive within those four corners.

So, think like a painter. Consider ways you can add foreground and background—in a word, *depth*—to create layers. You do that by pulling the eye in, by using color theory: warm tones that push and pull, cool tones that recede. You're trying to use every tool within your kit, every tactic to make an image more dynamic, to make it easy on the eyes and fun to look at!

Flex your angles—make your move

A unique perspective is so important. The most basic angle you will ever find is the one where you're just standing there looking at a scene. So consider every perspective. To fully appreciate that scene, you might get down on the ground and look at things from the lowest angle possible. Then go as high as you can within the given parameters that you have.

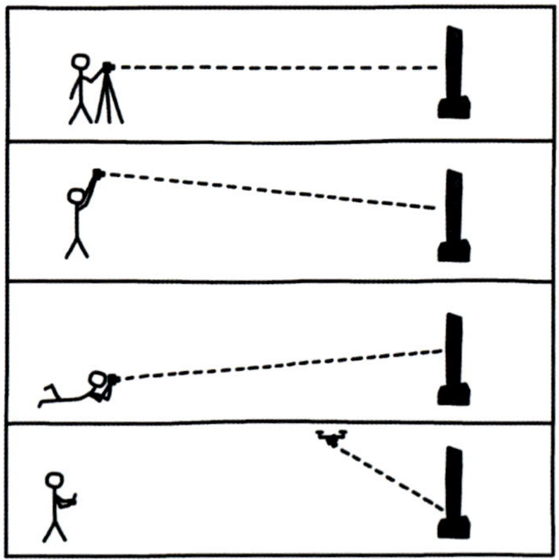

The *worst* thing you can do is start walking away from your scene and then realize there's an angle you didn't shoot and *that* was the best one. I try to give myself every opportunity to see my focal point, my subject, or whatever it may be, from every perspective that's offered to me within that space. Go wherever you can.

#NoFilter? No!

Filters definitely have a purpose, especially if you're trying to create a specific shot or a specific action. These are the types of filters I use the most:

- **Polarizer.** I like using a polarizer because it will cut through the clutter and reflection if there's dew or mist. It will enhance clouds and the blue sky if that's what I want. I use this filter a lot.

- **Graduated neutral density (GND) filter.** When placed in front of your lens, this filter allows less light to reach the camera's sensor. You can use it to darken the sky if you have a bright sky and a darker foreground. For example, let's consider a sunset: You have a sun ball. It's really bright and your foreground is beautiful, but it's kind of dark. A GND will even out the exposure. A normal neutral density (ND) filter will just darken the whole scene, which is great for video or if you want to shoot long exposures in the middle of the day.

- **Sunglasses.** It's good to try to use any available tools you have with you. If I'm using a point-and-shoot and don't have a polarizer but the scene really calls for it, I'll just place my sunglasses in front of my lens. Although the resulting image might turn out really warm and kind of funky, I can always change the white balance later. I've published images I've shot through a pair of sunglasses because that was the only polarizer I had.

- **Lens hood.** A lens hood is not a filter, I know, but to prevent sun flares I prefer using a lens hood versus a UV filter.

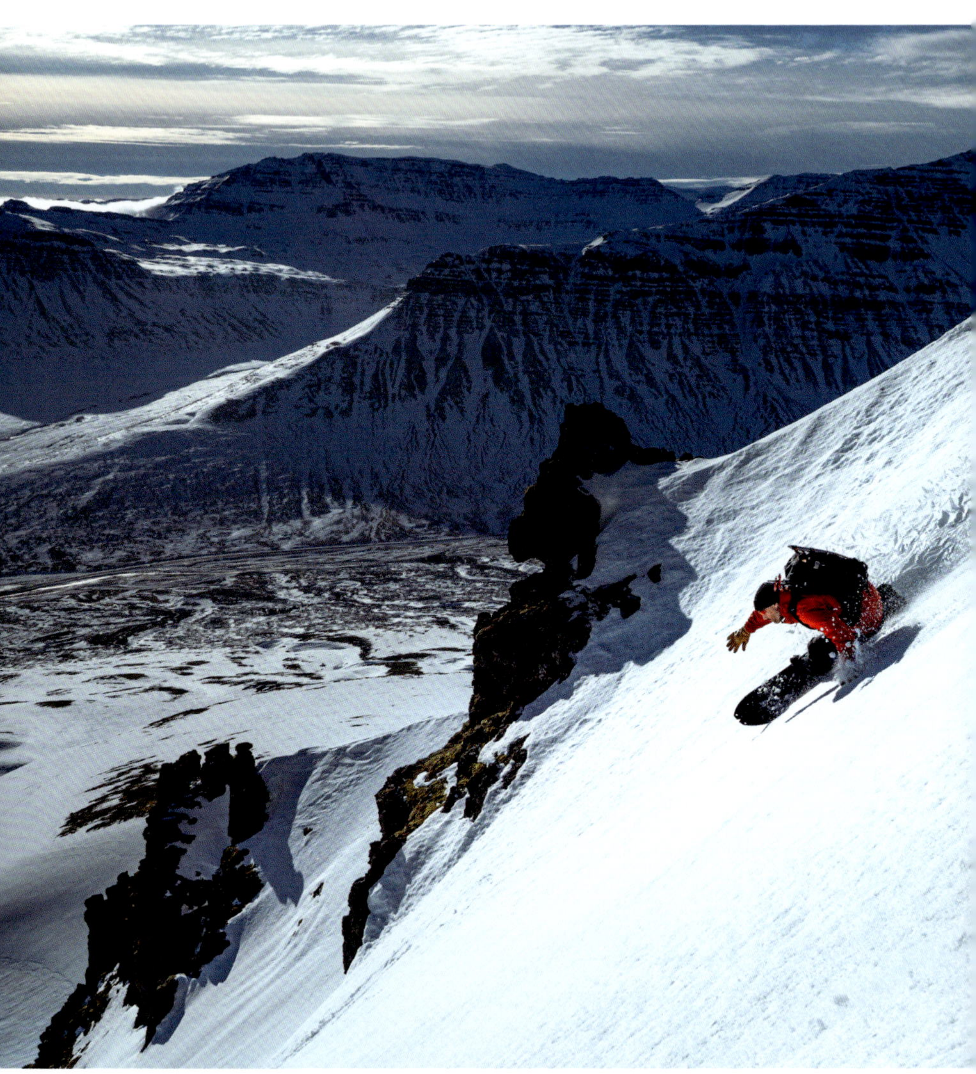

Burst onto the scene

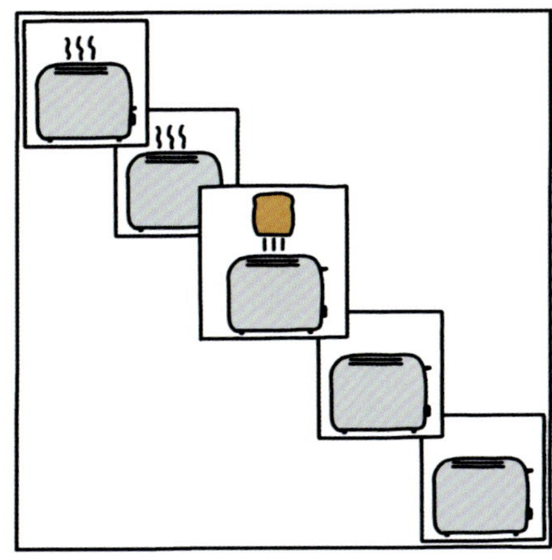

Burst mode is basically for when you're shooting action or for when something is moving toward you or past you, and you need to capture multiple frames. Burst mode is often unnecessary. With most scenarios you can just recognize the key moment and shoot it. But if the action is happening very fast—a surfer is doing a big air and there's one critical moment, or a snowboarder is gouging a big, fast powder turn, or a skater is doing a flip trick and their board is rotating—it's important to have the five, six, eight, nine, ten, or twenty frames per second that your camera allows. It's also critical to get comfortable using burst mode.

Back to the fore

Now, as far as positioning basics go, this is really where you start to take that secondary step. Getting low and getting high are useful, but they're not as critical as considering your foreground and background.

- **Foreground.** Add an element into the foreground to potentially create some depth. If the foreground is out of focus, it will obviously make what's *in* focus feel more important. If the foreground is in focus, it might lead your eye to another scene. The foreground is often meant to be complementary. If the foreground is a super bright color and your background is a muted pastel, that's going to do you a disservice because the brightness is

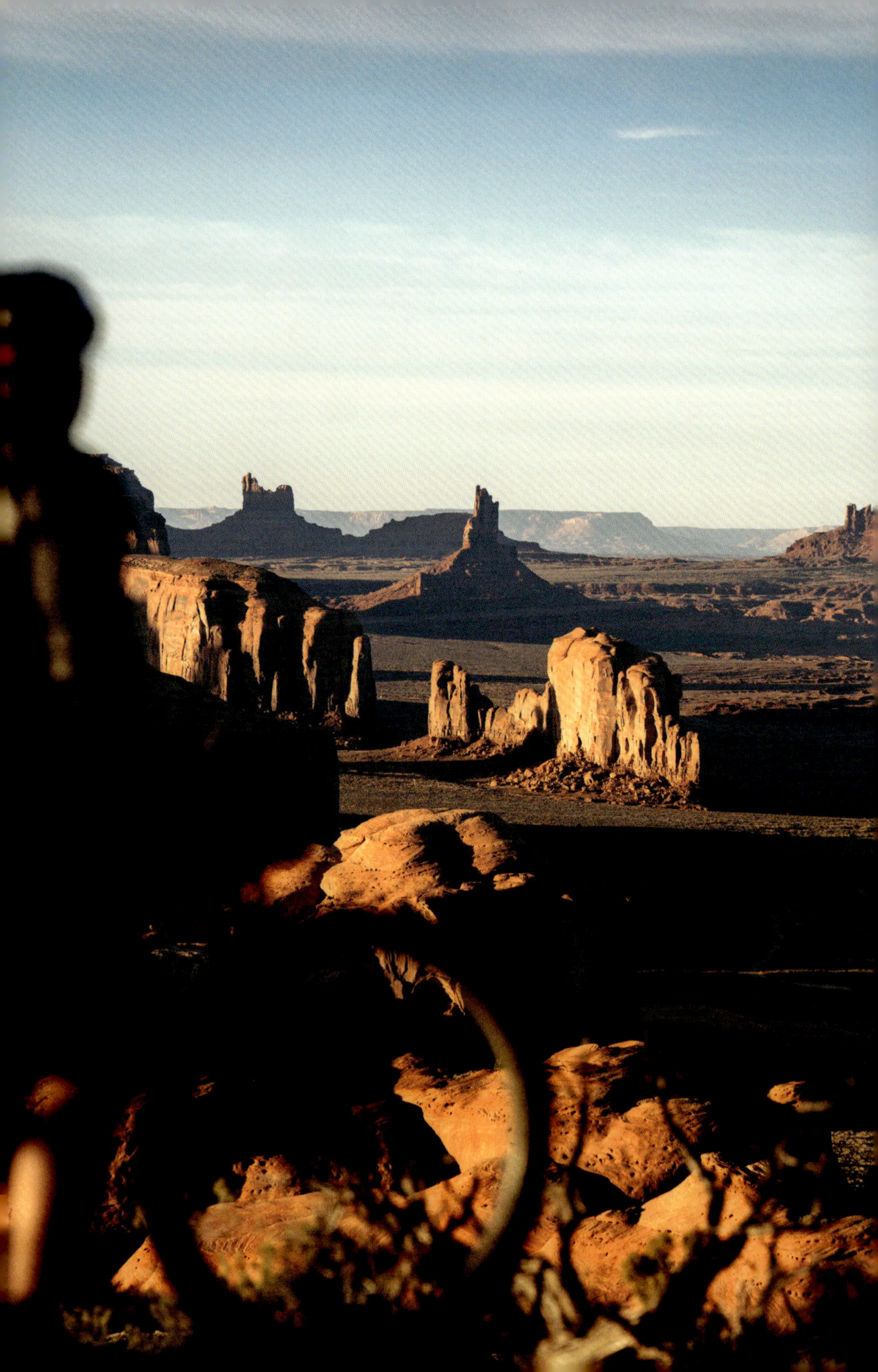

going to make your eye focus there. The same with background elements, right?

- **Background.** Maybe it's a surfer; maybe it's a landscape. Maybe you're framing things up so you have a key focal point behind your subject. Having something in the background is going to give your image some depth. Why? Because then the viewer is going to realize that this image has distance and context and scale to it: *Wow, look at that mountain waaaay out of focus in the distance!*

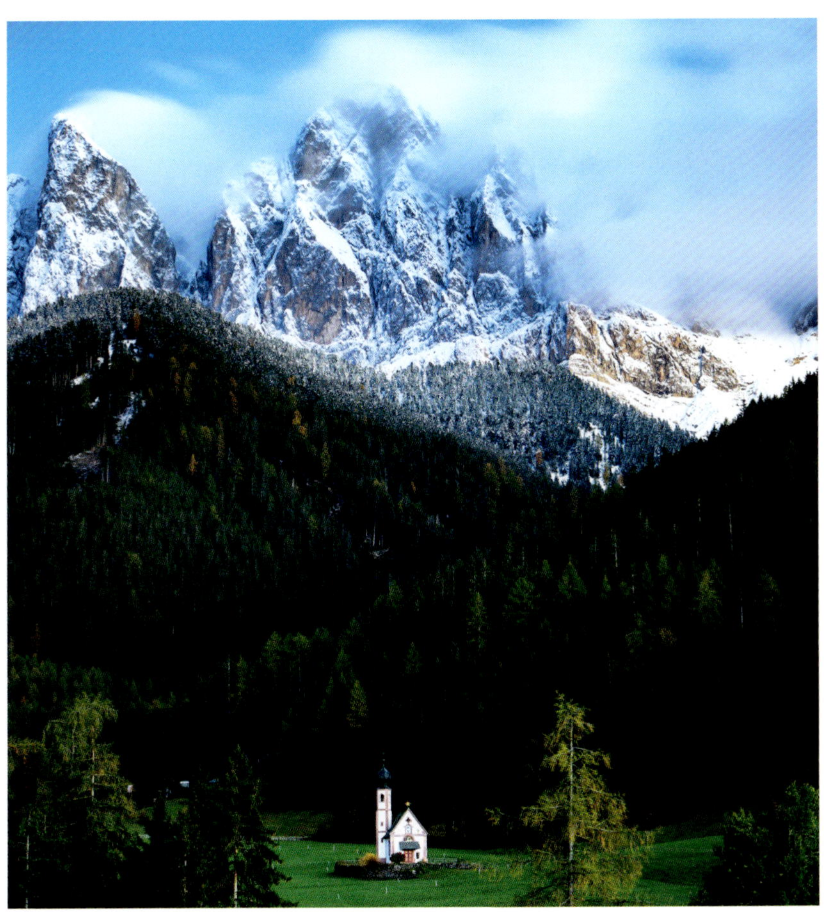

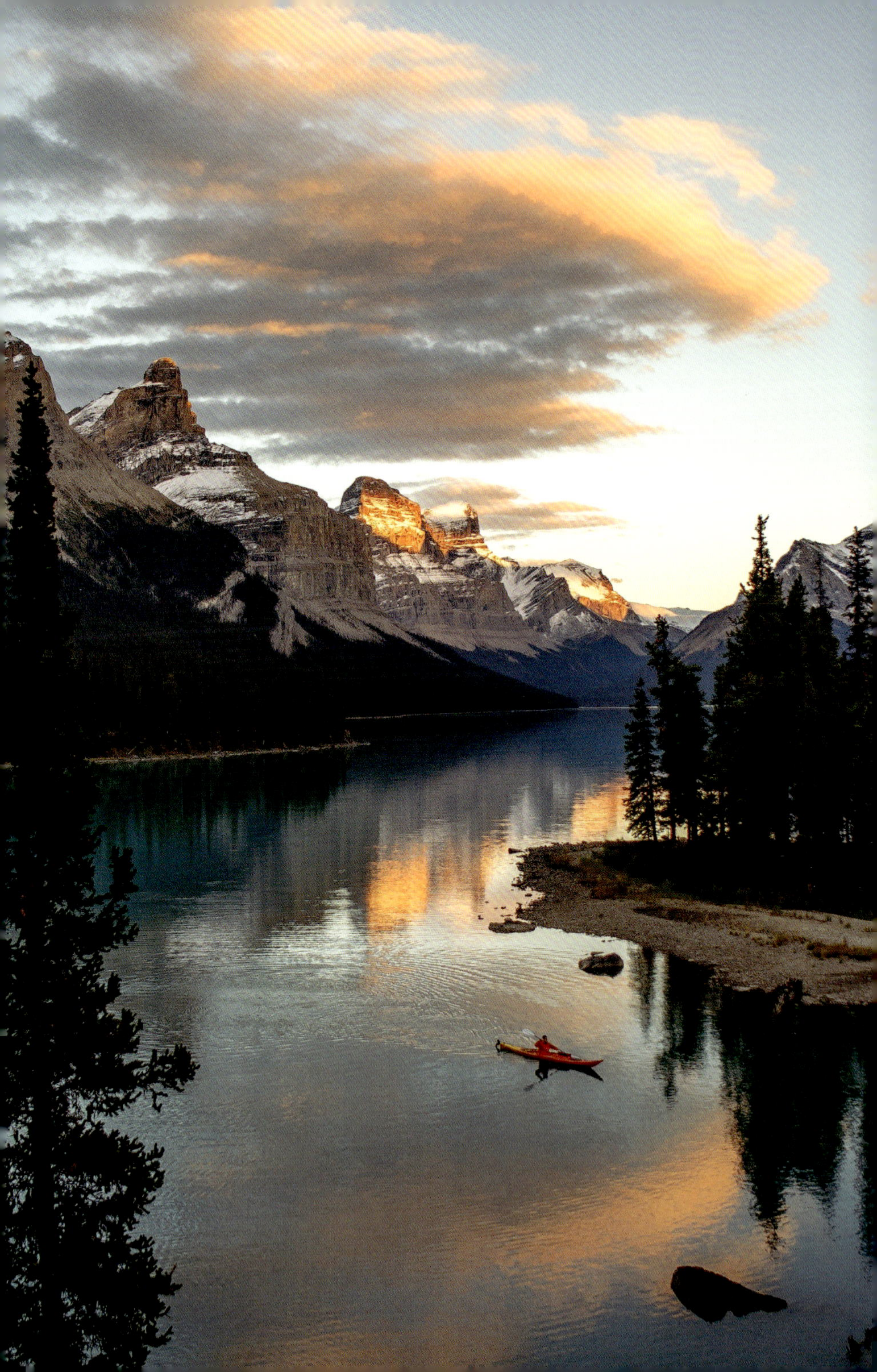

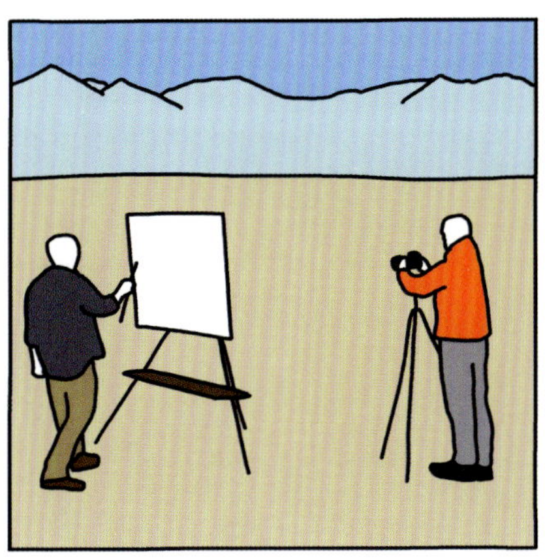

CHAPTER 7
Landscaping

The first rule of landscape photography: Never approach a subject or a place thinking that you're going to walk right up and make the best photo you've ever shot. Instead, ask yourself, *What do I want to see?*

A landscape artist has to create the depth on the canvas, create the distance of the mountains and the purple shadows and the orange sunset, all within the four borders of a painting. With a camera, you're doing the same thing. *You* decide what goes into your picture.

Soak in your surroundings

I tend to be a conscious observer—I enter a situation, evaluate what's happening, and think about the shots I want to make. I don't go into

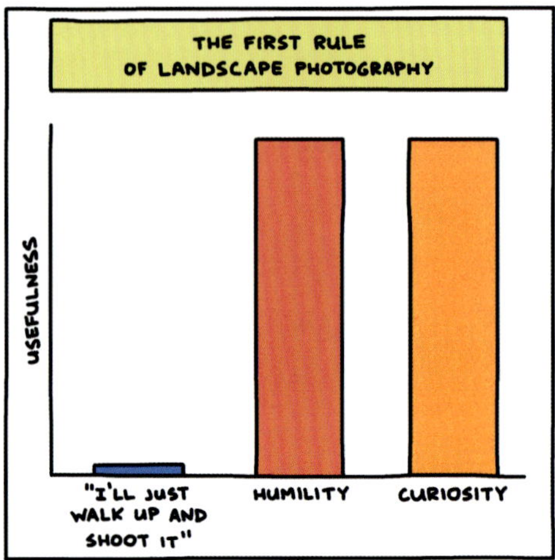

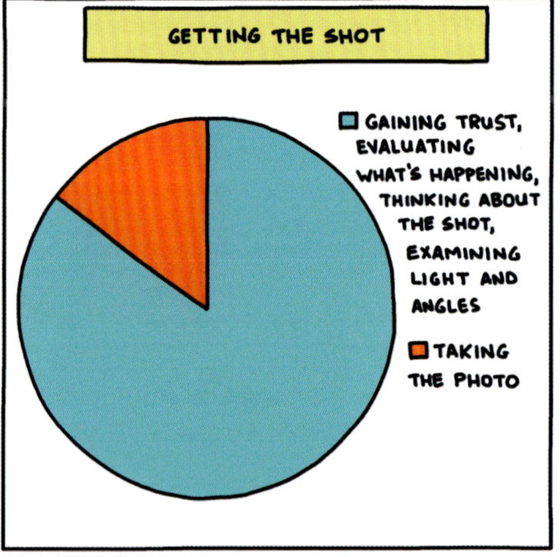

every moment saying "Yo, this is a full-blown photo shoot, and I'm Austin Powers, ready to do my fashion thing."

Instead, I'm trying to slow down. I'm wondering about how I can gain my subject's trust. I even ask that of a landscape: *How can I gain the landscape's trust? How can I give it the time it needs?* If I rush into something, my images tend to be subpar. If I allow enough time for the light to change, to just walk around and observe without my camera, I'm gaining a 360-degree perspective.

One of the biggest things when it comes to scouting or shooting a photo is time. If the sun sets at seven, am I going to show up at six, take my shot, and leave? Well, what I learned from Michael Fatali, a large-format landscape photographer I studied under, was to take my time: He'd allow two or three days to compose his images. I know that's not realistic for most people, but his mindset is important. While on location, he knew he only had two or three pieces of film because he was shooting large format, and he would go and scout around and get on his belly and look at that perspective and get up as high as he could. This is a critical thing to do when you're trying to compose an image, but when it comes to scouting and being there in

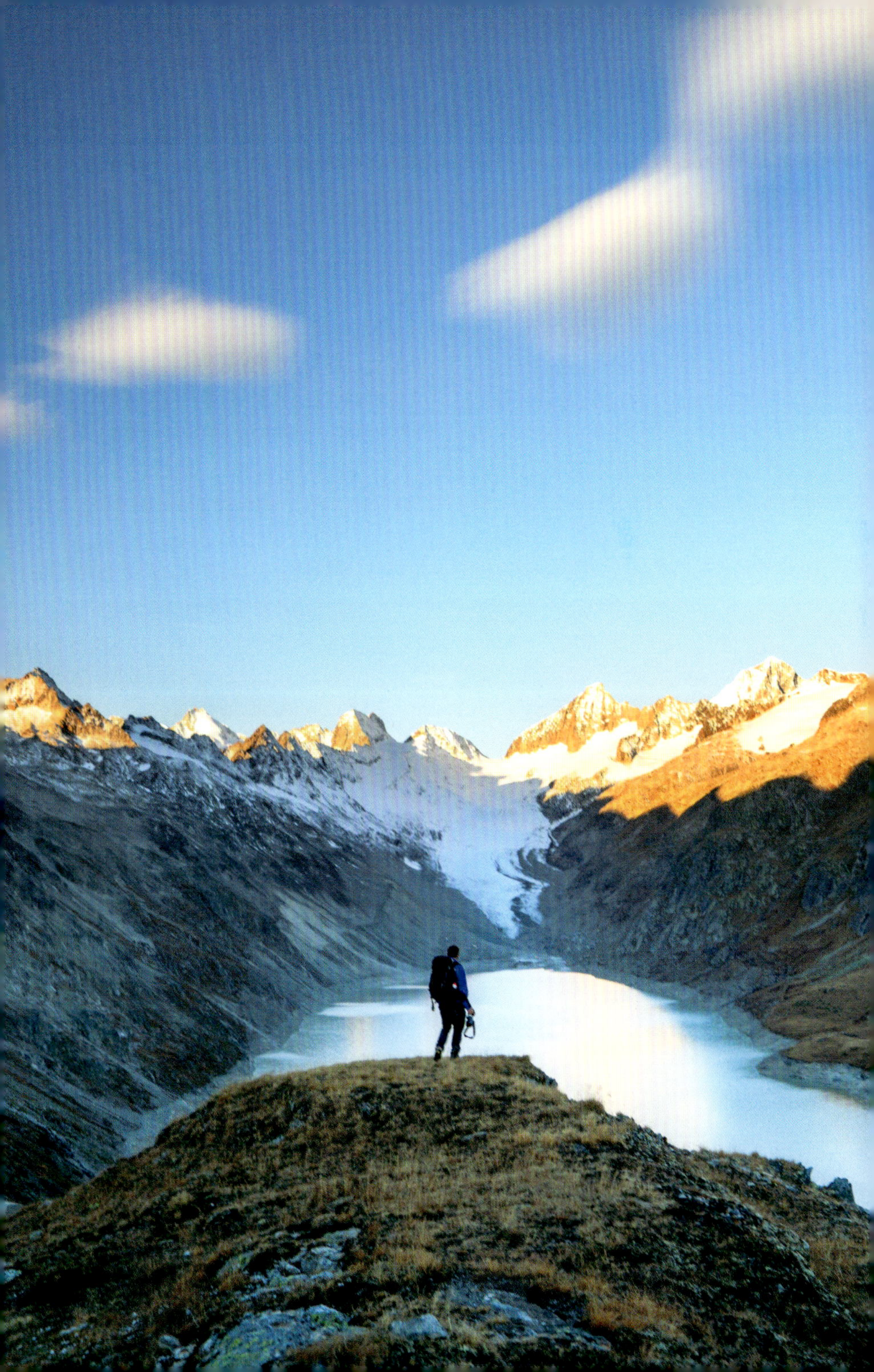

person, you want to think about how you can give these places all the attention that they—and you—need.

Get perspective

Let's say you're at Arches National Park in Utah, and you're going to shoot something that's been photographed a zillion times. Well, everyone else is going to stand 40 feet away and take a photo at eye level. How will you make your shot different? Even if you only have a couple of minutes, before you start taking photos, look around and frame your shot.

Fill the void

How can you make the uninteresting parts of a photo interesting? How can you fill that big blank foreground or background? Can you enhance that empty sky with some clouds or a tree limb? Can you fill that *blah* foreground with some rocks or bushes or a beach berm? Everything we do as photographers is to try to pull the viewer in. Sometimes the lowest angle might be the most interesting. What does a spider see? Or maybe the highest angle is the most interesting. What does a hawk see?

Laser in

But before we can do that, we must define an image's focal point, then find things that draw the viewer's eye to it. For example, a grove of trees can be a useful tool for framing a subject. Power lines can also be useful.

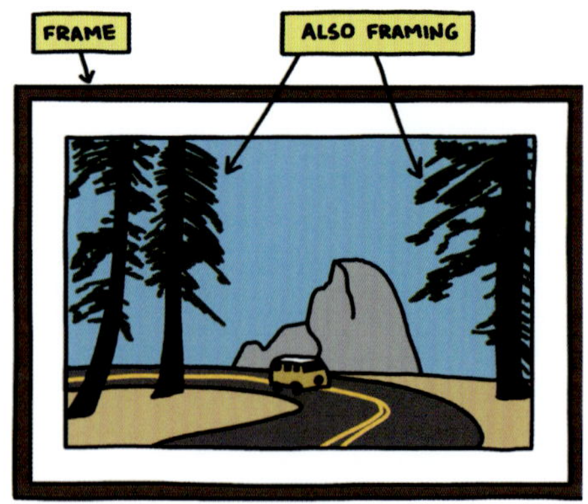

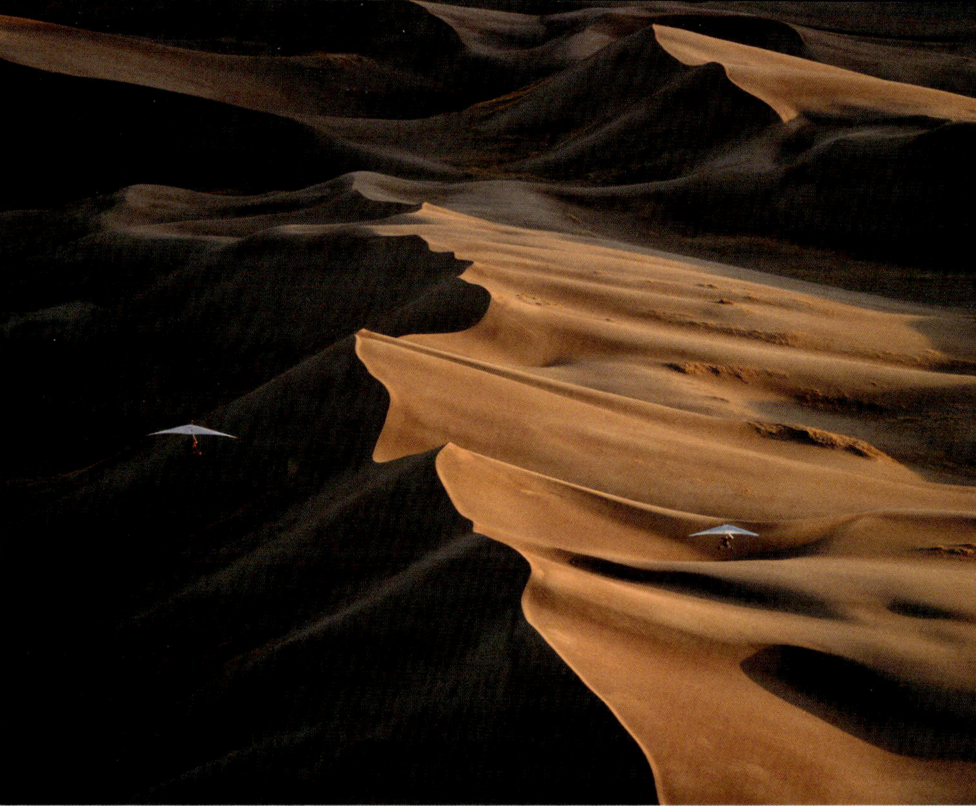

If there is nothing to draw the eye, this might be a sign to keep looking for something else. It can also be a good moment of clarity. Ask yourself, *Why am I even shooting this landscape? Is it to celebrate one single mountain peak, or is it to show the grandioseness of this river? Is it to focus on this flower or that perfect wave in the distance?*

Build your view

As I've said, identifying and finding layers is crucial. But this is not about simply having three layers (a.k.a. the rule of thirds). This is about having as many layers as you can because layers equal depth. If you were to think about it as an equation, more layers = more depth = more three-dimensionality. This is what makes a photo stand out, what makes it pop.

Go wide

I love shooting wide. This is when you're using a 35mm or "wider" lens. In landscape photography, you might want a 16mm or a 20mm lens so you can focus on that flower or on that little river or waterfall in the foreground and then have some beautiful mountain peak in the background.

A 16–35mm is my favorite lens because that's the way I see the world. When you're shooting wide, it's easy to find layers. You often have a foreground immediately because you have the width of a wide angle. And then you have your background farther away. That's what a wide-angle lens does for you. Shooting compressed is a little harder.

(Com)press your luck

Shooting compressed is more challenging because you're cramming all your subject matter into more of a flat frame. You're "flattening" the subject. So when shooting landscapes, it's nice to decide what will look good compressed. You might ask yourself, *How can I push this wave into this cliff face to make the wave stand out more? How can I push this beautiful grove of trees with their fall colors into this gorgeous mountain in the background?*

Shooting with a 70–200mm lens (or anything above a 50mm, really) is often where you start to get into telephoto territory. You start to compress and you can make the layers very contrasty. You just need to find that really important color that's going to work with the others in the frame.

Oftentimes with compression, you might be working with light and shadows. You might have a shadowy background with a light foreground, and that's going to create incredible depth because it will make the contrast go bonkers. That's what you're hoping for.

Keep time on your side

I always say that if you want to make your photos better, just shoot 20 minutes at sunrise and 20 minutes at sunset every day. I guarantee you'll create better images. Those are the times of day that resonate with us visually—the warm tones and the cool tones. They push and they pull.

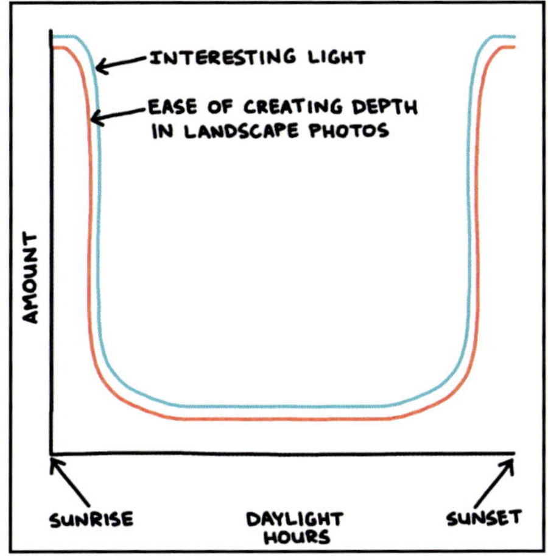

One of the key things I learned in my junior college art class was that if you want your mountains or your foreground to stand out or push away because you want to create that depth in a canvas, you need to work with colors. It can't all be orange. It's got to be different tones of cool to warm, warm to cool, pushing and pulling.

That's why finding those early mornings and those late afternoons is crucial. You want to shoot toward that more interesting light.

If midday is what you have to work with, it makes your life harder! It's difficult to create interesting subjects when the light is flat, which is what happens when the light is right overhead.

So think about the light that's available during various times of your day. Use it as a tool to help you create more contrast. Whether it's shooting into the sun or shooting sidelit, oftentimes that's going to make a more interesting frame than if you're shooting pure frontlit, where everything is perfectly illuminated and there are no shadows or contrast.

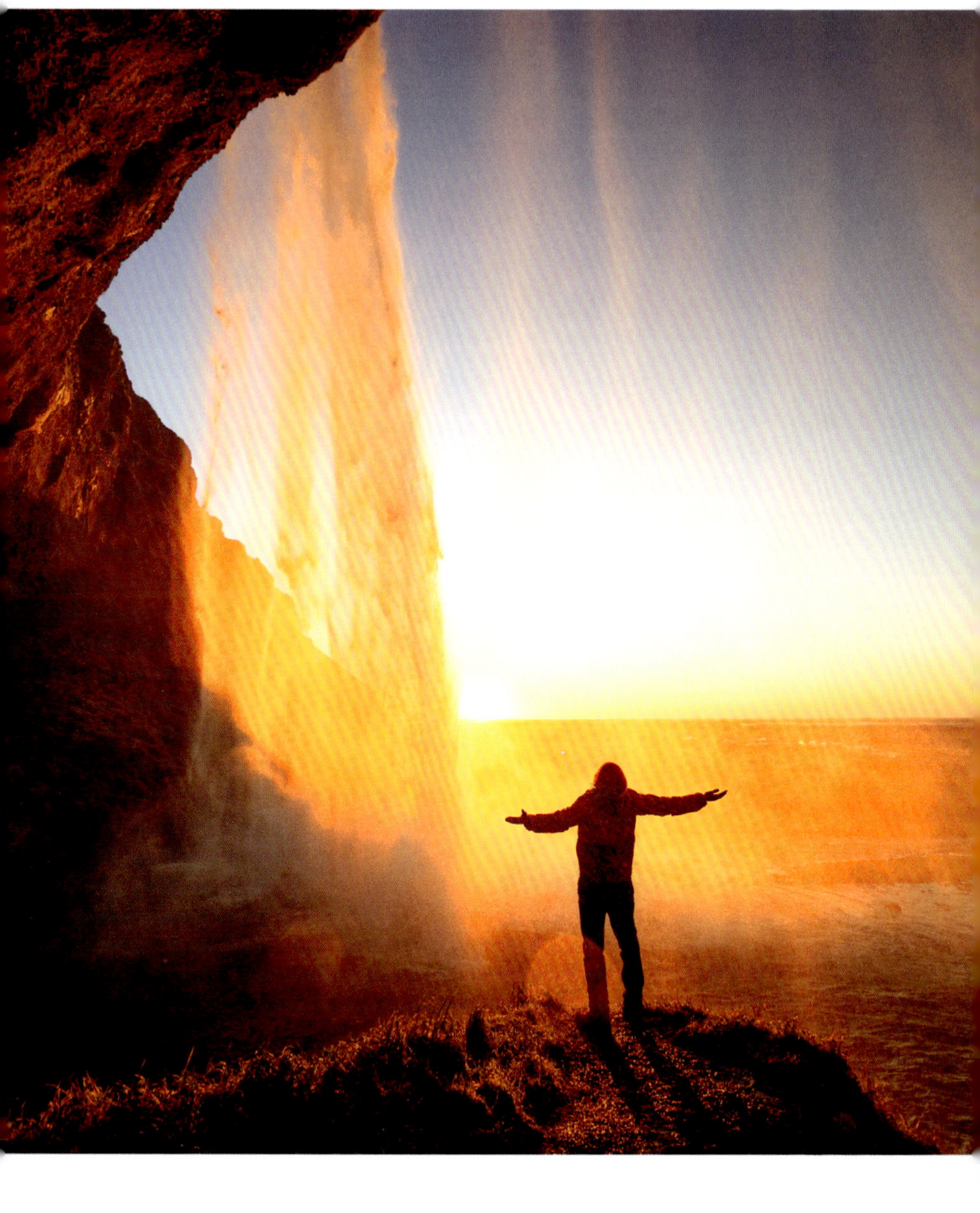

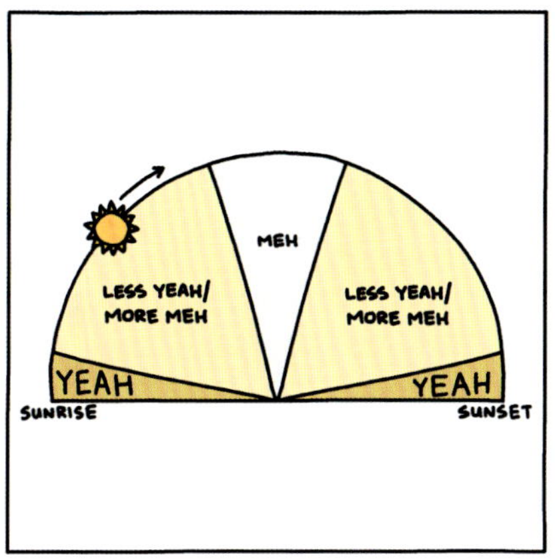

CHAPTER 8
Golden Hour

Like the sunrise and sunset, something happens every day: People are out holding their phones up to the sky because they're inspired by—guess what?—the epicness of golden hour. As I mentioned in the last chapter, these are the times of day most interesting to most of us. There is something visually pleasing about the contrast created in the subdued warmth of light. Let's pay attention to what it is we like about it and how we can translate those things into a frame. Then we'll discuss other considerations for shooting during golden hour.

Silhouettes

Silhouettes are common in photography because you can frame a subject that has anonymity. The lack of information about the subject makes a silhouette beautiful because the viewer can insert themselves into that photo.

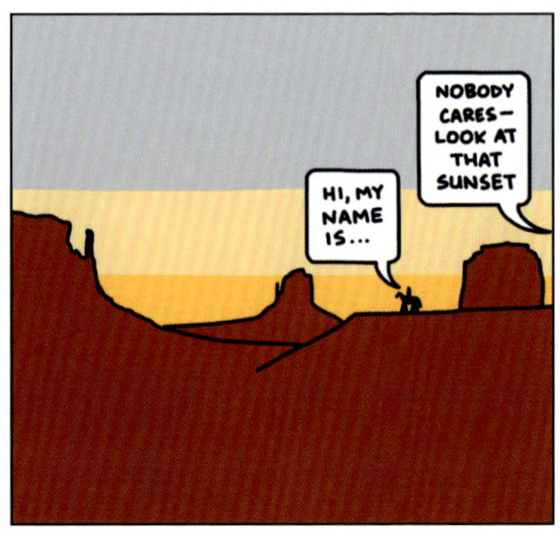

Guess what the viewer doesn't see? They don't know the color of the subject's skin, and often they don't know the gender. They don't know what clothes the subject is wearing. And they don't care! All of this stuff is irrelevant because they can't see it. This gives the photo timelessness.

Another reason silhouettes are so powerful is that they often simplify the subject down to a very genuine and easy palette, particularly with black-and-white photography. When we shoot frontlit stuff, there are more details to process visually, and the photo gets busier and more complex. A silhouette can be very simple, and simplicity is what we want.

Sun flare

UNPROTECTED HUMAN EYEBALL LOOKING DIRECTLY AT THE SUN	CAMERA LOOKING DIRECTLY AT THE SUN
CAN PRODUCE PERMANENT DAMAGE IN LESS THAN ONE MINUTE	CAN PRODUCE SOME REALLY NICE PHOTOS

Sun flare can be beautiful. It can make a sky that's relatively uninteresting *interesting*. To capture sun flare, you would typically shoot at f/16 or higher. Or you can shoot wide. The wider the angle, the easier it is to shoot sun flare, and the lower the sun gets, the greater are your chances of capturing something great.

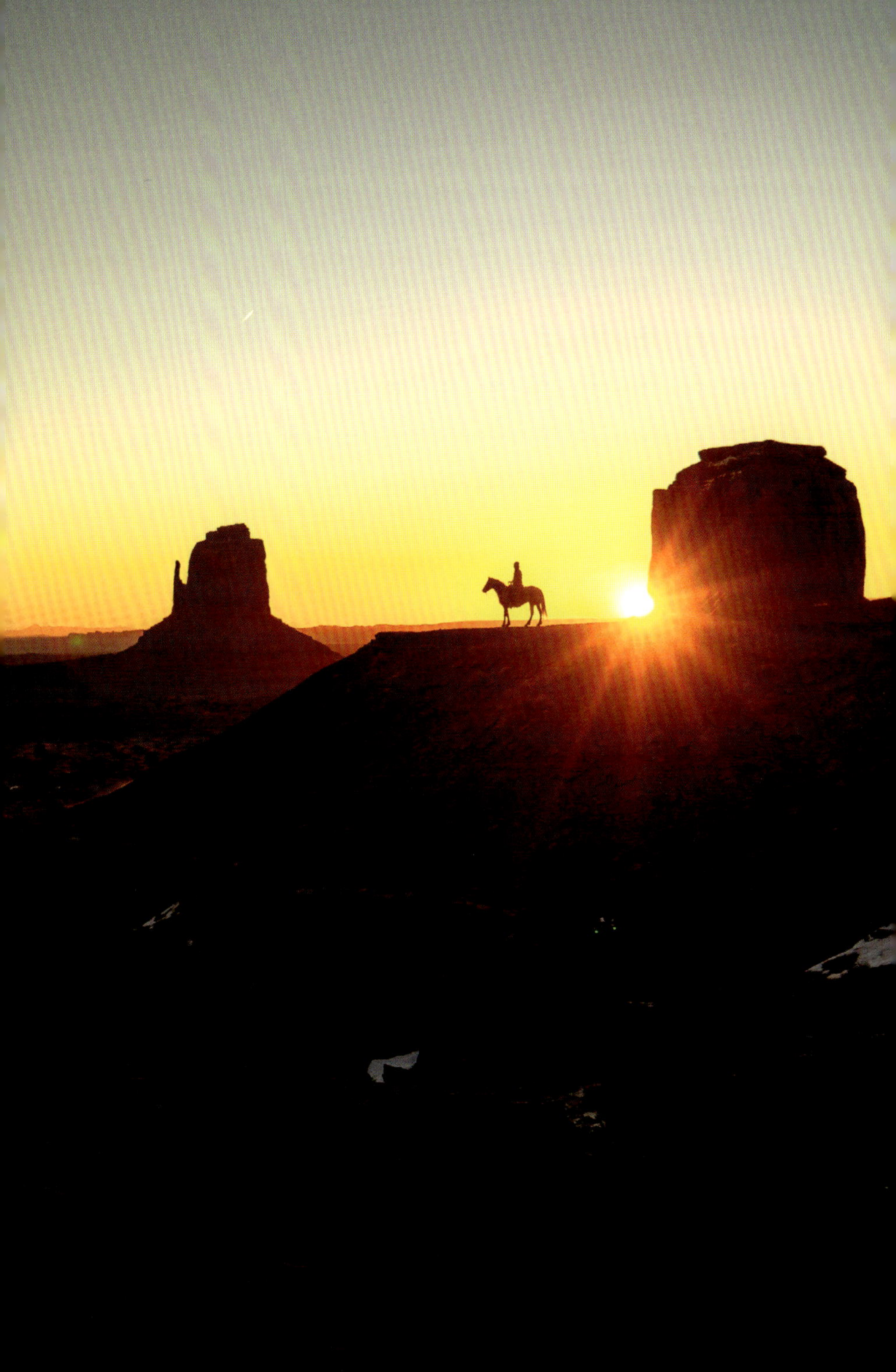

Shooting into the sun and playing with it as it crests around a pier or through leaves or through grass or over the ocean . . . that's my favorite thing to do. I'm almost always trying to shoot into the sun or make a sidelit image—something that creates more contrast. As we try to create more contrast, what we're really looking for are photos that are *timeless*.

Filters

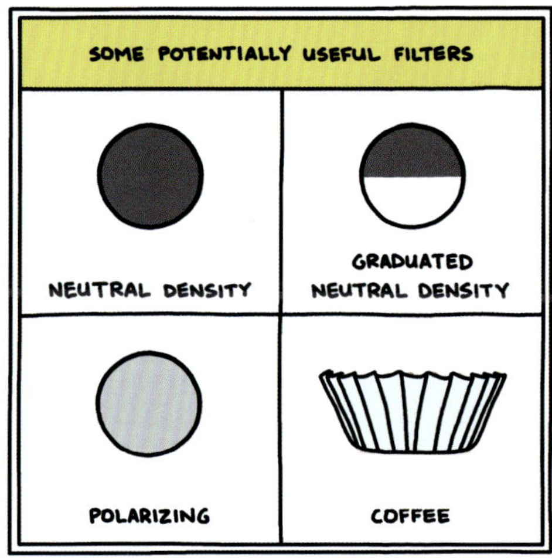

Filters can be quite helpful during golden hour. Imagine a beach scene. You have this beautiful cliff, and the sun is behind it, but the cliff is too dark and you can't see any of its textures. That's when you might use a graduated neutral density (GND) filter, which is basically dark at the top and light at the bottom. It's not really used to make something look perfectly frontlit, but it can equalize the exposure a bit so your shadows aren't totally black.

A neutral density (ND) filter is very different from a GND filter. You could use a neutral density filter if you wanted to shoot afternoon light or even midday light when it's super harsh and bright outside but you want to capture a long exposure of flowing water or a long exposure of the sky. That image is not going to be light on top and dark on the bottom—it's going to look dark all the way through.

What else? For me, using a polarizer is key. I use one all the time. A polarizer can at times make a wide-angle photo slightly obscured with darkened corners, so you have to be careful how and when you use

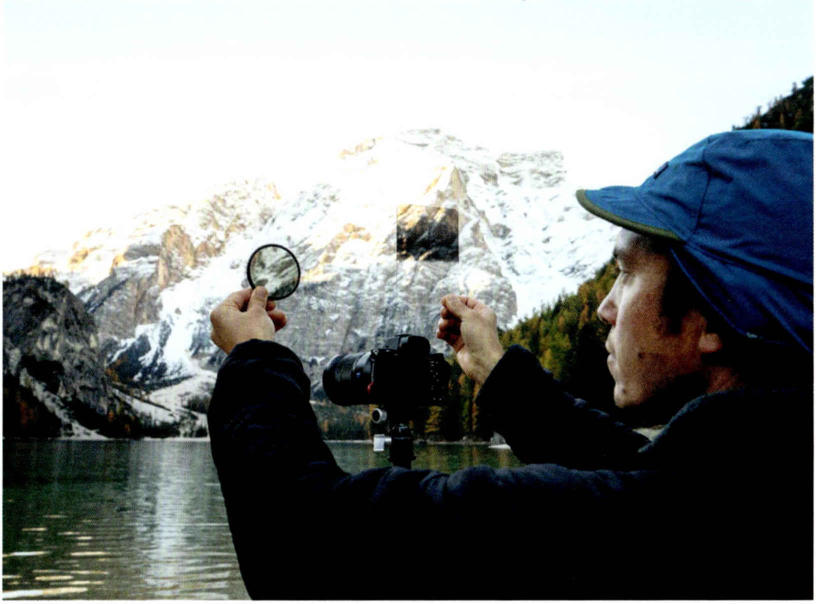

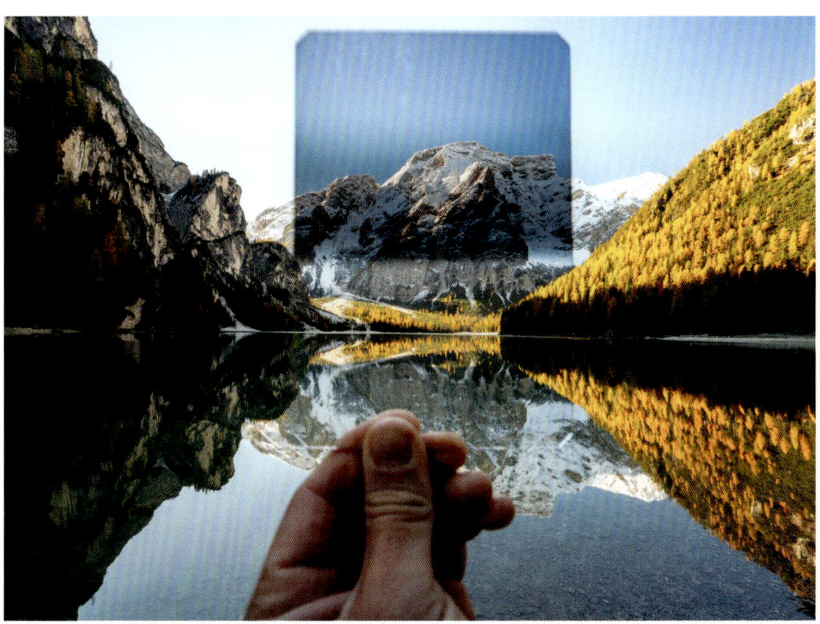

it. I find that there's a window in the afternoon—later afternoon and in sidelit scenes—that's really great, and a polarizer will tease out the sky and make the clouds pop. It'll also cut reflection. It's maybe one of the most useful filters I have. In fact, the polarizing filter is something that I always keep on my camera, and I use it probably 90 percent of the time unless it's evening, it's totally dark out, or I'm trying to shoot a long exposure.

Camera settings

EXACT RECIPE FOR A HAPPY, FULFILLING LIFE	EXACT RECIPE FOR CAMERA SETTINGS
DIFFERENT FOR EVERYONE (AND CAN CHANGE THROUGHOUT LIFE)	DIFFERENT FOR EVERYONE (AND CAN CHANGE THROUGHOUT LIFE)

During golden hour, you can strive for a shallow depth of field, but oftentimes it's challenging because as you shoot into the sun, both your f-stop and your shutter speed are going to be high. This is when having an ND or a GND filter can be really nice, as it will allow you to darken either the entire scene; or, in the case of a GND, the sky, allowing for an even exposure of the sky and foreground. If you want a shallow depth of field, you need to cut the exposure down *a lot*. This is where grads like the ND65 can be helpful, allowing you to diminish the light coming in and opening up your aperture to compensate. This gives you a shallow depth of field perspective, if that is what you are after creatively.

With these settings, I'm usually bumping my shutter speed up quite high and trying to decide what I want my f-stop to be, depending on what the subject matter is. *Do I need to set the subject matter apart from the backdrop?* Then I would need a shallower depth of field and a higher shutter speed. Or maybe it's the opposite: I want my subject to be a part of the backdrop, meaning that it's also in focus in addition to the backdrop. In that case, I might use a higher f-stop.

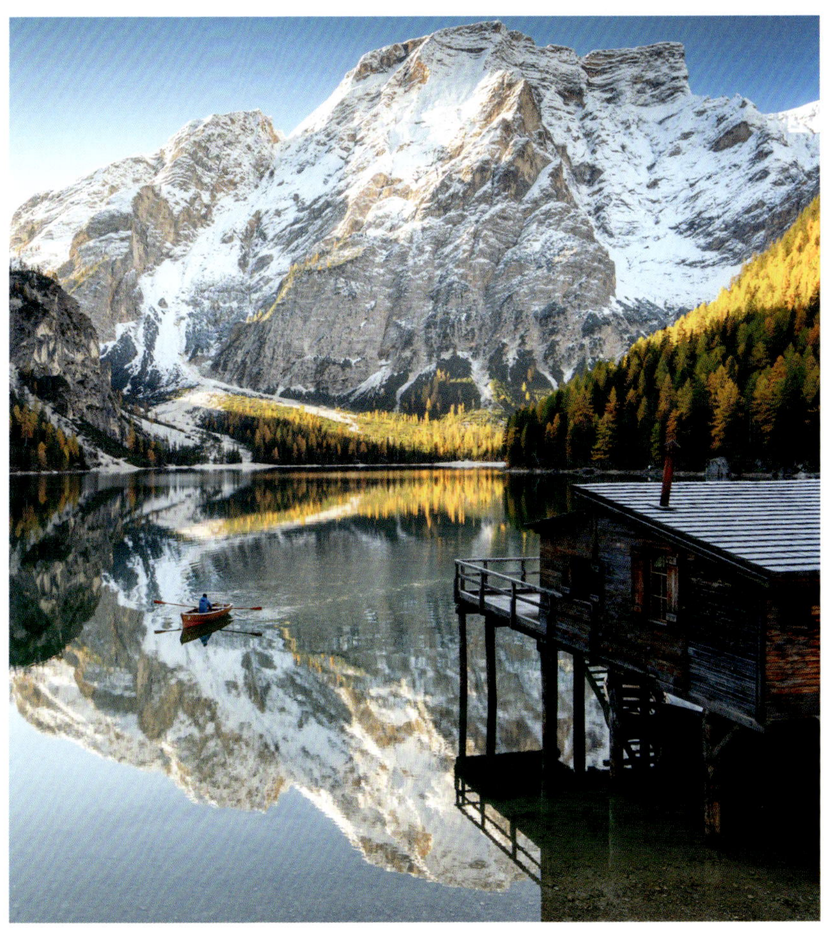

Remember: This is all personal preference. Settings are challenging. People want to talk about settings like there's a strict recipe for success when really every setting that you choose *is* a choice. It can be different for everyone. You're trying to do something that is meant to have a look. It's critical that you first know how to *use* your camera.

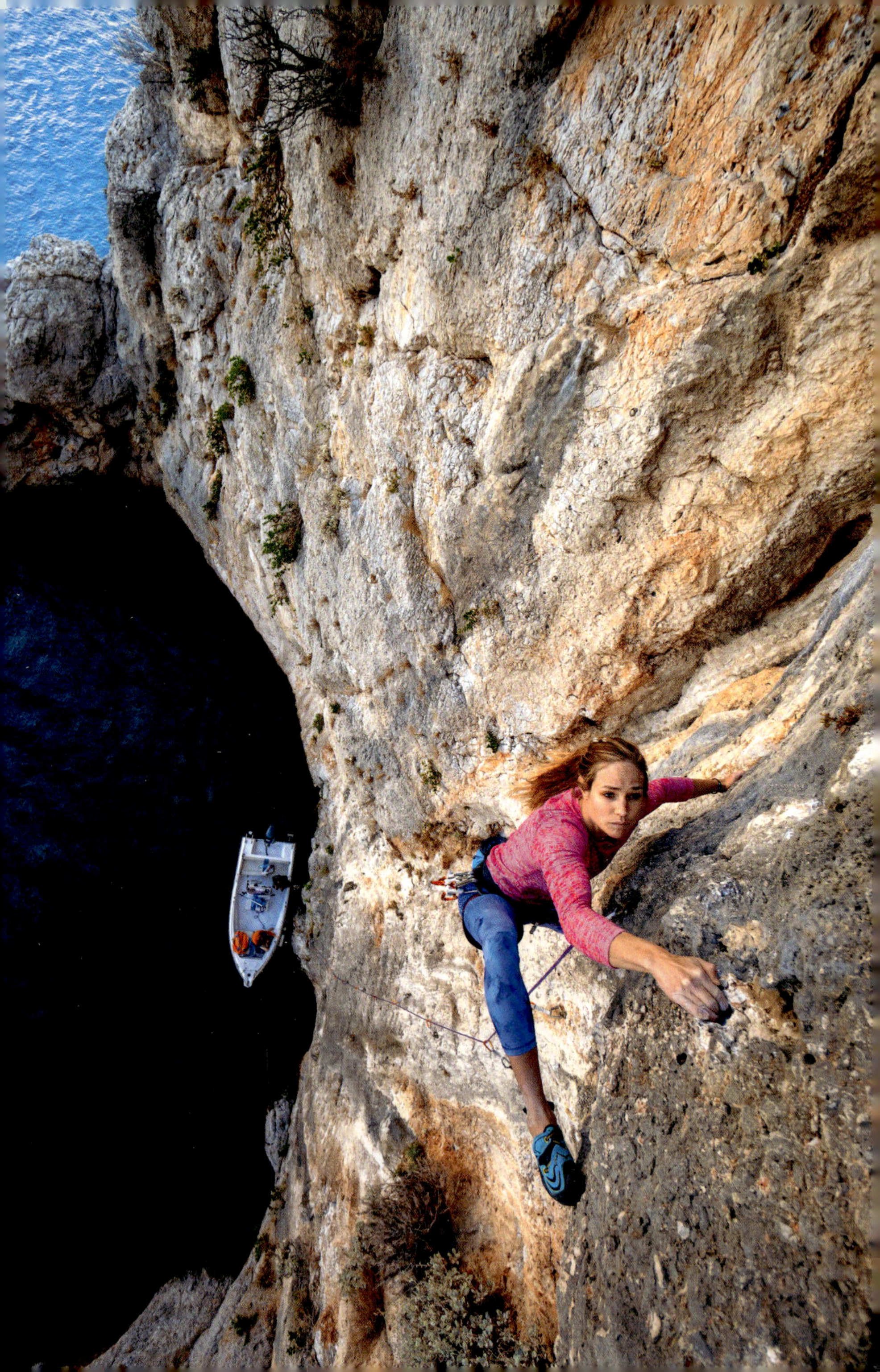

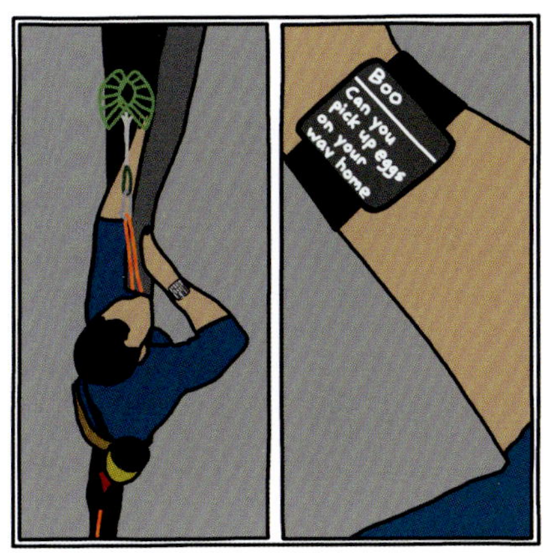

CHAPTER 9

Action Sports

This is a funny subject because there's a lot to be said about the way in which we shoot sports.

The best lens types for action are typically super-wide and telephoto lenses. This is the one area of photography in which these fringe lenses tend to work best. I find that 35mm, 50mm, and 70mm are not my lenses of choice for sports photography. If you're shooting surfing, you're usually in the water with a wide-angle or you're using a long lens on the beach. Most sports are like that. Or you're shooting with a zoom lens when things are happening rapidly, like in basketball where you need to be able to zoom in and out as the players go up and down the court. If you're shooting with a prime lens, you're usually premeditating the shot you want to get and nailing that shot.

Angles

Finding unique angles is crucial. What are you trying to show? Is it the action itself? Then you might want a tight shot. Do you want to show where the action is taking place? Then a pulled-back image might be best.

Shutter speed

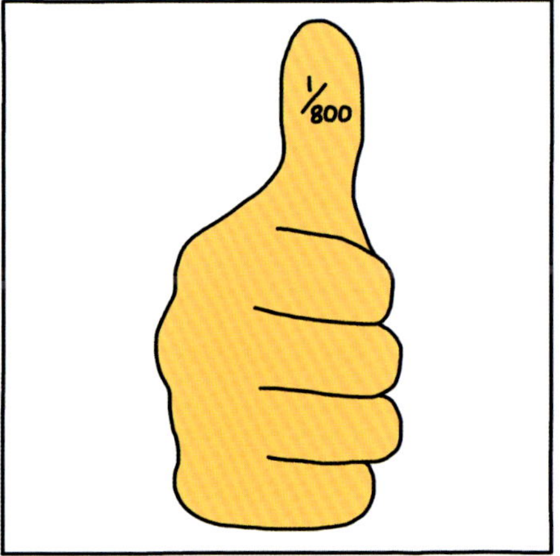

To capture the right image, the important thing is to make your life easier by shooting at a higher shutter speed (unless the desired effect is a speed blur). Typically, if you're trying to capture a runner on a track or a surfer on a wave, for example, you need 1/800 of a second or higher. That's a good rule of thumb. But if you're shooting an F1 racer and want a tack-sharp image of the car, that's going to require something faster than 1/800 of a second because otherwise you're still going to get blur.

So it depends on the look you're after. Do you want a little blur? Or do you want it to be tack-sharp through and through? Are you looking for a stylized image?

Focus

One thing folks seem to struggle with is focusing. Focusing is so tough. Over time, cameras have obviously improved a lot, and that's excellent—we're all very lucky to have cameras that can

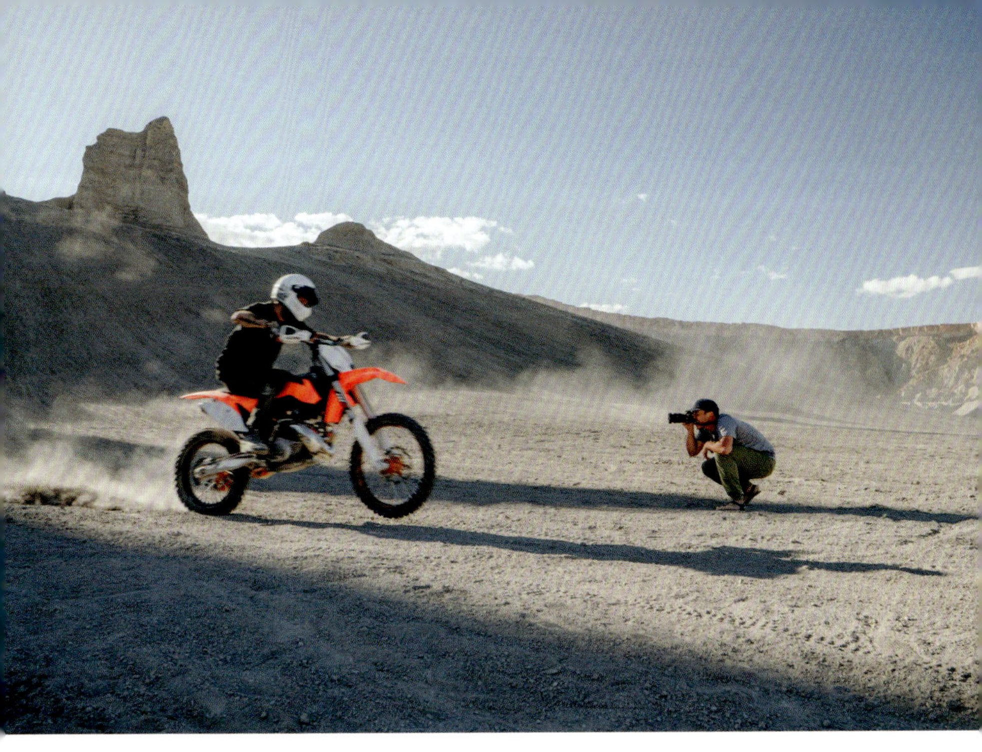

completely autofocus and prefocus and everything else. But the goal here is not to make your camera do too much of the work and oversimplify the process. If you're shooting a subject moving across a wave or around a racetrack and they're not getting any closer to you—which means that the focal length should be on one plane of view—you can simply shoot single-button autofocus, not continuous, because where we focus and how we frame an image are two different things.

If you want guaranteed bad images, set your focus in the center of your frame and shoot in the center all the time. I never do that because I often want my subject somewhere else. So typically I'm shooting single-button, and what I'm doing is something called prefocusing, which means that I'm anticipating where in the frame my subject will be—where they will end up.

Let's say you're shooting a surfer. You know they're going to be pumping down the line and doing the action, the move, whatever.

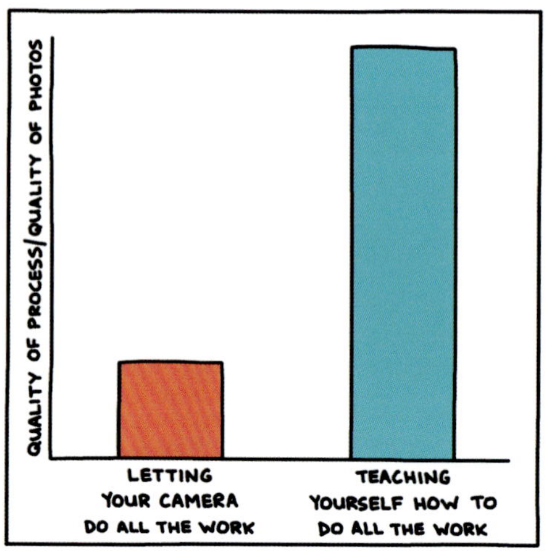

Or maybe your kid is on a bike soaring over a jump. What is your key frame going to be? Now we're getting into the logistics of composition—how do we *make* an image, not just *take* an image?

I'm not just shooting everything and hoping to capture something good. I'm prefocusing where I know my subject will occupy the exact desired spot in my viewfinder. Now, this prefocusing only really works when the subject is moving laterally, not toward you. If a subject is moving toward you, like a motorcyclist roaring down a track, and you're shooting down the barrel directly at that person, that's when you would need to have continuous autofocus, or an automatic autofocus where your camera is prefocusing on the subject and it knows where that subject is going. Some cameras do that, some cameras don't. Does yours?

Another thing to consider is that the closer the action, the higher the shutter speed needs to be, because as the subject gets closer to you, it's moving faster. In fact, I've shot many surfing photos where the surfer was pretty far away at 1/500 of a second. In that situation, I don't need to always be in the 1/800 range because

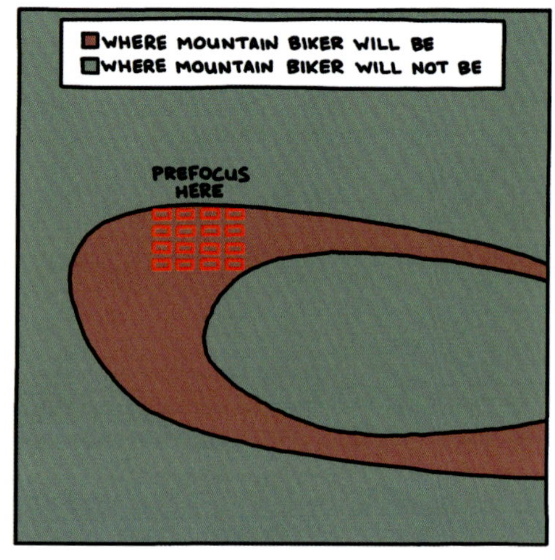

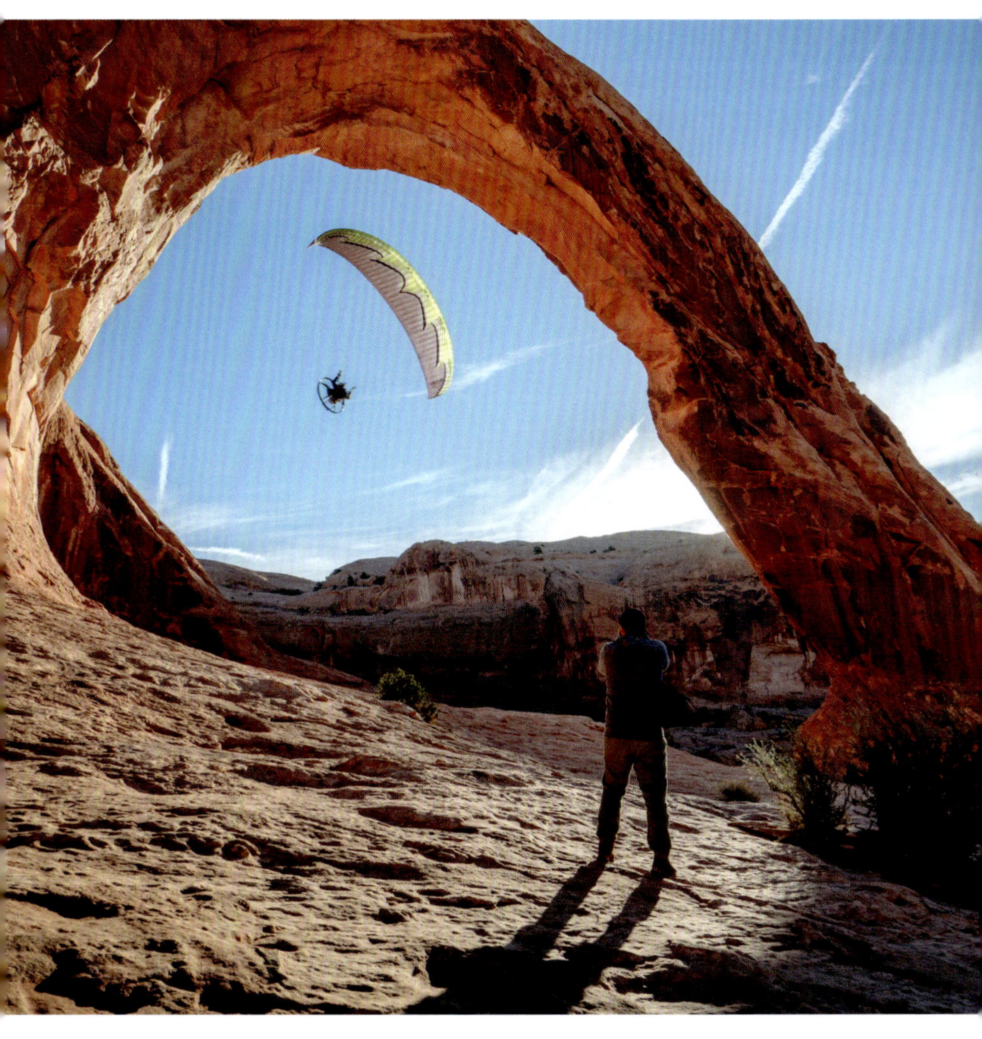

the subject is in the distance and they're not moving very fast, especially if they're longboarding.

If you use a fish-eye lens to shoot something that is very close to you and not moving that quickly, it'll look blurry every time. So that's where you need to bump your shutter speed way up to 1/1600 of a second.

Lenses

A telephoto lens—a 70–200mm, 300mm, 400mm, 500mm, 600mm—is great for compressing a shot. There are two ways to think about this. There's the tight action shot in which you're really getting the details—the leg movement, the muscles, whatever it is. Or you're really far away and you're compressing that beautiful Tahitian mountain backdrop with the surfer, or the palm trees with the wave, or a beautiful city

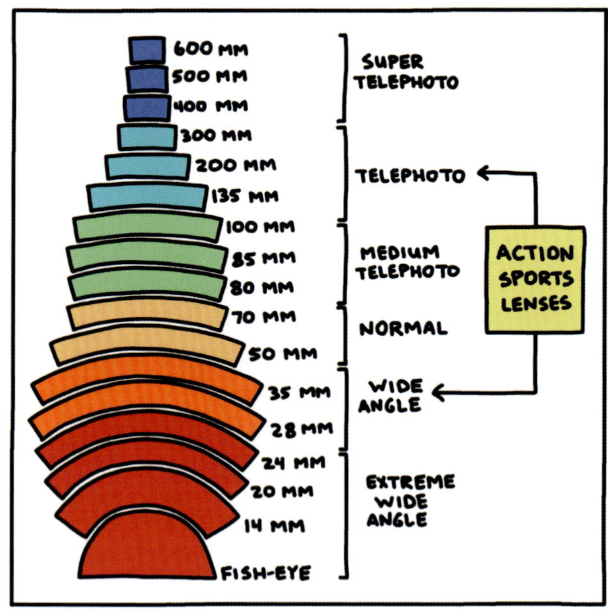

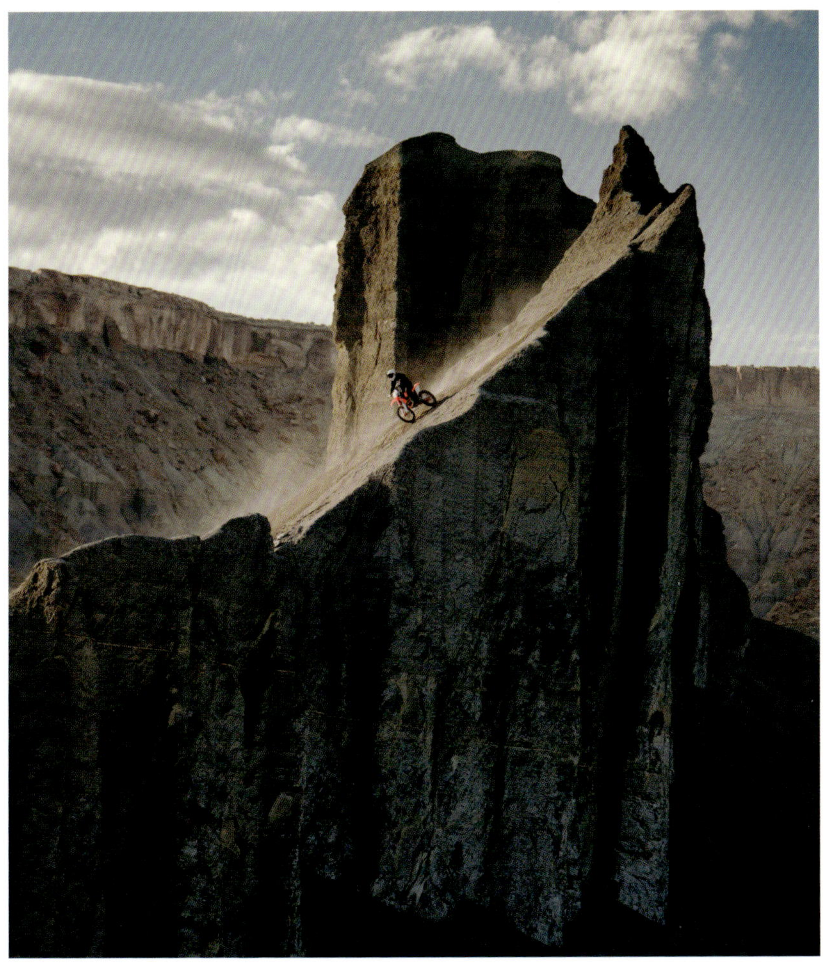

skyline with a motocross track below it. You're using the telephoto lens to compress the scene and pull it all together.

A telephoto lens can be a great tool for telling a story. You often feel removed from the experience because you're farther away, whereas a wide-angle lens will make you feel more a part of it. The result will feel more intimate and action-packed.

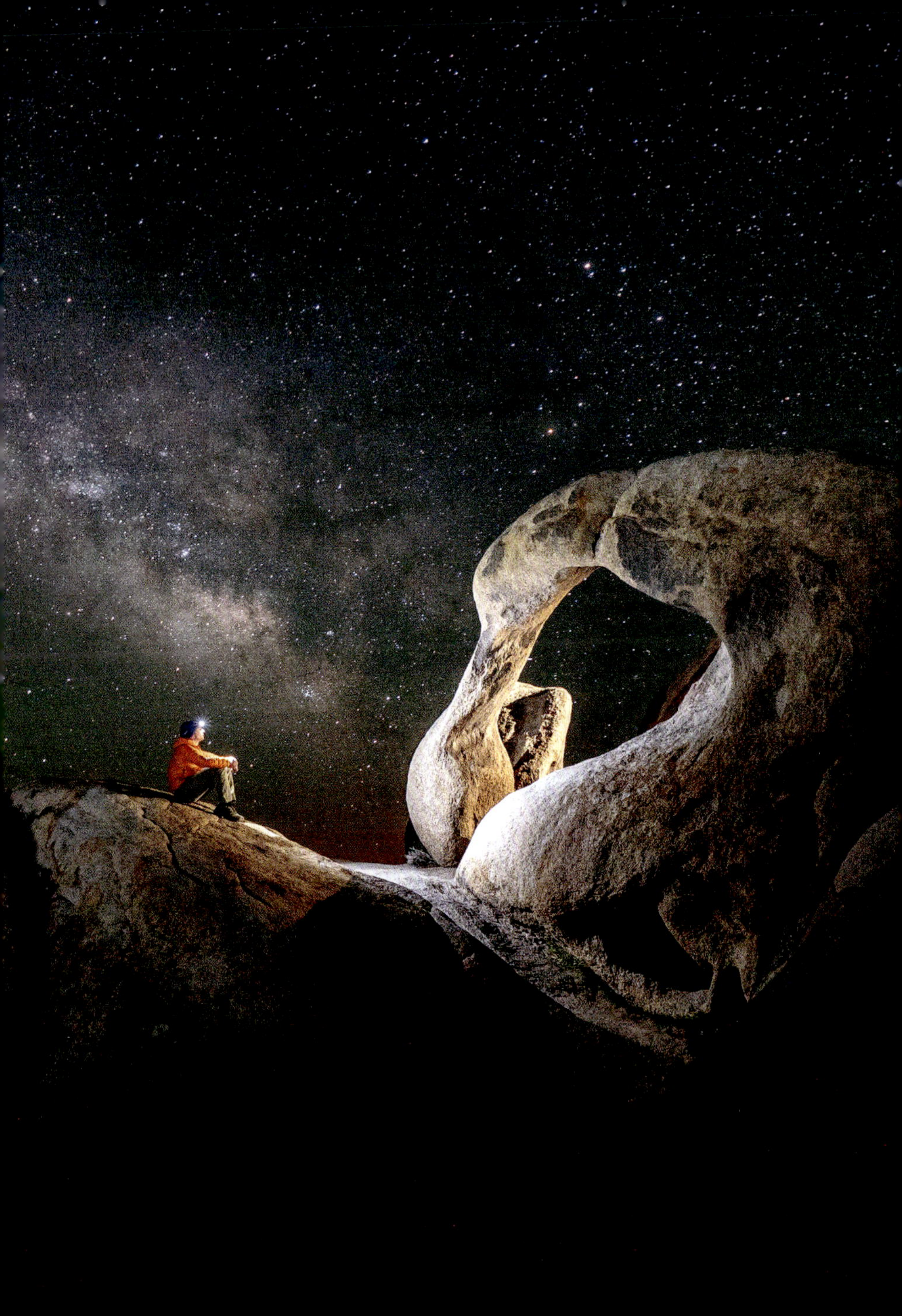

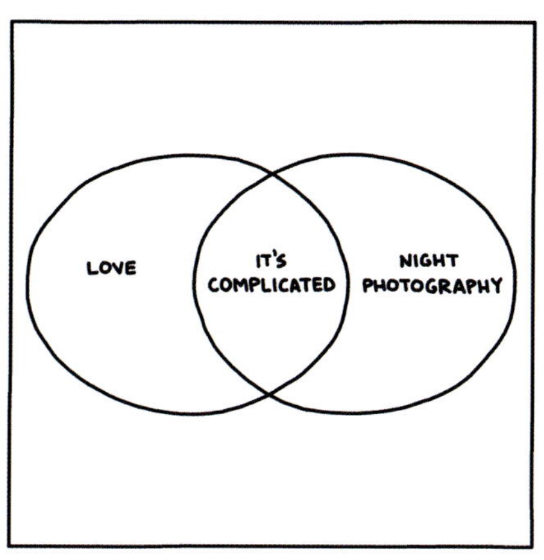

CHAPTER 10
Night Shots

I'm not gonna lie. Night photography is complicated!

So, first things first: *Let daylight set the scene*. Never try to shoot at night a place you haven't visited during the day. The very best images I've shot of the Milky Way or the aurora borealis are from places I've visited before; I knew the framing, and I thought about these images. I preplanned them.

NO HEADLAMP	YOU CAN'T SEE ANYTHING IN THE DARK
HEADLAMP	YOU CAN SEE THINGS IN THE DARK
HEADLAMP W/ RED LIGHT	YOU CAN SEE THINGS IN THE DARK; MINIMAL DISTURBANCE OF PEOPLE + OTHER LIGHT-SENSITIVE THINGS AROUND YOU

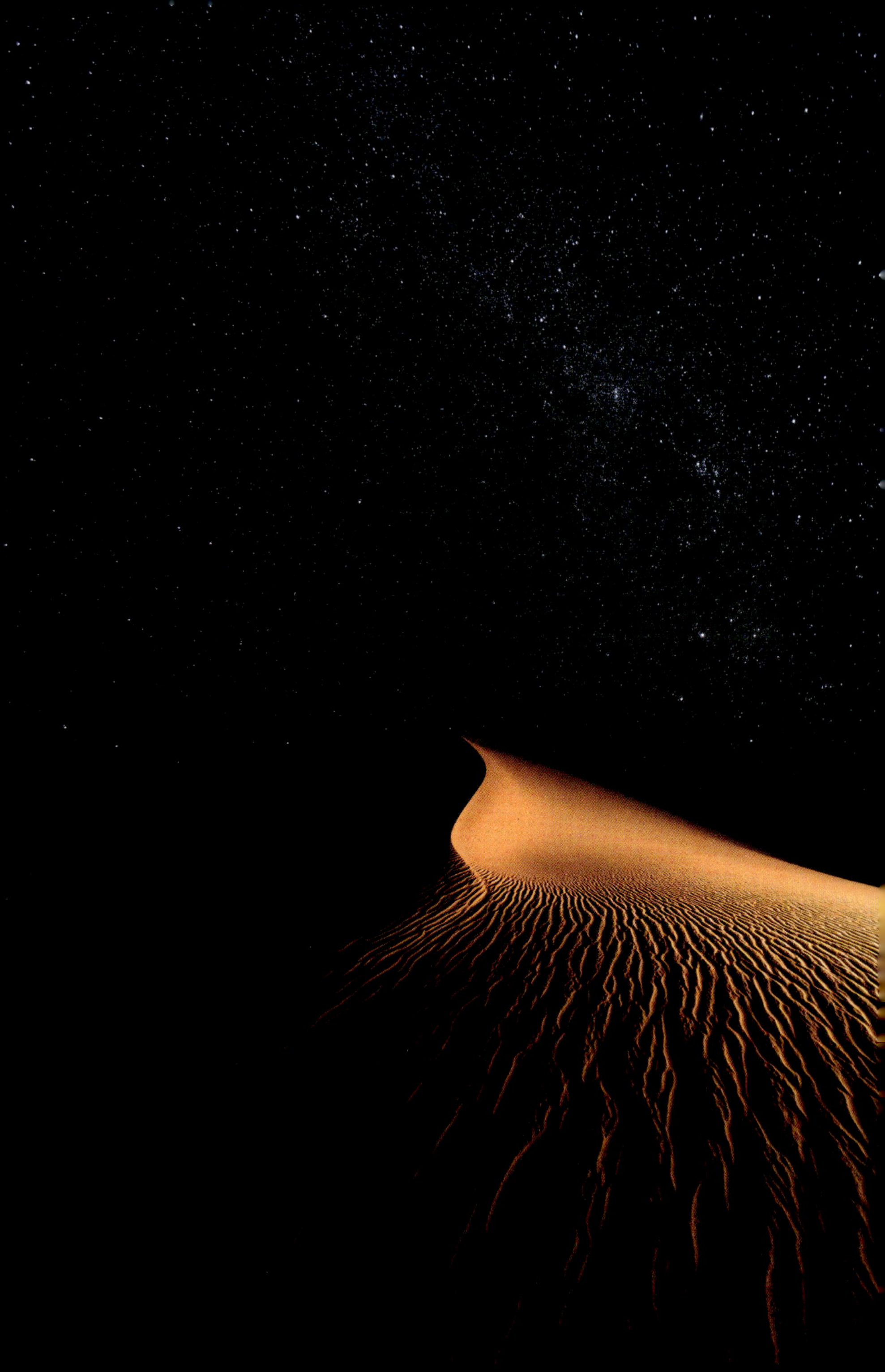

For example, let's say I want to shoot the aurora borealis over Skógafoss in South Iceland. I've visited the waterfall before, and I know the setup. So I'm looking at the weather forecast, and I've already got my reference image all framed up. Why? Because then I'm not trying to connect the lens while wearing a headlamp when it's freezing outside and the Arctic wind is blasting. Do you know how many times I've seen people have no success, or accidentally step into an icy river, or get too close to the edge of a cliff, or worse?

Equipment

From a safety perspective, definitely bring a headlamp or a small flashlight, ideally one that has a red mode so that you won't disturb other photographers or other things happening—something you can make small adjustments with and can operate with your gloves on.

If I'm bringing a multitude of cameras and a big kit, I will have one bag or pouch that has my low-light camera / light-sensitive camera (like a Sony a7S) and my low-light lens. Usually that low-light lens is a wide-angle—a 14mm or a 20mm.

The key with any low-light lens is that the f-stop has to be very low, usually under 2.8, ideally under 2.2, even 1.8, 1.6, or 1.4. Why? Because that's going to let in the most light, which allows you to have the lowest ISO, which in turn allows you to shoot the cleanest long-exposure image.

All said, there are specific cameras and specific lenses to do all of this. If you're really serious about night photography, I recommend getting the specialized gear.

Aside from a cable release, a Bluetooth trigger or a wireless remote can be great—something simple to trigger your shutter without touching it and causing vibration, especially if you want to be in the photo yourself. Almost all new cameras have touchless release now.

A quick note about lenses: The faster ones are prime lenses, not zooms. They're typically ideal for shooting night stuff. They're also ideal for shooting portraits when you want to have a lot of beautiful falloff. They have great bokeh. The background separates from the subjects, so they're popular for shooting concerts or weddings and other situations you might typically shoot at night.

The Milky Way and the aurora borealis

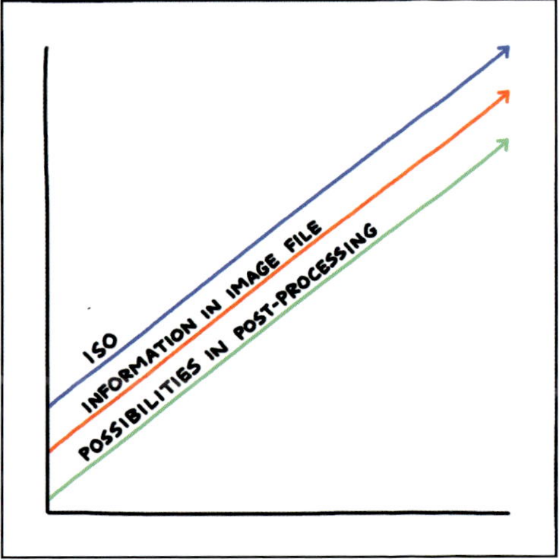

OK, let's dive (not literally!) into the Milky Way and the aurora borealis (a.k.a. the northern lights). These are the two subjects for which most people go out and shoot at night. There's also moonlit landscapes, night street photography, weddings and concerts, and such, but oftentimes the stars and the aurora are the big draw, right?

One key mistake I've seen a lot of photographers make is thinking that they can use Photoshop or Lightroom to take a dark image and brighten it up because they were afraid to raise the ISO. I'm here to tell you that it's better—and I've seen it from post-processing myself—to shoot the right exposure and, if you have to, darken it a little as opposed to lightening it up a little. In fact, the digital image itself will have more information to work with. Now, this is never going to be an excuse for not just shooting a nice clean image with a fast lens and a good camera. I always recommend that even if you shoot ISO 8000 or 10000, or if you want to shoot a much longer exposure, you can have that bit of post-processing as an option.

Another option we have when compensating for the lack of light or for our fear of high ISOs is shooting a longer exposure, like 20

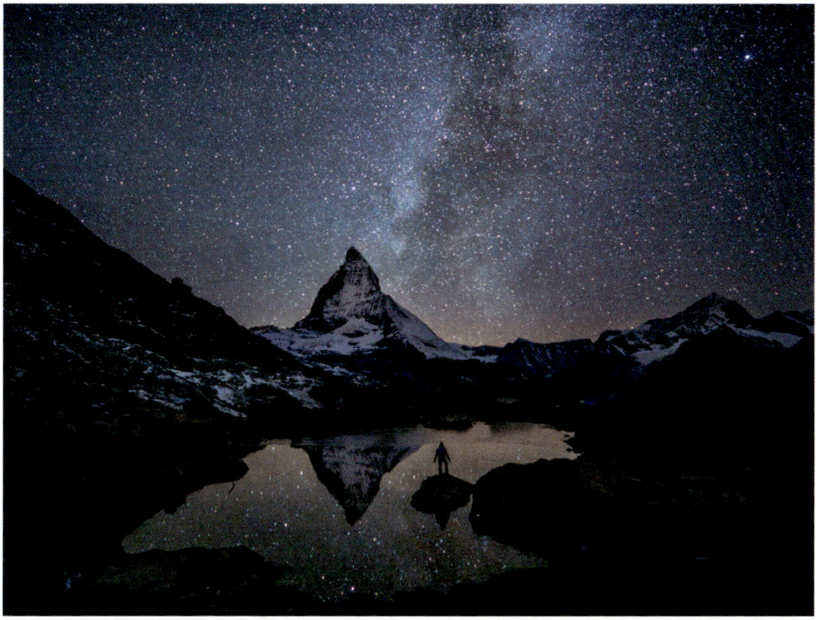

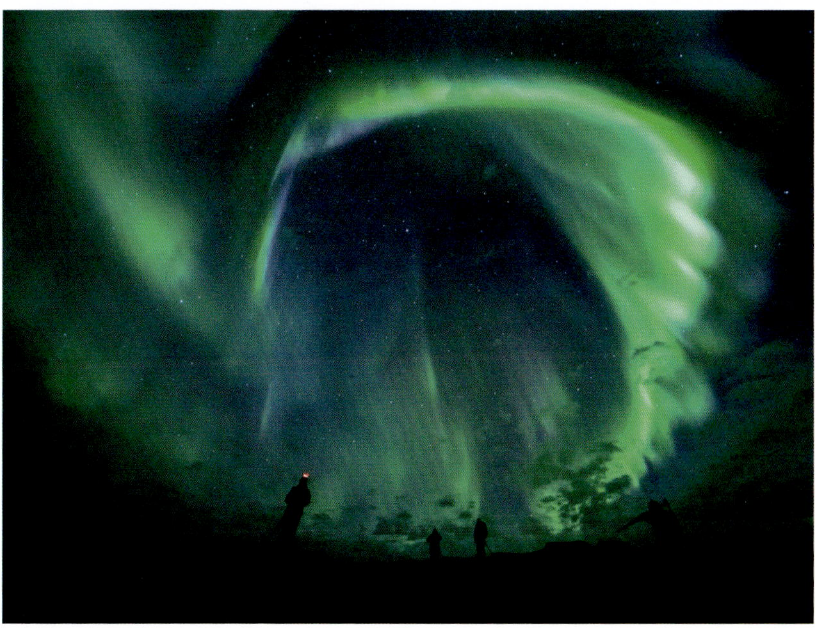

or 30 seconds. That's great, but you'll find a lot of star movement, or you'll get a blurry green sky. The best northern lights photos and the best Milky Way photos are usually shot in 10 seconds or less. This makes the aurora look vivid. It also makes the stars look very sharp. As a side note, you can definitely find a formula to figure out how much star movement you'll get as your lens widens, because the wider the lens, the less movement you get. It's kind of the inverse of action sports. But that's not really something we're going to discuss here because it requires actual math.

To tripod or not to tripod?

A tripod is *always* going to make your life easier. Putting a puffy coat over a rock and finding a way to balance the camera with a 10-second timer might work, but it sucks. I've had to do it. If you don't have a tripod, you can experiment. Find a way to balance your camera. Put it on a delayed 10-second shutter so the camera can stop its vibration (from being handled) and find its balance before taking the shot.

What I really recommend is having a tripod you trust and one that you can handle well with gloves, because usually when you're shooting at night, the air is cold. So make sure that everything you need to do, you can do while wearing gloves.

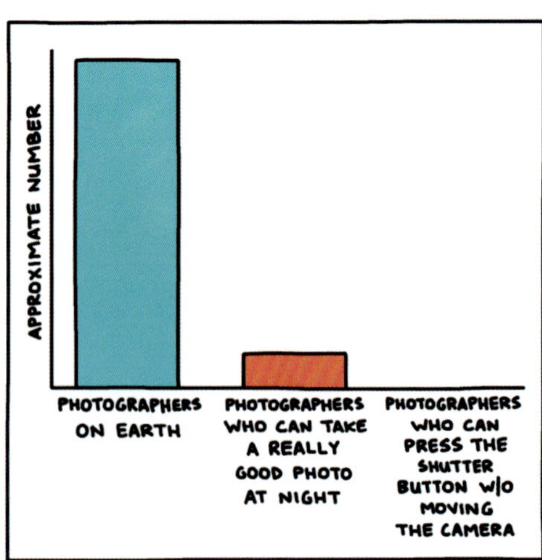

I also recommend a 2-second timer or a 10-second timer. Even if you have the camera on a tripod, the point is to push the shutter and move away from the camera so it can stop vibrating by the time the frame is shot. As a

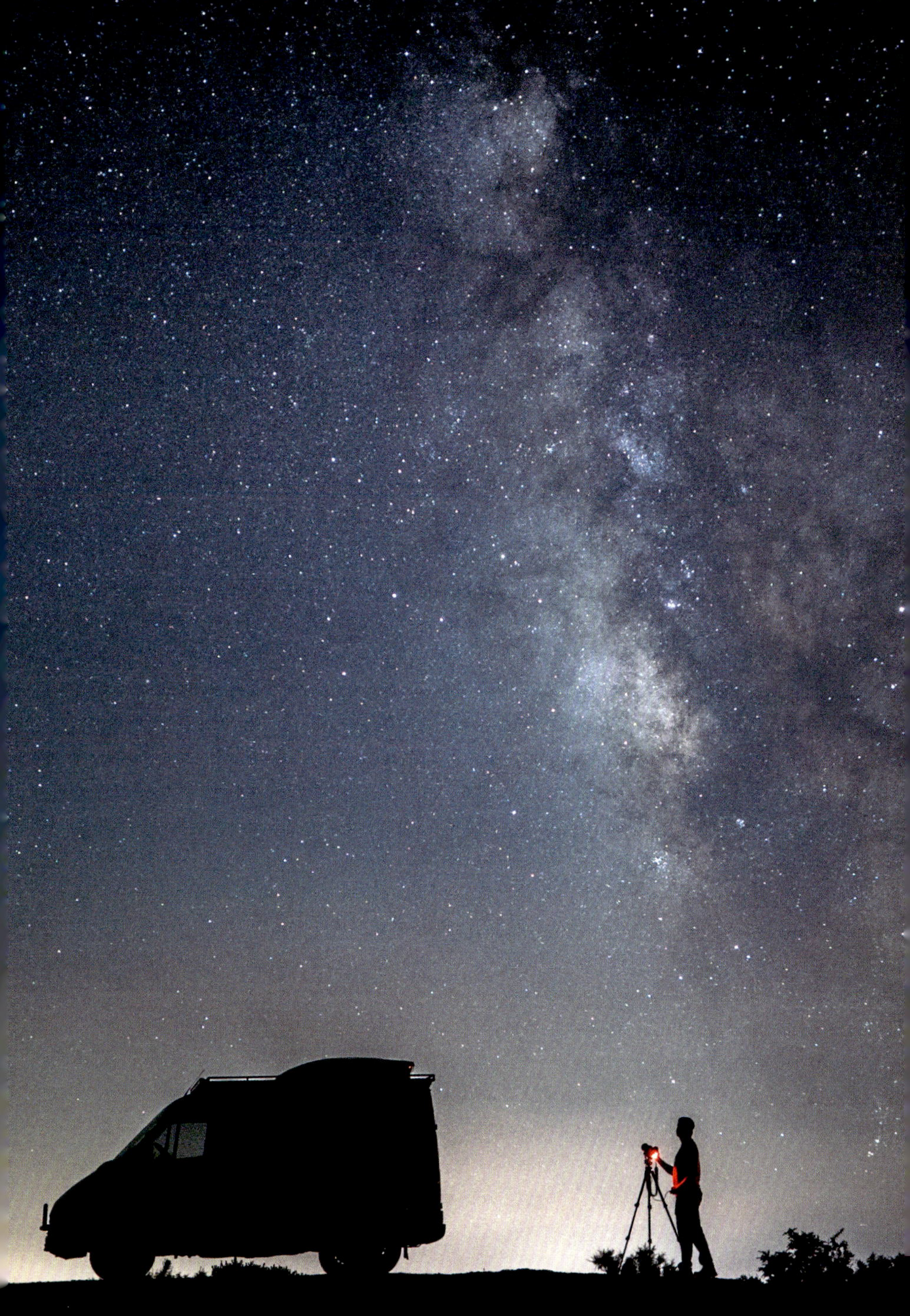

human, no matter what, you *will* make the camera vibrate—even just a little—when you manually push the shutter button.

If I'm just framing up my shot or doing my test shots, I don't really need to use the timer. But once you've locked in your exposure and locked in your frame—that's when you really start being serious, and that's where the 2-second timer comes in.

My process

Whenever I begin a night-photography session, my process is very simple: I usually don't start with a tripod. I bump my ISO *way* up, and I crank my shutter speed down to 1 or 2 seconds. Maybe I'll just hold the camera or put it on a rock. I'll crank my lens all the way open: f1.4, f1.6, f1.8, whatever. And then I take a couple of test frames. That's it. These are throwaway photos to simply show me whether the frame is cool. Maybe it's not. And then what I typically do is start the subtle arithmetic, the lock mechanism, of going back and forth: ISO down, shutter speed up, ISO up, shutter speed down. I will dial it in. I'm going back and forth between a higher ISO and a longer shutter or vice versa. I'm trying to work on a couple different ways of having images. Because when it's dark and you're looking through a backlit screen, it's really hard to understand if that image is going to be as clean as you thought. So having a couple of options is great.

Focus

Focus can be challenging. What I recommend is that when you're shooting with a wide-angle lens, remember that if the shot or the action or the landscape is more than 3 to 10 feet away, everything's in focus. So you can oftentimes push the lens to infinity and maybe back it off just a little bit, and that will give you almost dead-on focus.

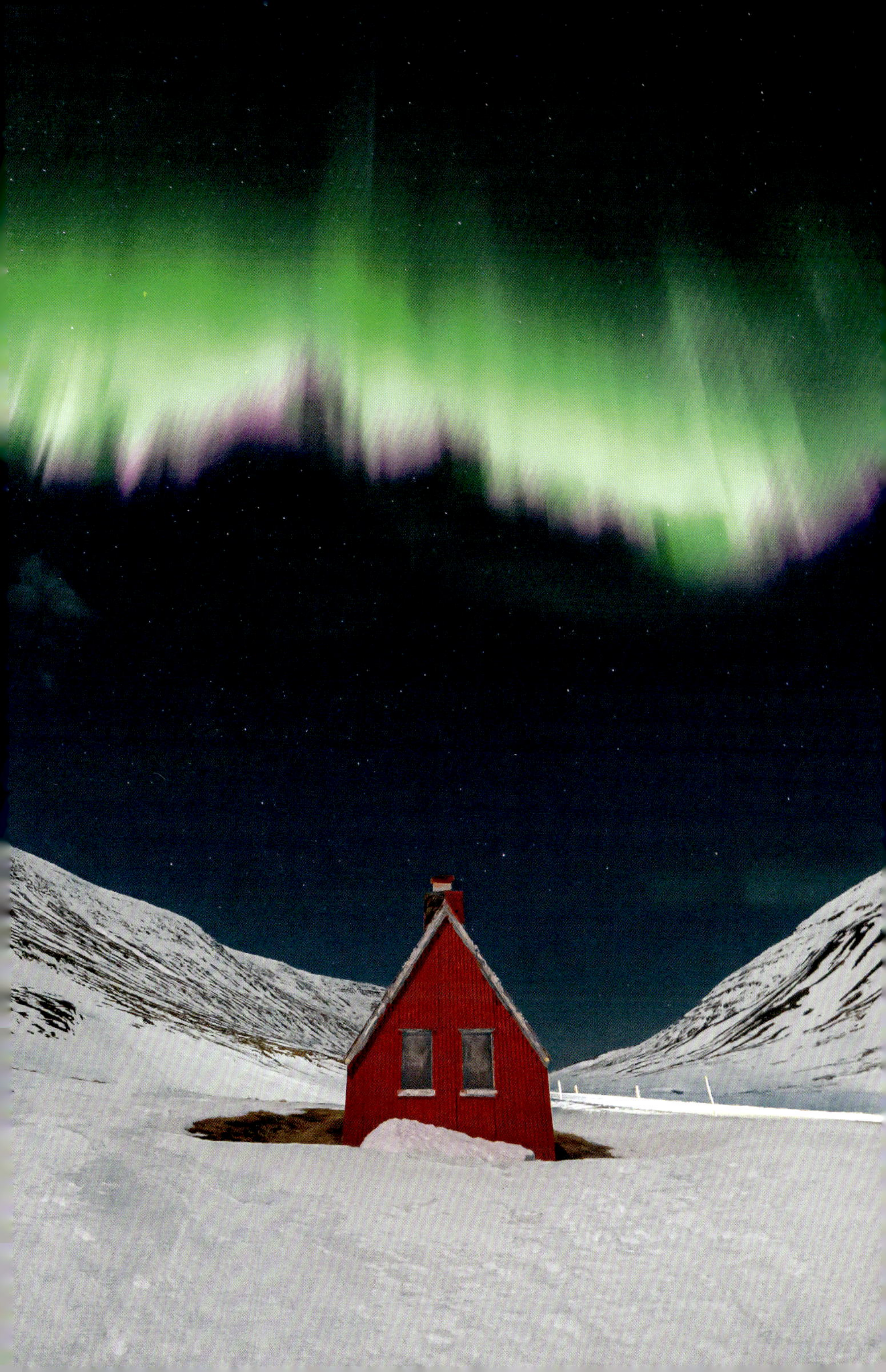

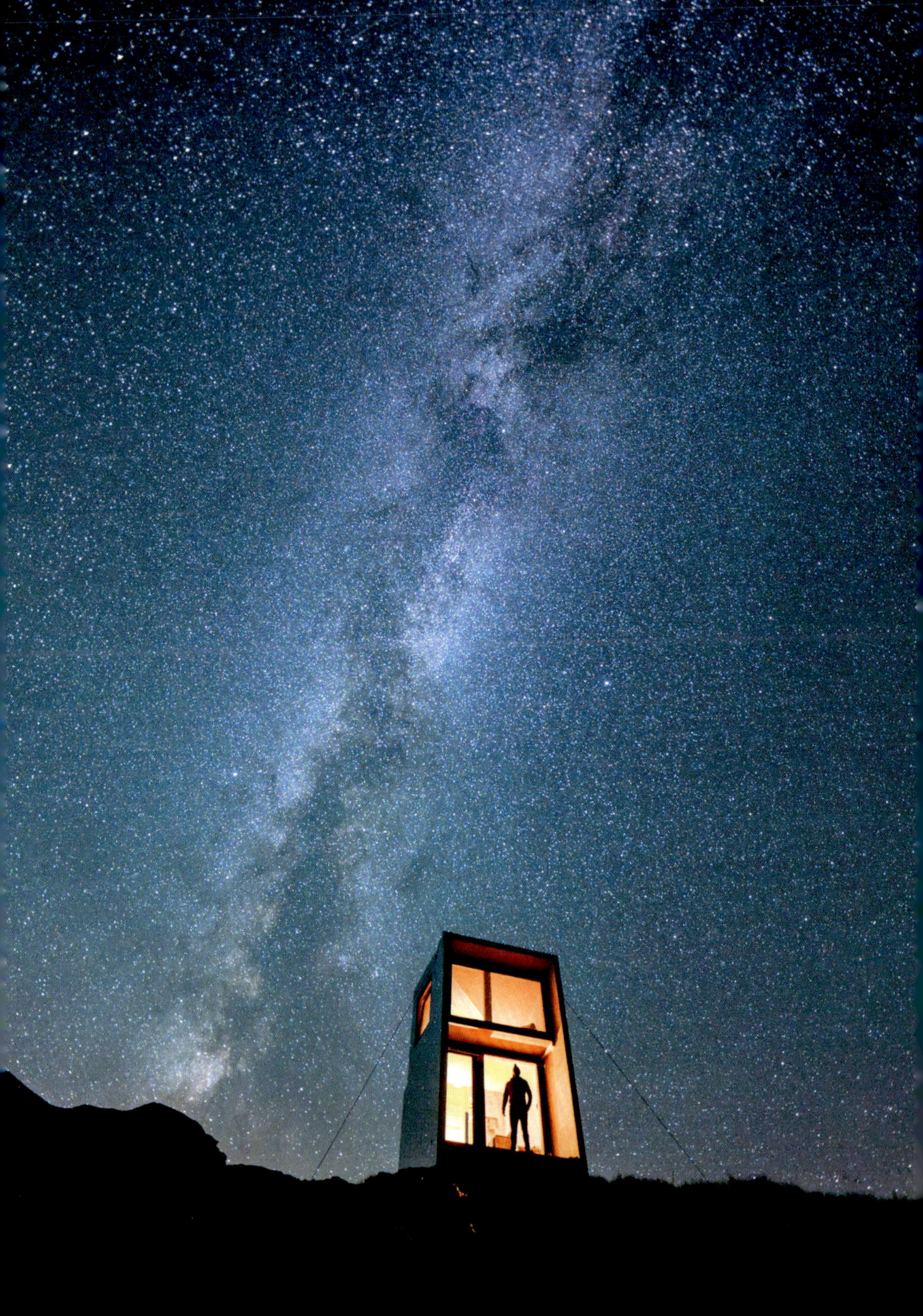

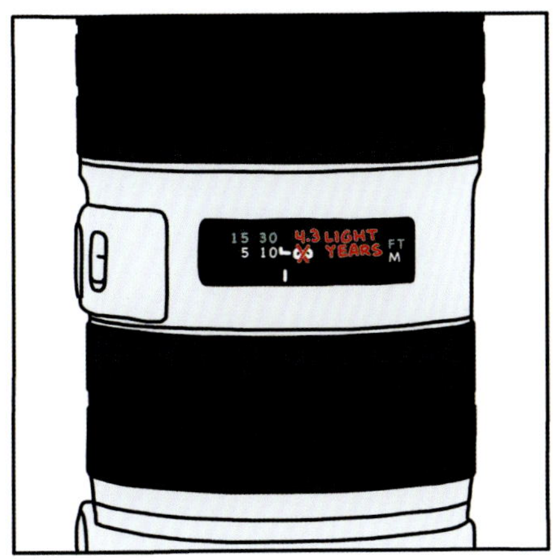

A great tool in a mirrorless camera is the ability to have a digital readout on the lens—this allows you zoom in or focus on a faraway star or a light in the distance and make sure focus is locked in. Often, I'm setting mine to infinity (∞) focus, and then I can ensure the focus is perfect for a night exposure or any kind of long exposure setting when I'm shooting a wide angle. Or I'll rely upon the digital readout if I want something closer.

Make sure to set your lens in manual focus. That is key. Many modern lenses have a direct manual focus option, which allows you to zoom in digitally, get your focus, and then take your hand away, and your camera's in focus. That is the best way to do it.

Another option is to ask a friend to stand 30 feet away, focus on their headlamp or phone light or whatever, and you're good. But this only works when you have a wide-angle lens. And the reason you normally would shoot with a wide-angle lens is you want to be shooting the sky *and* the ground, and that will require a wide angle. A 50mm lens is usually too close. Even a 35mm lens can be too close. I've found the best approach is to use something fairly wide.

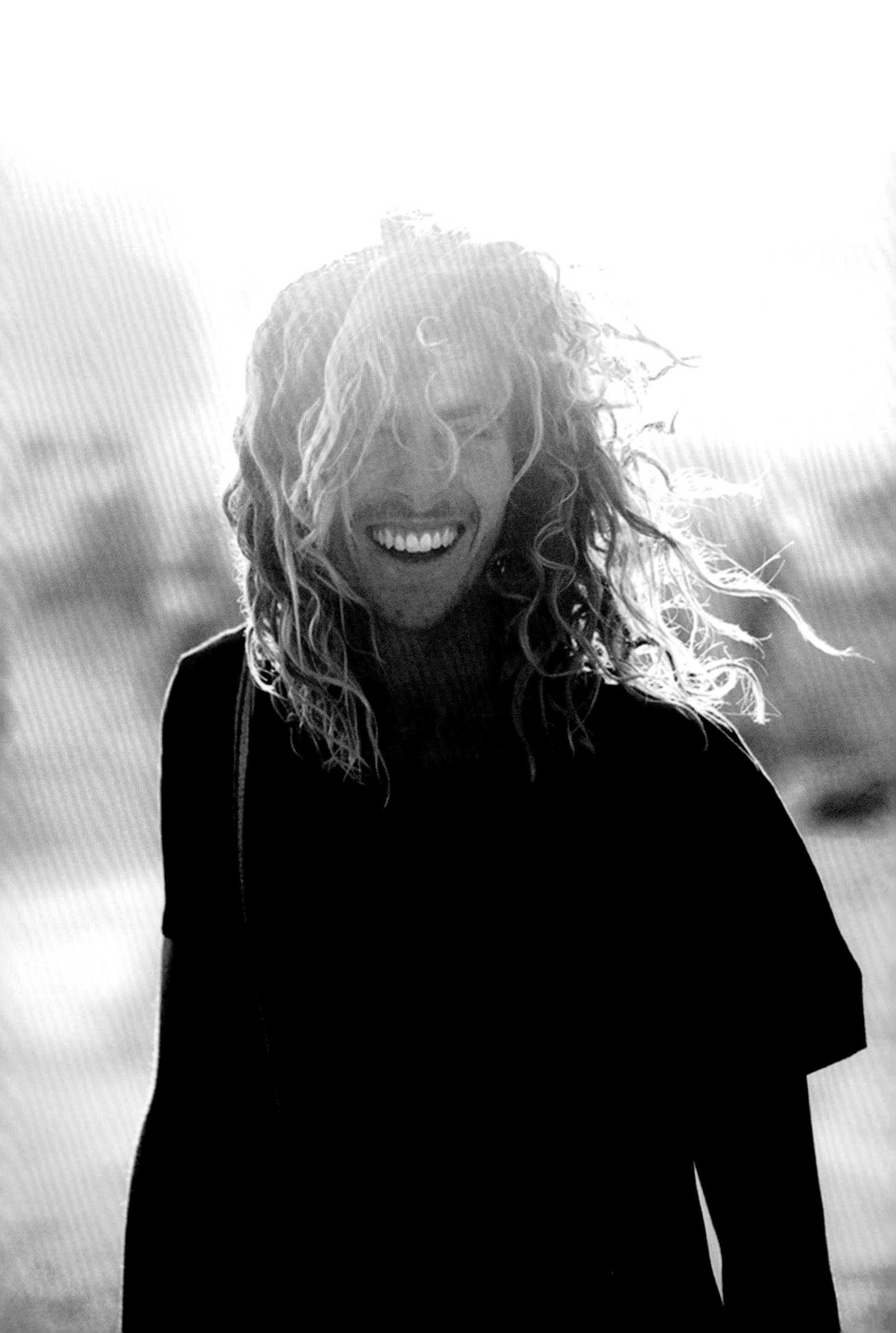

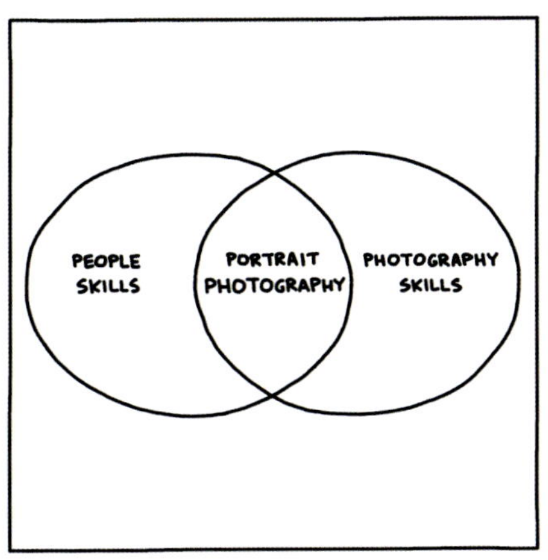

CHAPTER 11
Portraits

Apart from the obvious, what defines a portrait? It's not time. Sometimes a portrait "session" will run less than one minute. You might see somebody on the street and snap a quick photo of them that ends up being a keeper because you happened to catch their countenance perfectly by chance. Those are my favorite. Or maybe you'll have a preplanned sit-down session with a subject and get to know them on several levels.

Essentially, being a good or great portrait photographer entails being a people person. You've got to enjoy chatting to and getting to know others. The world's best portrait photographers are fluid conversationalists. Dale Carnegie's classic book *How to Win Friends and Influence People* is a great tool for portrait photographers, who often need to win their subjects over in a short period of time.

Tips for great portraits

- **Connect with your subject.** This is not about telling them how you're going to shoot or about them getting to know you. This is about *you* getting to know *them* and finding ways in which their conversation is something you can both relate to. Chat with them. Be interested. Ask questions. Learn about your subject and make them feel safe so they can trust you. Express to them what you'd like to capture and why.

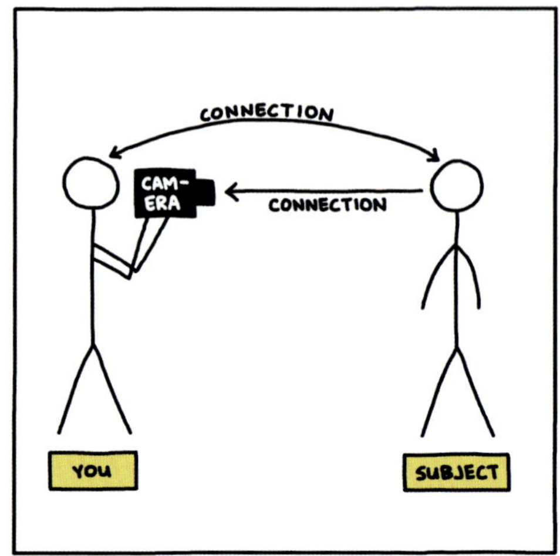

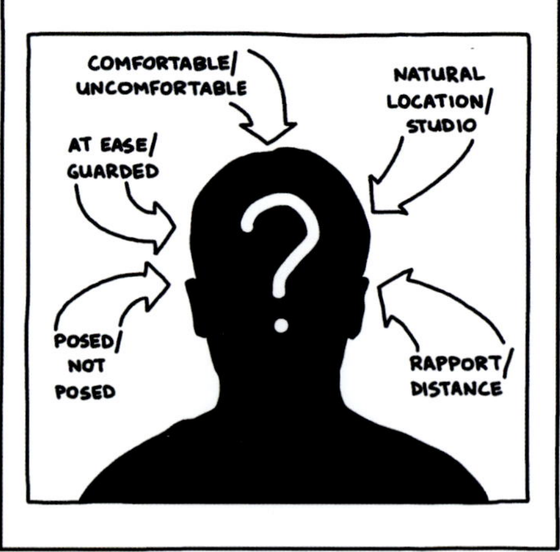

- **The best portraits are usually not posed.** We've all seen the shot where the kid is sitting there smiling and staring at the camera. That's what you go to Walmart for. That's not what we're here to do. We're here to capture our subject's natural ambience in whatever setting—natural or unnatural—they may be in.

- **Capture your subject where they feel comfortable.** Oftentimes, if you're photographing someone on the street, you're already in their space—you're in their home, where they play, where they work, and that's a comfortable zone. And it's usually very honest. But if you have to pick a location, try to choose somewhere you think your subject can feel comfortable or a place that means something to them—a place that can get them talking and surveying the landscape. For an environmental portrait, figuring out a location that's going to be meaningful to that person goes a long way toward creating an impactful and meaningful portrait of them. Obviously, if you're in a New York City studio, that's a very different situation, and you need to be able to make your subject feel comfortable there too.

POTENTIAL PORTRAIT LOCATIONS	
COMFORTABLE	UNCOMFORTABLE
IN THEIR HOME/ STUDIO/ NEIGHBORHOOD	DURING A DENTAL CLEANING
WEARING THEIR FAVORITE CLOTHES/ OUTFIT	WEARING AN ILL-FITTING SUIT
WITH THEIR DOG	IN A POND FULL OF ALLIGATORS
AT THEIR FAVORITE TRAIL/ CRAG/ BEACH	AT THE DMV

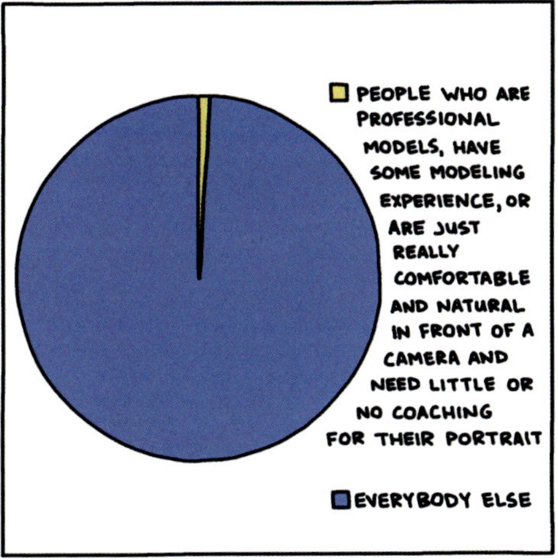

- **Find emotion in your subject.** Sometimes the best portrait could be somebody eating an apple or caught in mid-sentence. Sometimes it's them appearing to be deep in thought or striking a pose that feels like you caught them doing something.

- **Their eyes tell the story—right?** Everybody knows this old adage. But sometimes the subject doesn't need to be looking straight at the

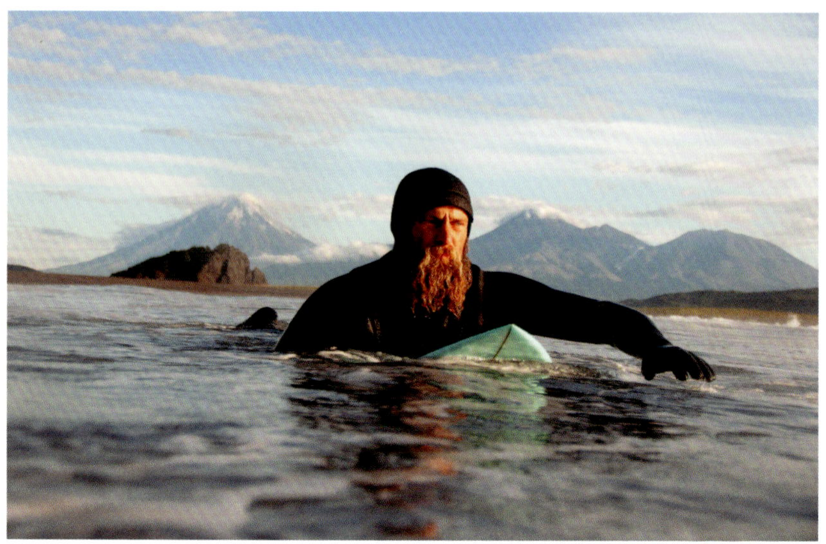

camera. In some situations, having the subject look *away* from the camera can be just as important.

- **You define the mood.** Sometimes we get lucky enough to work with models who are really comfortable doing all this stuff; they're used to it. In that situation—a professional portrait session, not just photographing somebody on the street—you need to learn how to articulate what you want: *Hey, I want your body to look like this*, or *I'm really looking for this*, or *I need your eyes to be like this*. You define the mood—the feeling—you'd like them to convey. You want to give them more than just physical prompts.

A word about gear

Here's a quick and dirty list of camera lenses and preferential settings I have for photographing people and portraits.

Portrait lenses are usually shallow depth-of-field primes.

The wider your lens, the more challenging it will be to make your

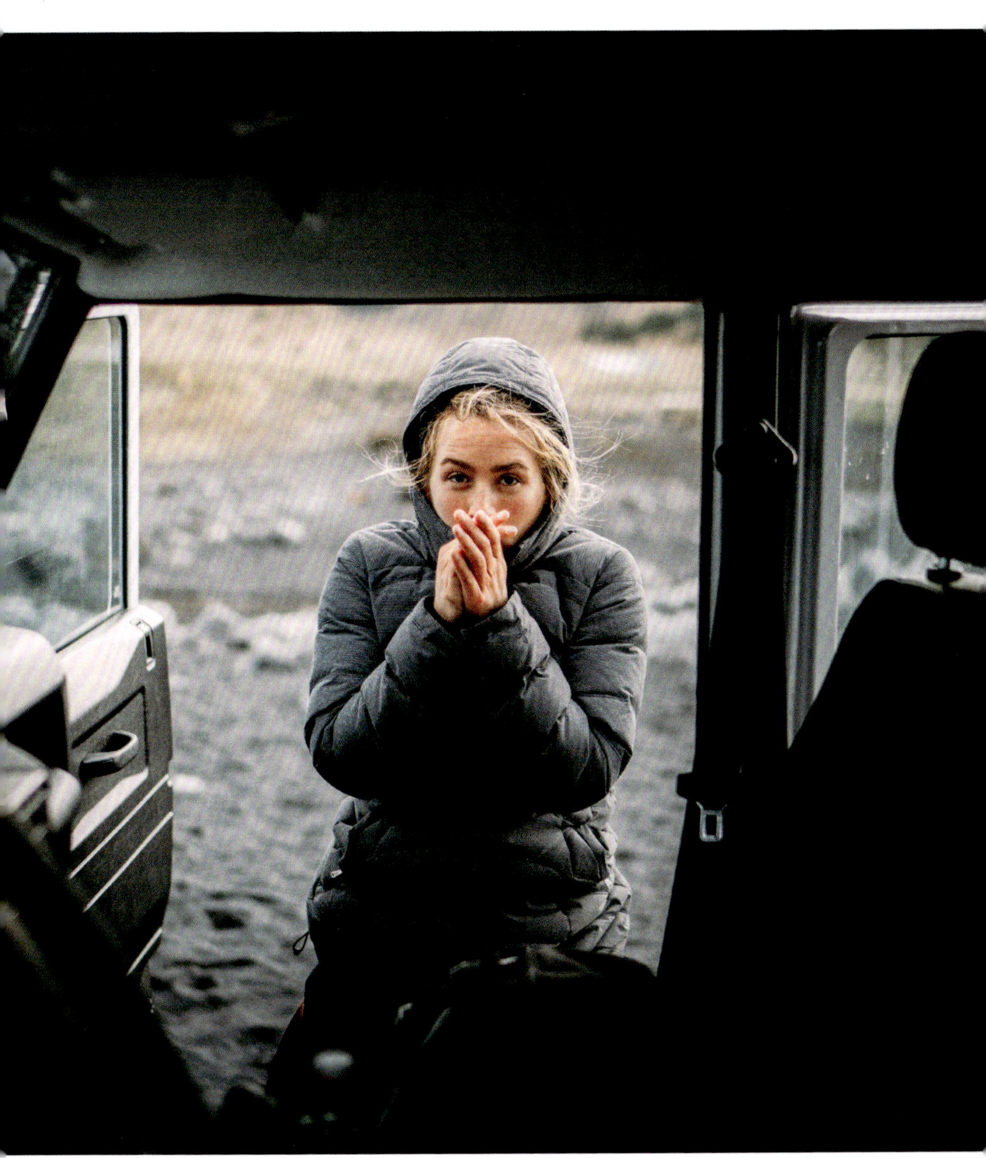

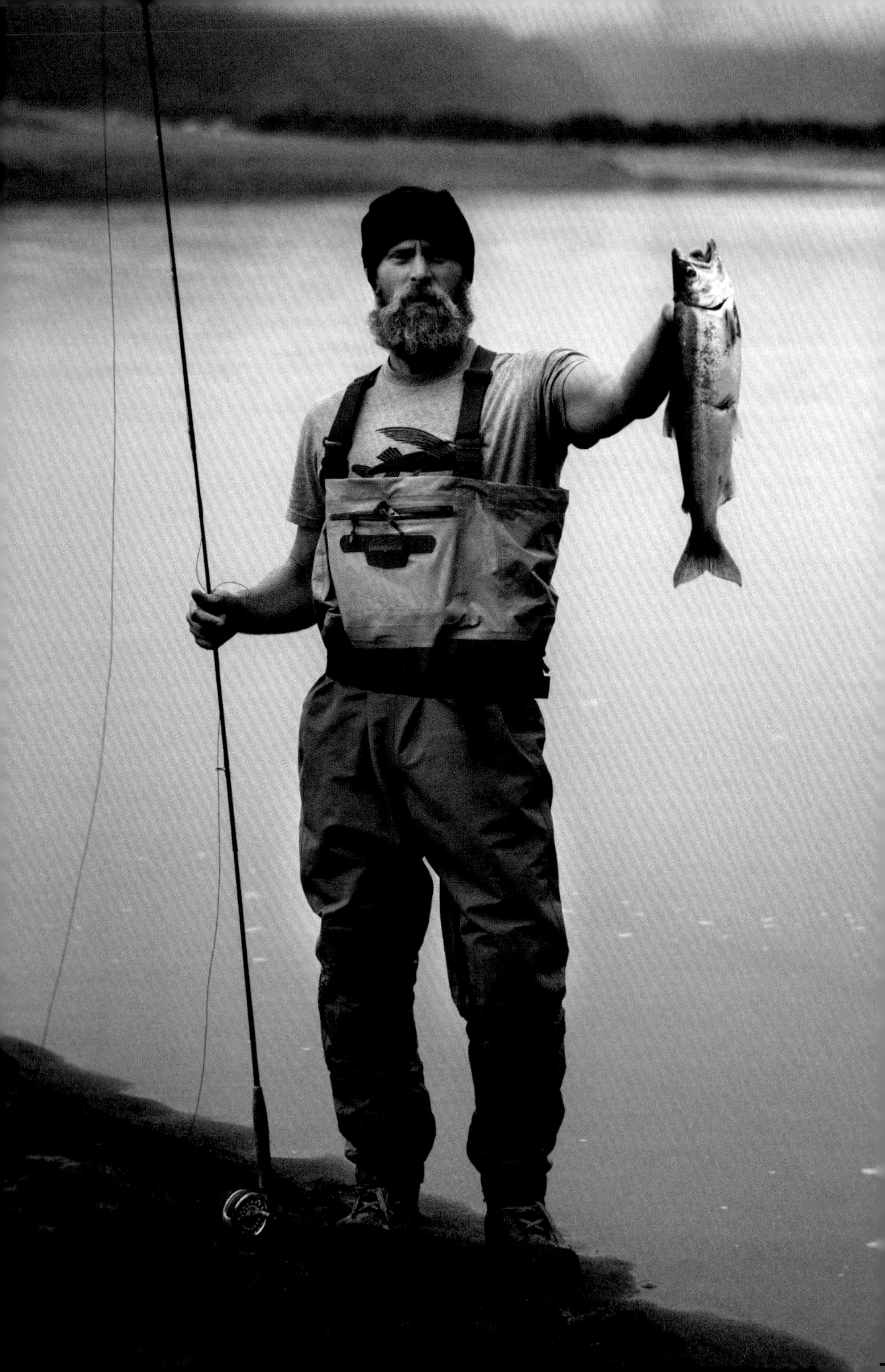

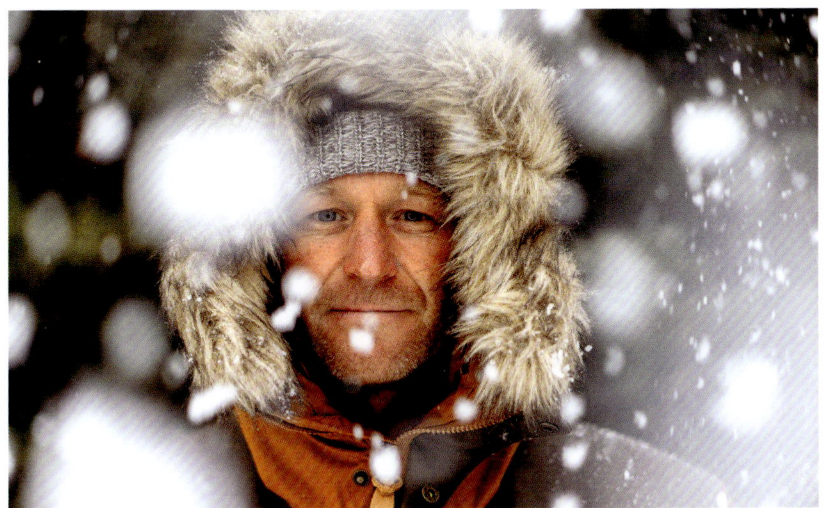

subject's body look natural because a wide lens will start to make things appear wider (imagine that!) and more bowed (or distorted) than they actually are.

A shallower depth of field will separate your subject from the background, which is important if it's a busy scene. Let's say you're in the middle of downtown NYC and you shoot a portrait at, say, f/11. Everything's going to be in focus, and it's going to look terrible. If you shoot at f1.4, it's going to look milky. It'll be harder to nail focus on your subject, but it will look like the person is popping out of the background. A shallower depth of field will make your subject stand out more and is a really beautiful way to create contrast.

Environmental portraits are often my favorites. Perhaps you're shooting a photo of an environmental advocate in the place they want to save. You might use a wider lens, like a 24mm or a 35mm, but shoot from farther away and show parts of a tree or parts of a cliff.

For headshots, as you need to home in on the subject's face, you might use a 35mm, 40mm, or 50mm lens—or even a 70mm or 100mm. But I would say that the sweet spot for close-up portrait photography is in that 35–70mm range.

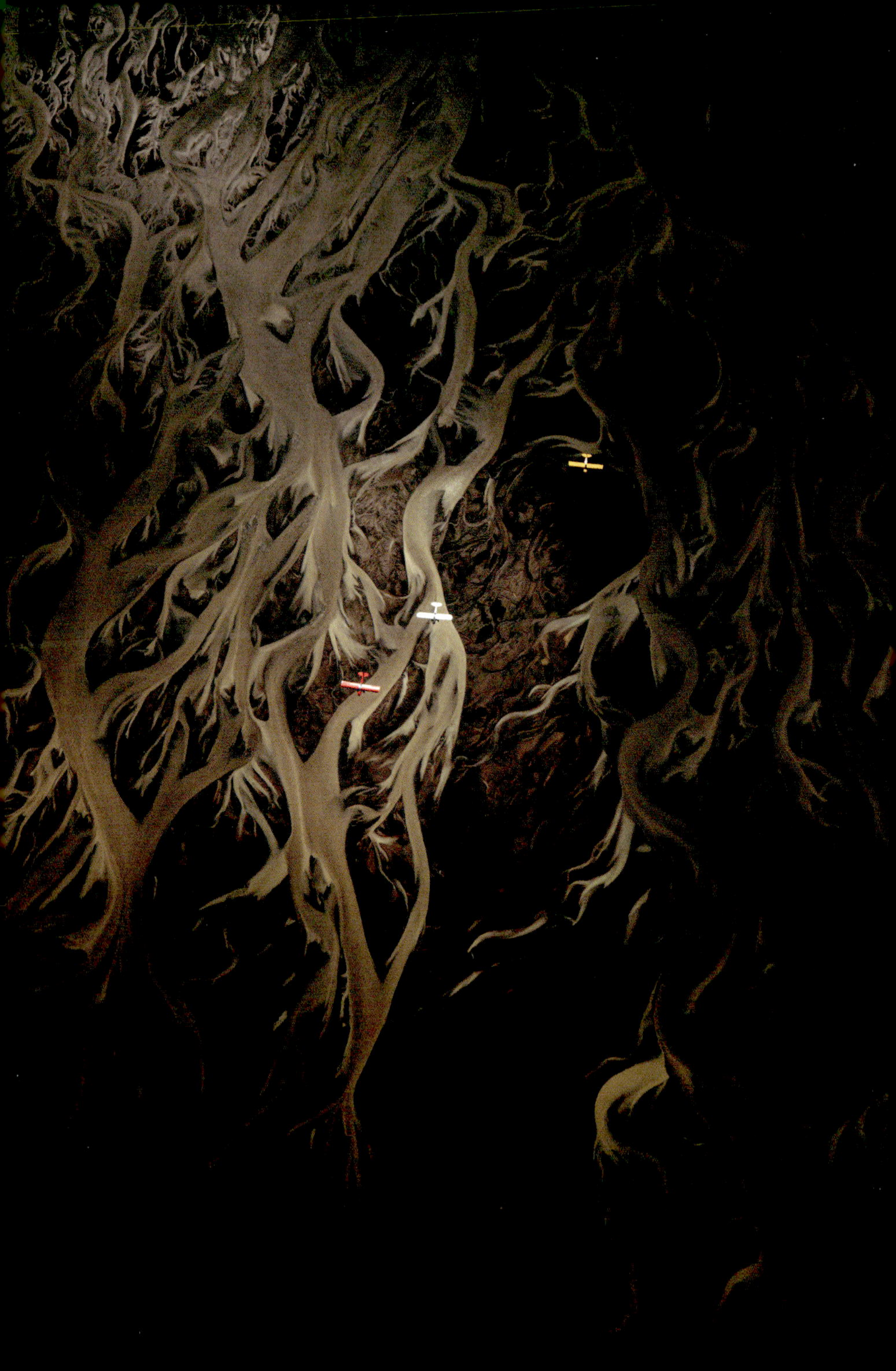

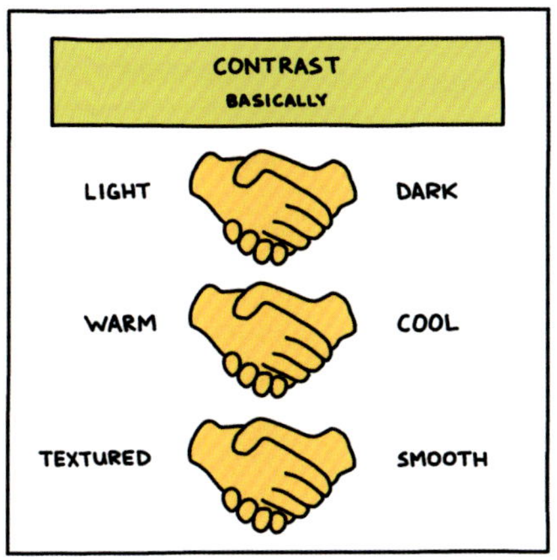

CHAPTER 12
Contrasts

Guess what? Contrast can be more important than composition because contrast is really where your image springs to life.

Sometimes contrast occurs naturally. You're shooting at sunrise or sunset. Try to find ways in which you can make the landscape feel more three-dimensional because that's really what we're after.

Contrast can be achieved through tone and color, texture, shadow, and silhouette.

Tone and color

Look for warm tones on cool tones. Why do we feel so drawn to Christmas lights during blue hour (twilight)? It's because those warm Christmas lights give us some feeling of safety. They elicit an emotion, and we like that.

Sometimes there's contrast you can control. For example, you can curate opposing colors. If you want your subject to stand apart, maybe have them wear a yellow jacket against blue water or a red shirt against a green forest. Things like this make a big difference. Maybe it's the makeup you put on somebody, or the types of tools or gear they're using—the backpack or the sunglasses.

BACKGROUND	CONTRAST IDEA
BLUE WATER	YELLOW JACKET
GREEN FOREST	RED BACKPACK
WHITE SNOW	ORANGE PUFFER
ORANGE + YELLOW LAVA FROM CURRENTLY ERUPTING VOLCANO	ACTUALLY, JUST EVACUATE

Texture

Texture is an interesting topic. In a photograph, it means something to us and can evoke a feeling. The texture of sand, of an ice cream swirl, of a ripple on a wave—these are things that we often try to capture. Then again, the lack of texture can also be beautiful, like gorgeous milky water that's really glassy and reflective.

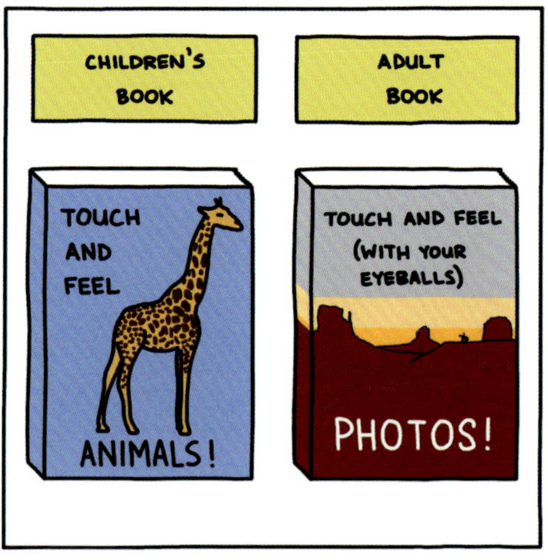

Sometimes when I'm shooting sand dunes, I look for a specific texture to home in on. This becomes my foreground. Focusing on that

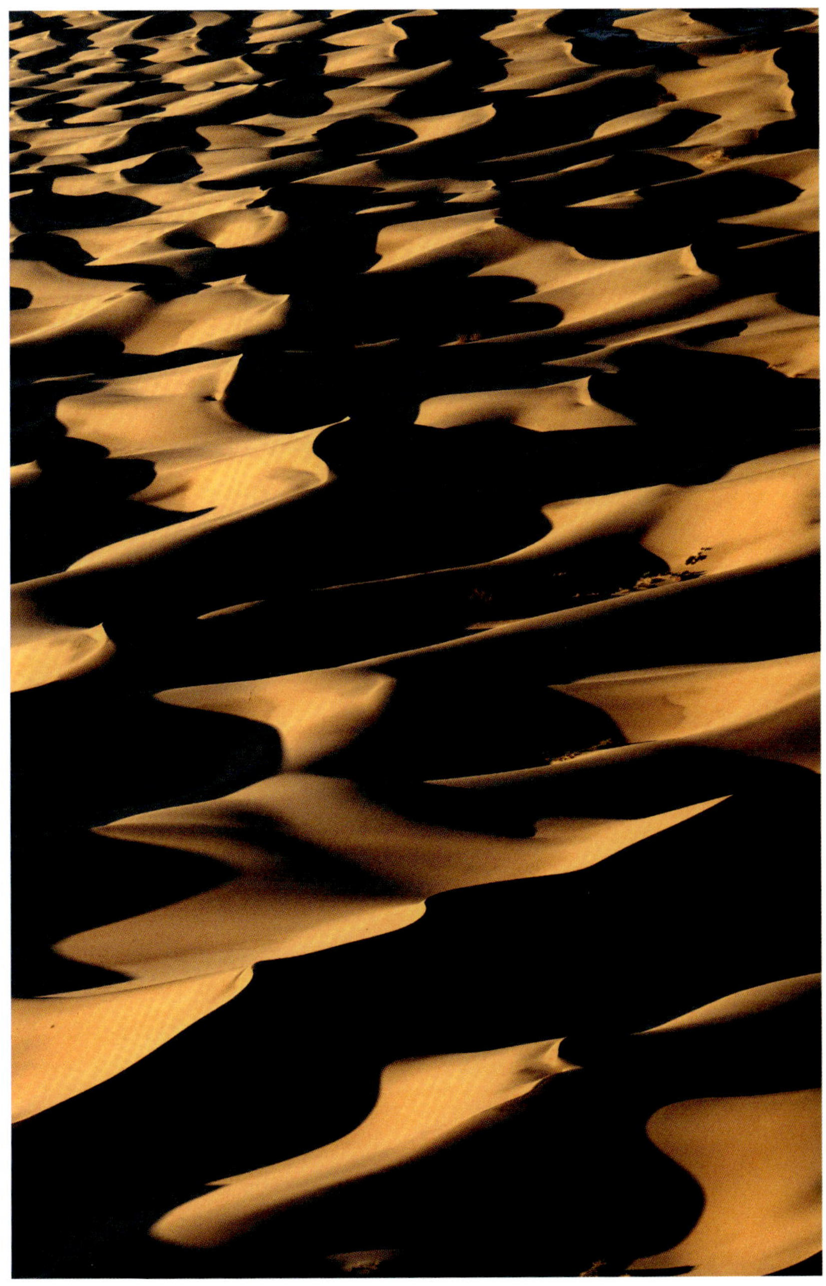

texture and letting it fade off into the background of my shot allows me to create an anchor point for my image.

Texture allows people to relate to something because it gives us one more visual cue: something we remember, something we've felt before. Viscerality—basically anything we can see, smell, taste, or touch—is what we're looking for in an image. When we show texture, we can conjure that.

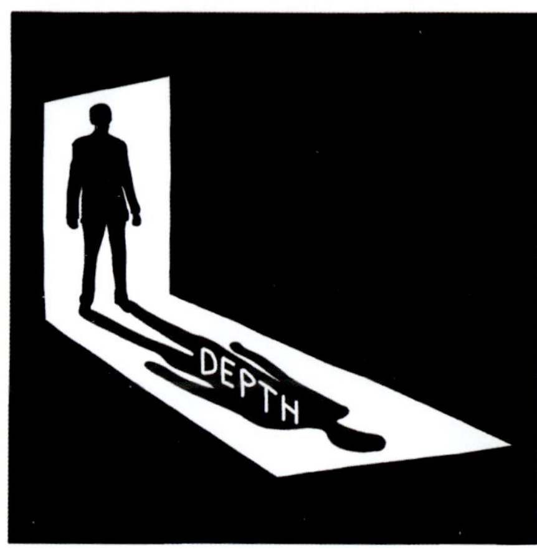

Shadow

Shadows are beautiful things. They can lend depth to an image. You can explore long shadows (early or late in the day) or short shadows (mid-day). You see some great street photography that utilizes shadows as a way to tell a story, to create contrast, or to add a little mystery or wonder. Shadows can also steer the viewer's eyes toward something they wouldn't normally see.

When I'm shooting from the air, I'm always looking for shadows. The shadow of a mountain, the contrast of a tree. Look for the color in the shadow because the color can be darker—more blue, more purple—as opposed to that warm orangish tone that's on the landscape.

We often use shadows as a way to create depth or falloff. One analogy might be a prop town or a ghost town that was set up on stilts. You're making these houses or structures dynamic. You're adding or decreasing depth, shadows, lighting, angle, lift. Instead of making things look flat and propped up, you're giving the scene life.

Silhouette

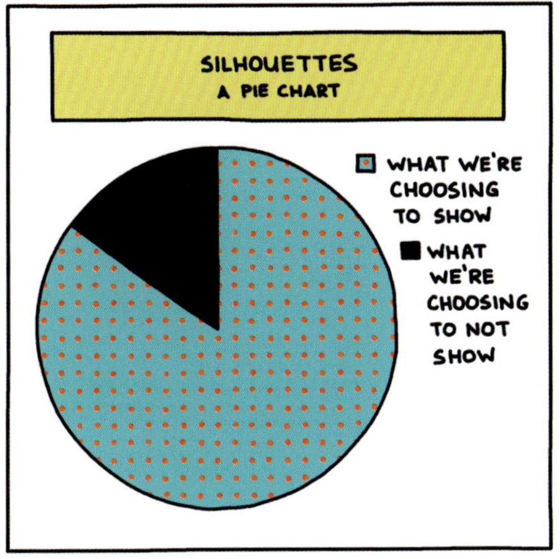

To me, perhaps the most timeless and most important aspect of creating and shooting photographs is learning to work with silhouettes. Silhouettes can be anything. You might wonder why we work with them. It's because when you capture something or somebody in silhouette, there's a sense of anonymity. A silhouette is about what we're not showing. We're not showing the color of the subject's skin or the logos or brands they're wearing. A silhouette simplifies everything, almost purifying the image to its basic form, and I love that. I love when an image can have one or two tones instead of midday light or frontlight, where there's a thousand different colors all competing for attention.

So maybe you're shooting a yoga pose on a mountain somewhere. A silhouette is going to be a stronger way of implying what you're trying to shoot. Maybe you get really low so you can contrast that silhouette against the sky—sometimes it's about contrasting something with other parts of a background. It's about working with layers of dark and light and figuring out why you want to shoot whatever it may be.

A silhouette is akin to a black-and-white photo. It begs for less of your attention, and what's important often stands out the most.

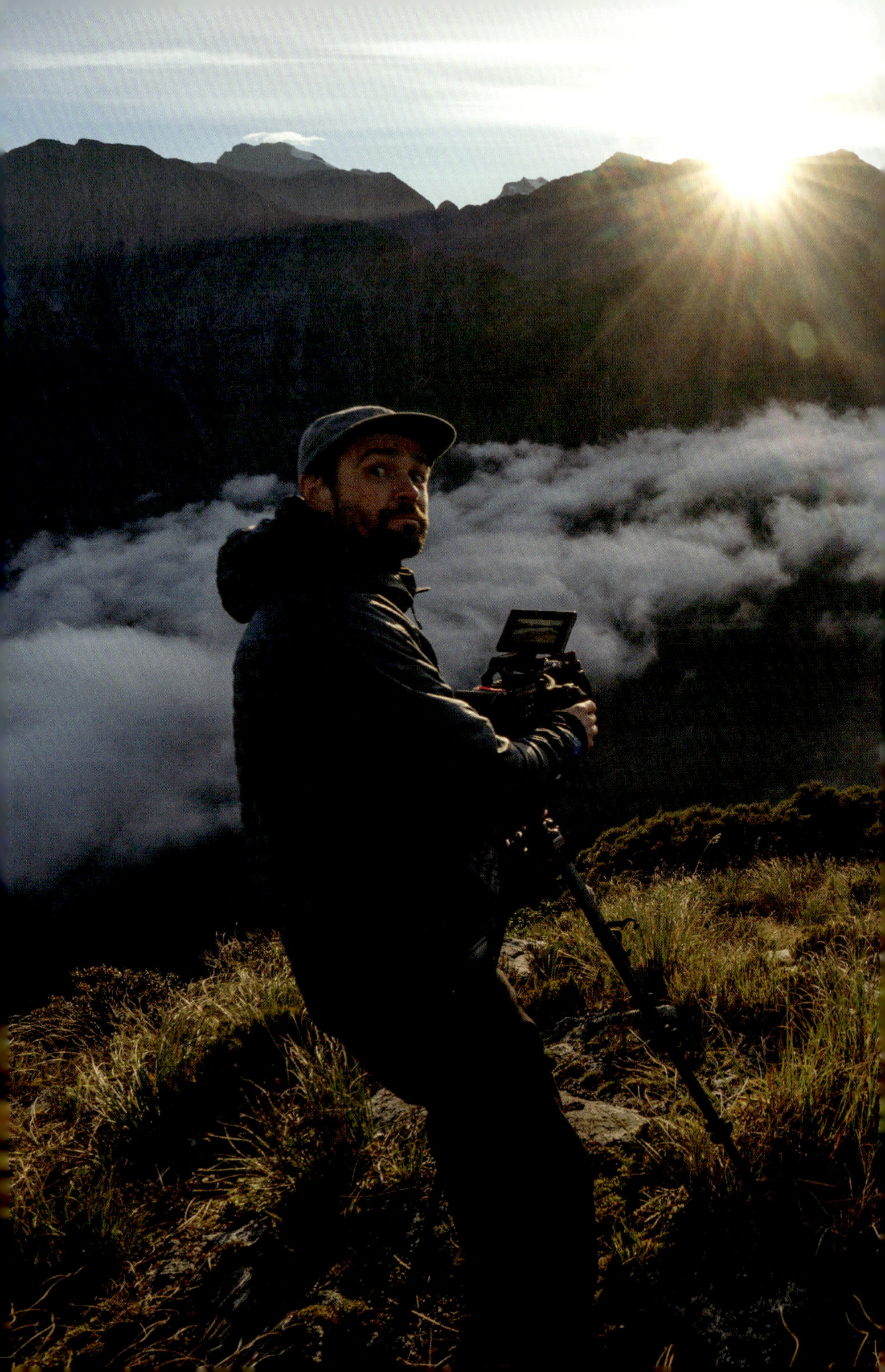

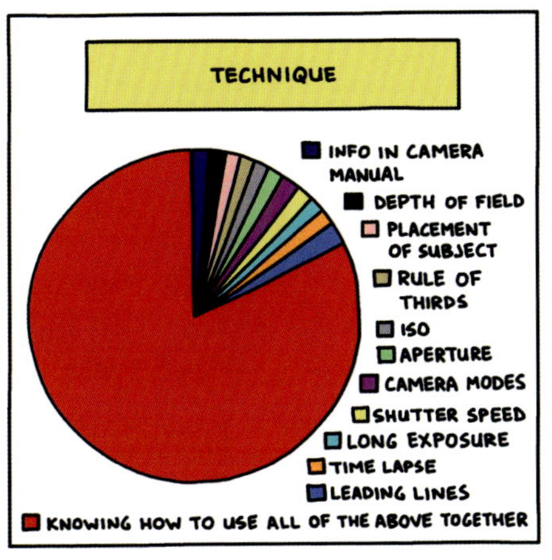

CHAPTER 13

Technique

First and foremost: Read your camera's manual. Every camera operates differently—especially within the vast and overwhelming sea of modern digital bodies. I know the manuals can be painful to read. I get that. But the reality is that a light-sensitive camera, like a Sony a7S, is going to operate differently from a Sony a7R, which has no anti-aliasing filter and is built for high resolution.

Here are some tools you need to get used to. Once you have mastered the most basic functions of a camera—shooting a light or dark image—you can capture your subject with creativity and make the photo you want. In a word, you can create something beautiful.

Depth of field

You can manipulate depth of field in multiple ways. You can just do it with the lens, giving yourself a shallow field where you're going to create a lot of visual depth.

If you want to have falloff, you would use the widest aperture, which is usually f2.8 or more.

If you want the depth of field to be very shallow and just have your subject in focus, you would shoot usually at f11–22, which is standard.

And if you want a large depth of field with everything in focus, you would shoot at f/22 or f/11.

Composition

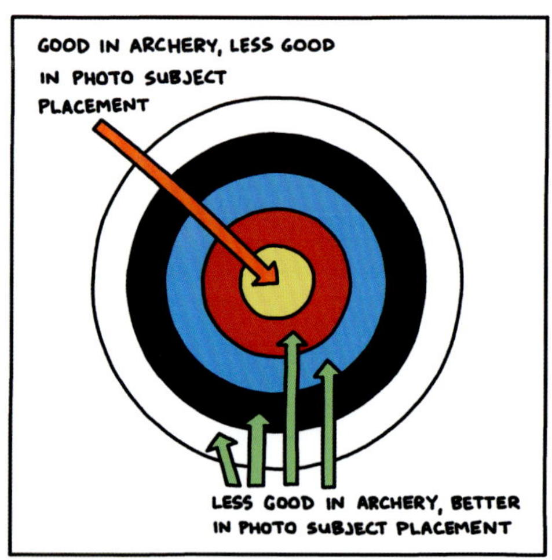

The overall *purpose* of your image defines your composition, and the more advanced you get, the more you will start to compose your image based on what exactly you're trying to create.

To bull's-eye or not to bull's-eye? That is the question. As you may have guessed, to bull's-eye is to place your subject in the frame's dead center—boom!—which is challenging because often when you're trying to tell a story, you want to show either where your subject has been or where they're going. You could be shooting a plane in the sky or a person paddling across a lake.

Spoiler alert: You never really want to have your subject dead center. I think a lot of this comes from not wanting to have the subject of your image fall into the gutter of a magazine. Nowadays, we use social media and other things, but still, it's an important rule. Because it's nice to allow space—breath!—for where your subject is going or could go. Try to animate a still-static subject and give it some life.

The rule of thirds is a common guideline for composition. If you create three layers in your image—a sky, a mid-ground, and a foreground—it's going to be more interesting. Well, that's great for the most basic composition, but if you're looking to do something a little deeper, I suggest you go for five layers. Or go for ten layers. Create an image that has lots of depth and gives you a ton of space to actually create more layers than you think you need. In doing so, you're going to make the image feel like you can reach out and grab it, and you're going to create distance between each one of those layers.

Camera modes

I highly suggest you avoid using your camera's auto mode unless you're in the very first stages of coming to grips with a modern camera. Yes, it's nice to have auto mode to fall back on, but I really rely on shutter priority mode. When I'm shooting action of any kind, I use manual mode as much as possible, and sometimes I use f-stop priority (basically AV mode), which allows me to focus on what kind of falloff I want. Do I want everything in focus, or nothing in focus?

	AUTO	MANUAL
CAR	EASY, STRAIGHT-FORWARD, SUITABLE FOR MOST PEOPLE	MORE DIFFICULT TO LEARN, CAN BE REWARDING, EXCITING, + USEFUL FOR SOME PEOPLE
CAMERA	EASY, STRAIGHT-FORWARD, SUITABLE FOR MOST PEOPLE	MORE DIFFICULT TO LEARN, CAN BE REWARDING, EXCITING, + USEFUL FOR SOME PEOPLE

Leading lines

Leading lines can be confusing. This is where you want the viewer's eye to go. People often think a leading line should be a physical line, like a trail or a painted line in the middle of a road. It can be, but sometimes it's a mountain that can pull you into the shot. I often find that if I can push my frame (zoom in or out) or frame the edge of my image to where there is the line of a mountain, the line of a sky, the line of a horizon pulling in—any line that can help the eye go somewhere specific—it's going to help the image become more centrally focused.

ISO

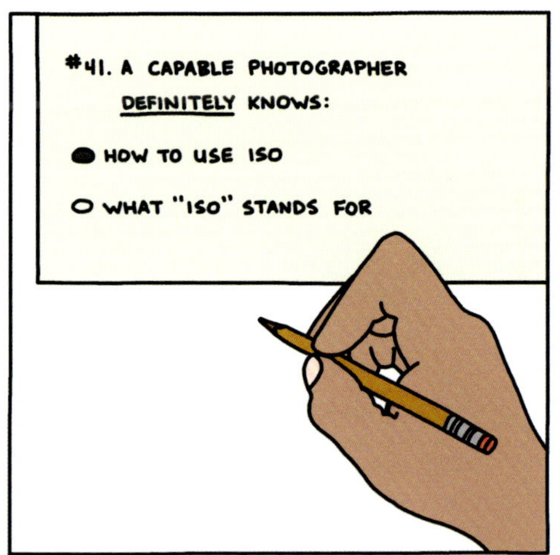

No, *ISO* does not mean "in search of." Originally devised for film, it's the standard of light sensitivity set decades ago by the Geneva-based International Organization for Standardization. There are general rules of thumb here, yes, but it's important to know the differences within digital cameras. In the past, all cameras were equally "sensitive," and the film stock was what determined how much light would be allowed into the camera for the exposure. But with modern-day digital cameras, some are hyper light sensitive. This doesn't mean that the camera will operate or function differently in terms of ISO setting, but it does mean that it's going to give you a better-quality image at high ISO. One example is the Sony a7S III (the *S* stands for "sensitivity"), which is a preferential tool for shooting in

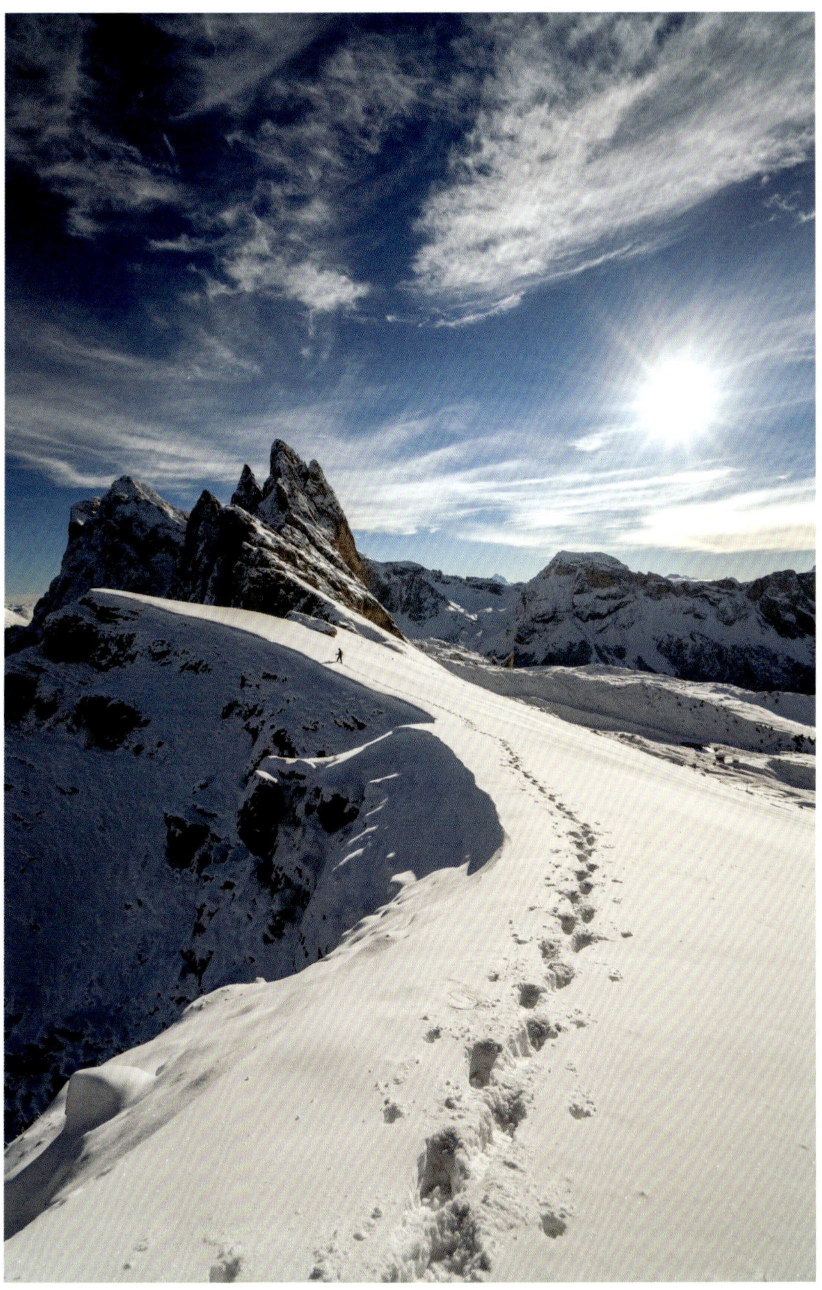

low-light situations. These cameras can yield more contrasty, brighter feeling images when compared to other non-light-sensitive cameras.

More ISO = more sensitivity to light. Choosing more sensitivity will vastly change two things: the brightness of your photo when shooting at certain shutter speeds and f-stops, and the grain or the noisiness of your photo. Relatively speaking, as ISO goes up, the image quality goes down.

Aperture

Aperture can change your depth of field, which means as you adjust it, either on the lens or on the camera dial, it will make the images have a shallower or greater depth of field. The wider the aperture, which on the camera looks like the smaller the f-number, the more light is allowed in the camera, but the shallower the depth of field. You might shoot at a wide-open aperture, say f/2.8, so just the subject's face is in focus and the landscape falls away and gets nice and smooth and blurry. Or you might shoot at f/22 so everything is in focus, from the foreground to the background. That will result in more of a traditional landscape-style image.

Shutter speed

Set your shutter speed low if you're handholding the camera and you aren't shooting any action, meaning nothing's moving. Set your shutter speed high if you're shooting action and it's moving across your frame or coming toward you. For trail running or surfing or mountain biking, you might be shooting at 1/800 of a second or at 1/1600 of a second. If somebody is climbing a rock (climbing *is* an action sport!) but they're not moving fast, you might only be shooting at 1/250 of a second.

As you slow down the shutter speed, you can start to manipulate your image, such as by showing shutter blur or movement in water or the movement of trees from wind. The slower the shutter, the more

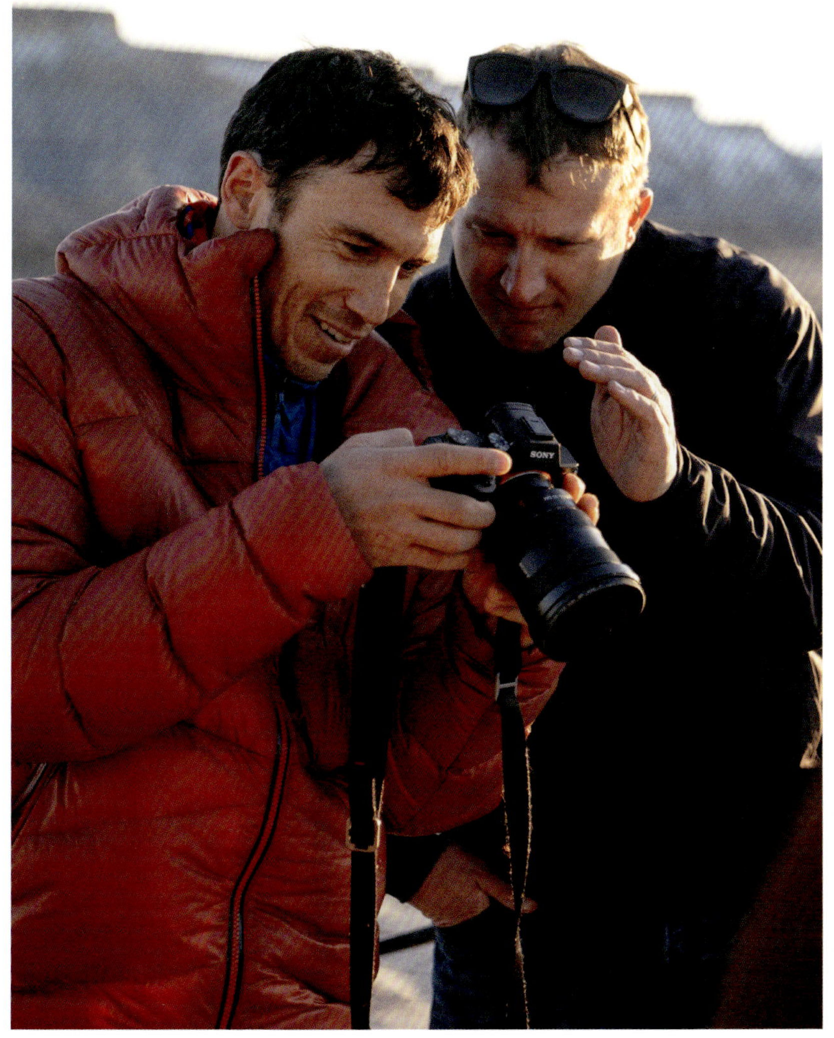
SONY

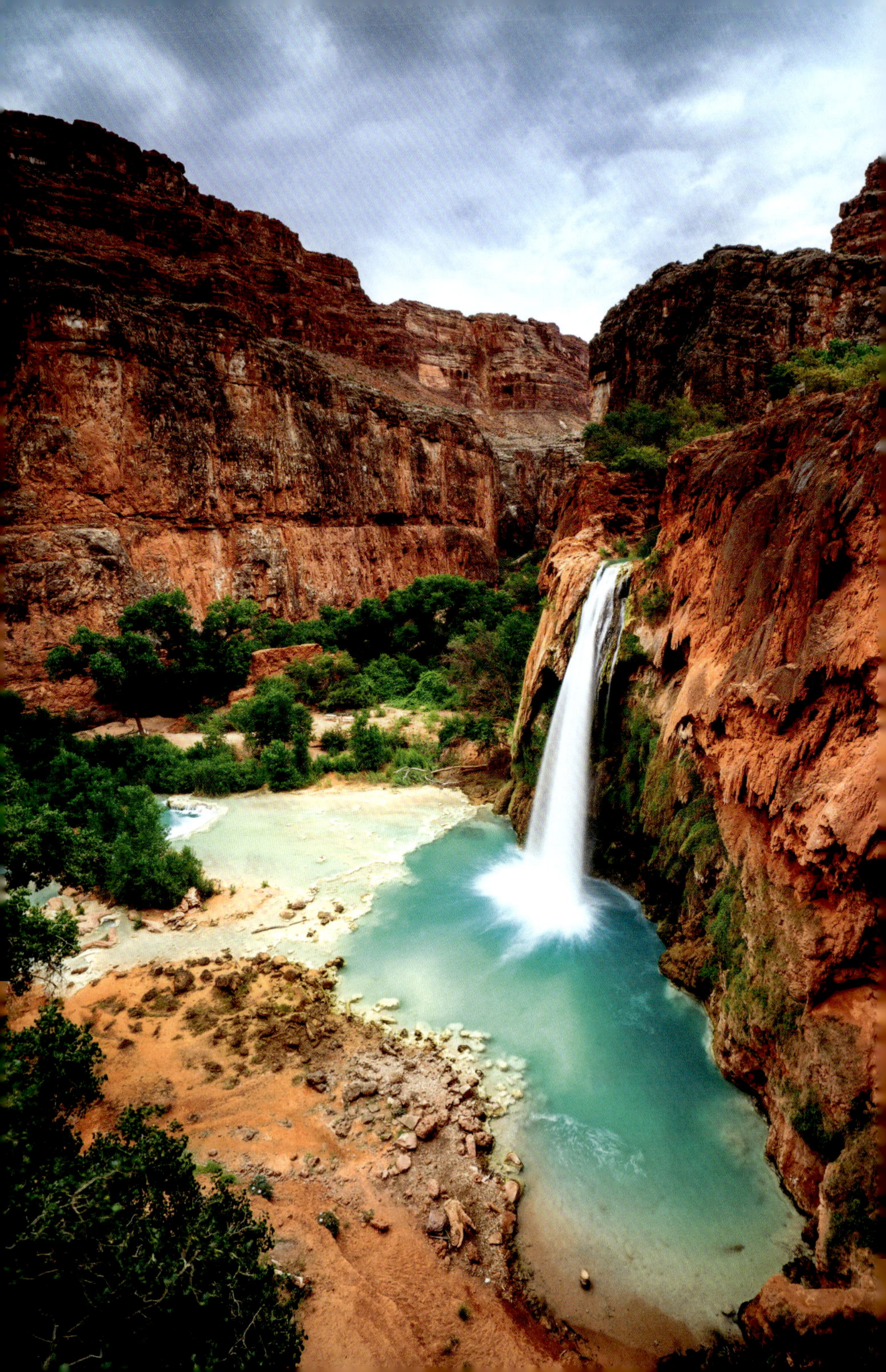

light you're allowing into the lens, and sometimes you're saturating the image slightly with more color. For night exposures, shutter speed plays a big role.

So, these processes create a *style* of image. They just make an image brighter or darker. That's all they do.

Time-lapse images and long exposures are merely a result of shutter speed. A time-lapse is produced by shooting multiple images over and over. It's a setting within the camera usually, or within a time-lapse tool, like a little remote that would allow for the camera to continually shoot-shoot-shoot and keep shooting so you can stack images or play them back in a video.

A long exposure would be when you're shooting anything that can't be handheld. So if the exposure is set for 1/2 of a second or 1/10 of a second, you have the camera on a tripod for 2 seconds or 5 seconds or 30 seconds. That's a long exposure. And the longer the exposure, the more manipulated the photo is going to be. The image is going to have star trails or moving water that's actually blurred. These are things you cannot see with your eyes. That's why the image is "manipulated" and looks and feels different.

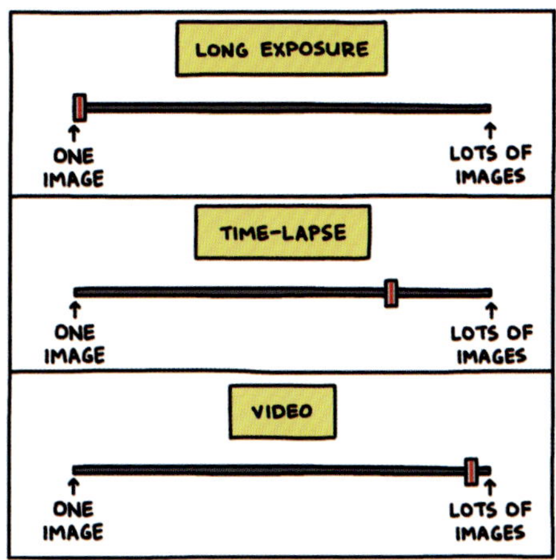

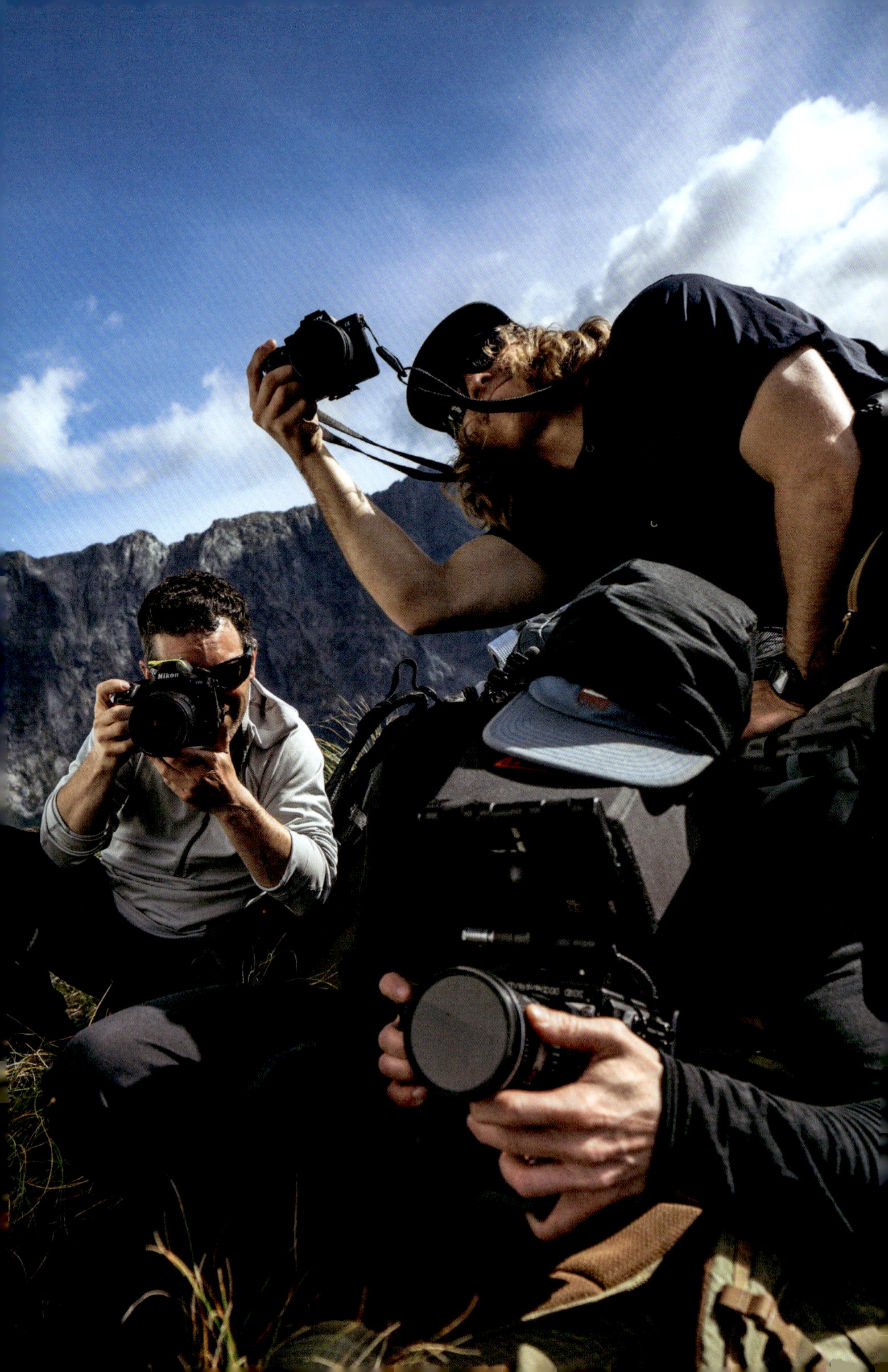
Nikon

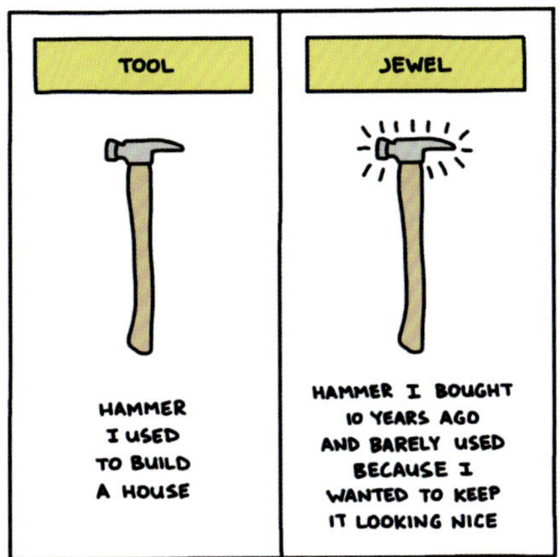

CHAPTER 14

They're Tools, Not Jewels

Cameras

Everyone wants to know: Which *one* camera will do it all?

Answer? None of them. No modern camera does everything. And so my personal mantra has always been: *It's not about the camera—the best camera is the one you have and are willing to use.* If that's your iPhone, then your iPhone's the best camera. If it's a high-resolution medium-format camera, then that's the one. If it's a camera that's simple and easy, that's going to be it. I tend to relish opportunities where I can use the Xperia smartphone or my iPhone to shoot a film, or a GoPro, or an RX100 (a small basic point-and-shoot). I oscillate between all of these because I like to remind myself that I don't need fancy equipment to shoot something really special.

Every company makes something different, and the light-sensitive cameras are the ones that really are specifically built for certain purposes. For example, if you want to shoot the northern lights, the a7S is going to be a good setup. Or if you need high-resolution, the a7R is a great camera. But for the most part, I really love to shoot with the most minimal equipment possible.

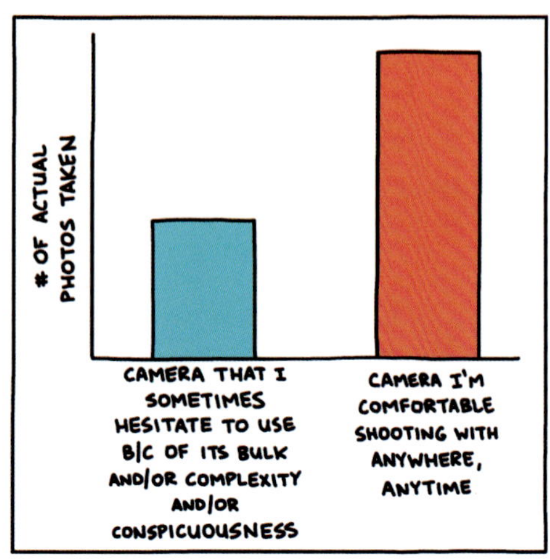

The biggest thing with cameras is understanding not only the multiple styles available but also their sensor sizes. Whether it's Micro Four Thirds, APS-C, or full-frame—they're all going to give you a different look. A larger sensor provides better low-light sensitivity and better bokeh (a.k.a. better falloff). If you're shooting f/1.8 or shallow depth of field, a larger sensor will give you a better depth of field.

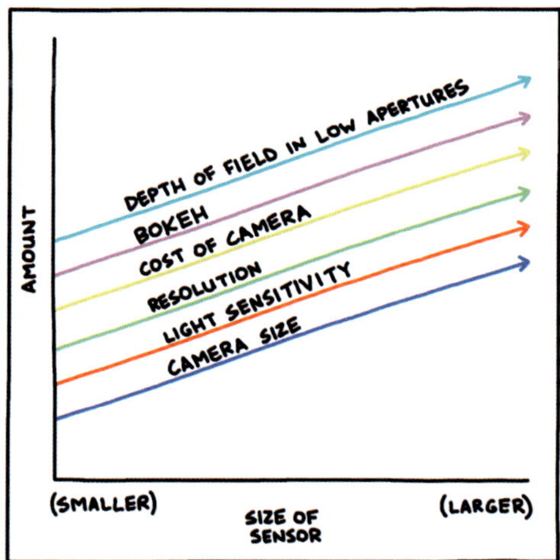

A smaller sensor has other advantages. More things are going to be in focus because it has better focusing capacity. The resulting image is lower resolution, though. So there are pros and cons. Another advantage of a smaller sensor is a smaller package—a smaller camera. A bigger sensor requires a bigger and usually more expensive camera.

Personally? I really like Sony's full-frame compact camera, the a7C series. Because the camera is small and easy to use, I carry one in my backpack at all times. But if I'm going on a professional assignment, sometimes I'll bring a larger, more expensive full-frame body. It just depends on what I'm after.

Lenses

OK, enough about cameras. What about lenses? Lenses are a personal choice. The 16–35mm is my all-time favorite length. I love wide-angle perspective the most.

PRIME LENSES VS. ZOOM LENSES		
CATEGORY	PRIME LENSES	ZOOM LENSES
BETTER F-STOP RANGE	👍	
BETTER FOR ACTION PHOTOGRAPHY		👍
ZOOMS ~~BETTER~~		👍
BETTER FOR PORTRAITS	👍	
BETTER FOR NIGHT PHOTOS	👍	
WINNER	👍	👍

I try to start every shoot with the same lens so I can operate in a cyclical fashion and know what else I can get my hands on. This doesn't mean that using a prime lens is a bad idea. Primes are great because they give you the ability to make a sharper image. I use primes anytime I'm shooting portraits or in a low-light scenario.

With a prime lens, you're limited, though. This makes them highly valuable for beginners because, for example, a prime will force you to walk toward your subject for a proper focus field. You've got to dive right in—get up close and personal.

Zooms are excellent for action photography. I use them when I'm facing varied, uncontrollable conditions, and I'll have to move around—to be up close and wide and far away. When I do commercial jobs and shoots where I don't know what's going to be coming up—perhaps I'll be shooting a landscape and then a portrait and then a product shot—a zoom is what I'll go for.

A 16–35mm and a 24–70mm are always in my bag. Usually I'll have one prime with me, depending on the job. It might be a 35mm, a 20mm, or a 24mm, depending on if I'm shooting a landscape assignment or people or whatever. Additionally I might bring a 70–200mm or a 100–400mm and maybe some specialty primes (again, depending on the job). You must build your lens kit based on the job you're doing. That's the key takeaway here. You need to evaluate the situations you're going to be in and go from there.

Specialty photography

Aerial photography is a special situation. As far as lenses, I prefer a 24–70mm, or if the pilot's really good and I know they can get me in the right position, I'll use a 16–35mm. It's much harder to shoot wide

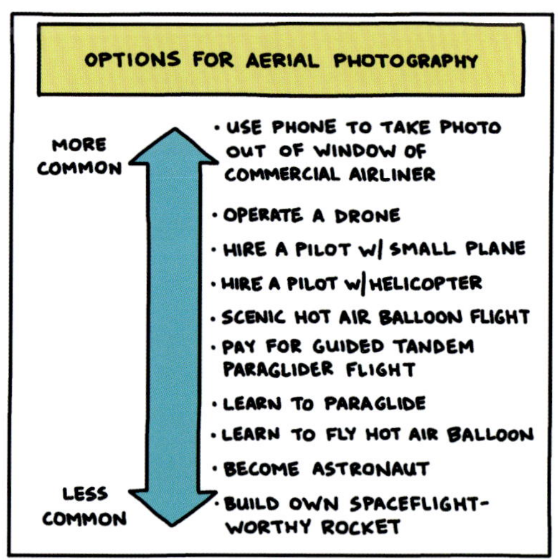

in the air without getting the wing or the tail in the shot. The easiest thing for aerial photography would be a 70–200mm, but I think the resulting images look less interesting because they're flatter instead of wide and dramatic.

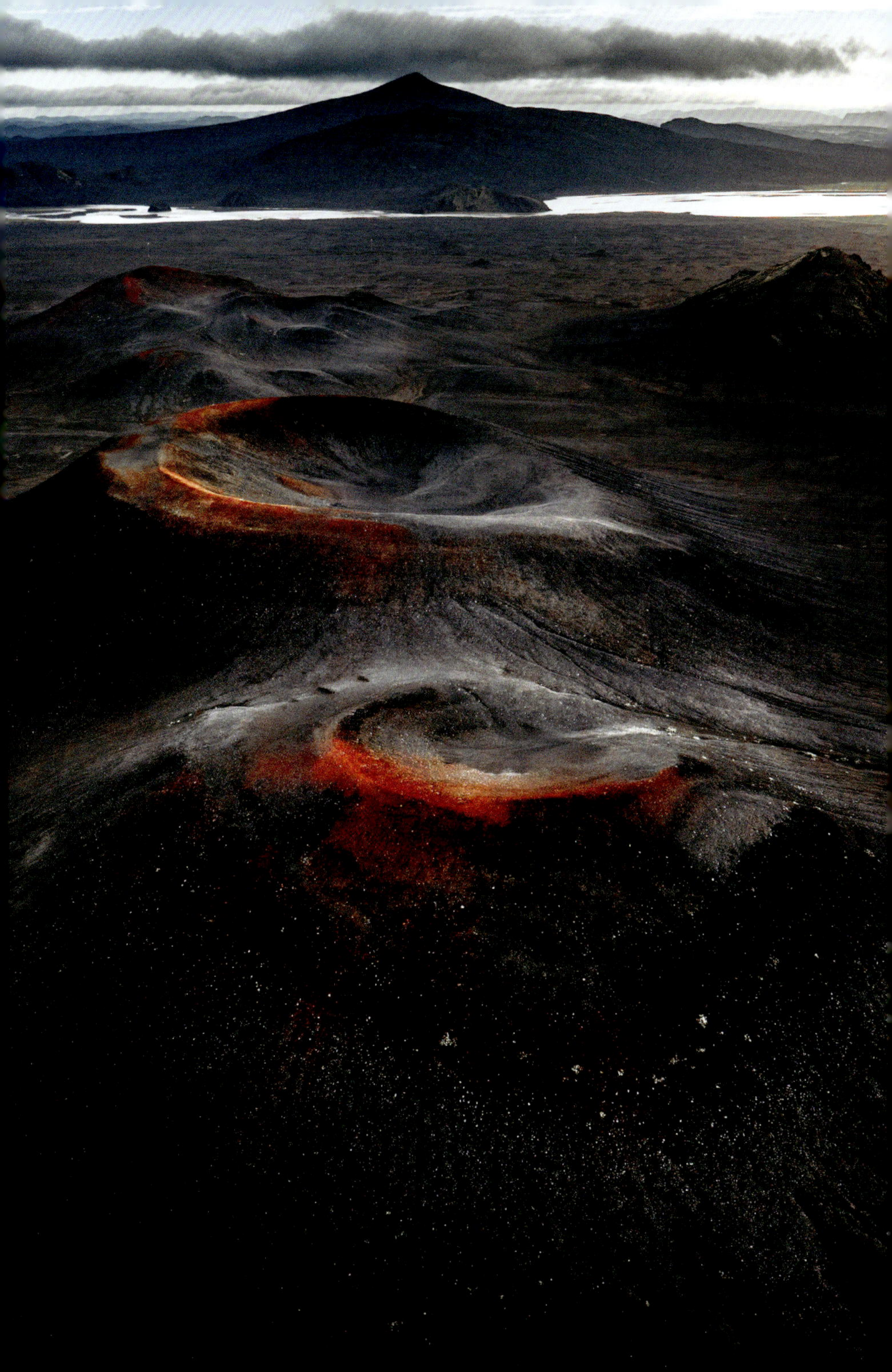

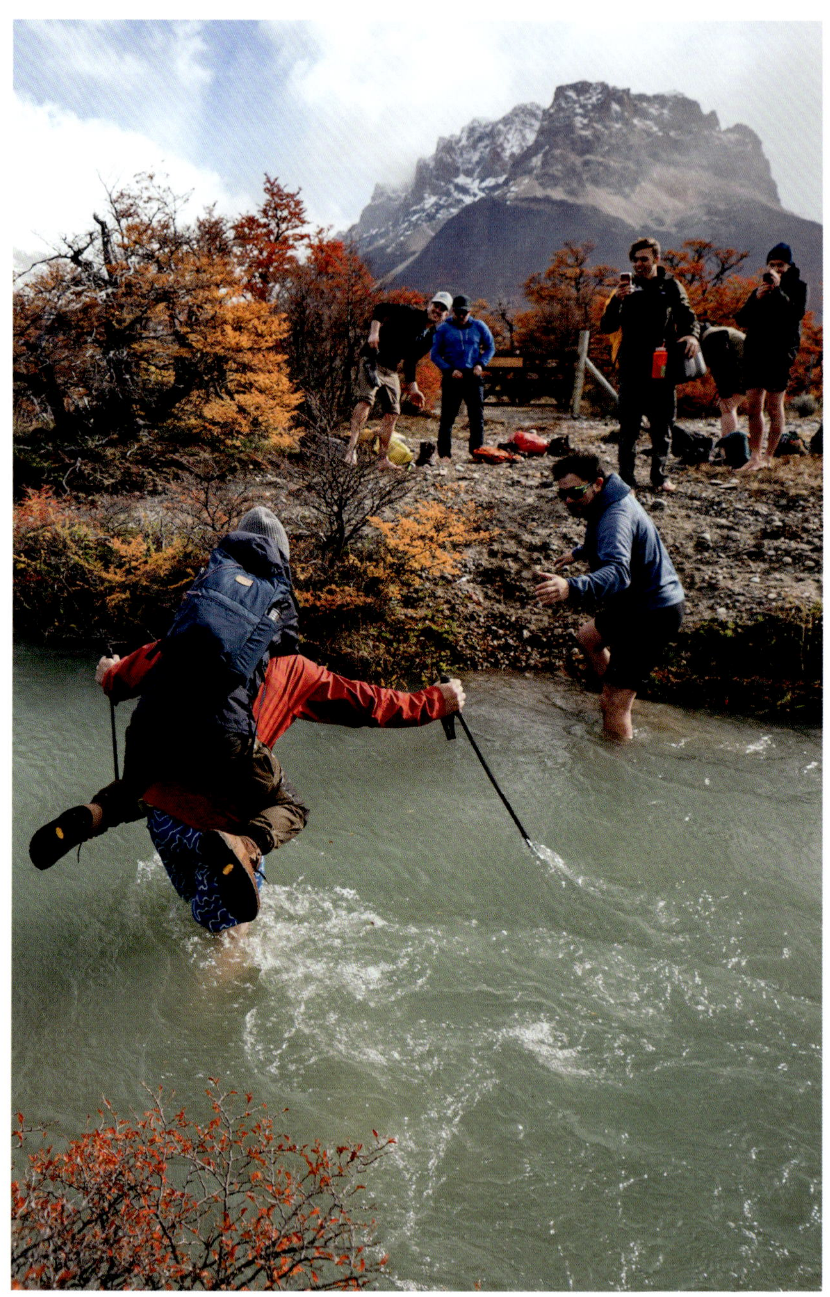

Drone photography is kind of what you make of it. If you spend time shooting with a drone, you're going to get really good at it. It's not my favorite type of photography, only because it takes you out of the moment a lot and makes you feel less connected to the subject.

Camera phones

When it comes to mobile devices, the key thing to know is that a camera phone is pretty limited. You're often restricted to one lens length or maybe a few lens lengths, and you can't have a quality zoom. A phone is a fun tool and useful for grab shots, but it's never going to be great for low light and the bokeh you want for portraits. Some phone cameras incorporate AI features that can make an image interesting, but it's never going to be great. Camera phone photos are not going to be high-quality because the sensor is so tiny.

Overall, I recommend shooting at the lowest ISO setting you can. If you're shooting with a phone, you can shoot in RAW file format if you want to upgrade your imagery. There isn't really a way to ensure better quality out of a mobile device, but if I'm shooting with an RX100 or a GoPro or something like that, I'm always trying to shoot it in the lowest ISO. Other than that, some cameras offer image stacking, which creates multiple images and higher resolution. That's a really good option too.

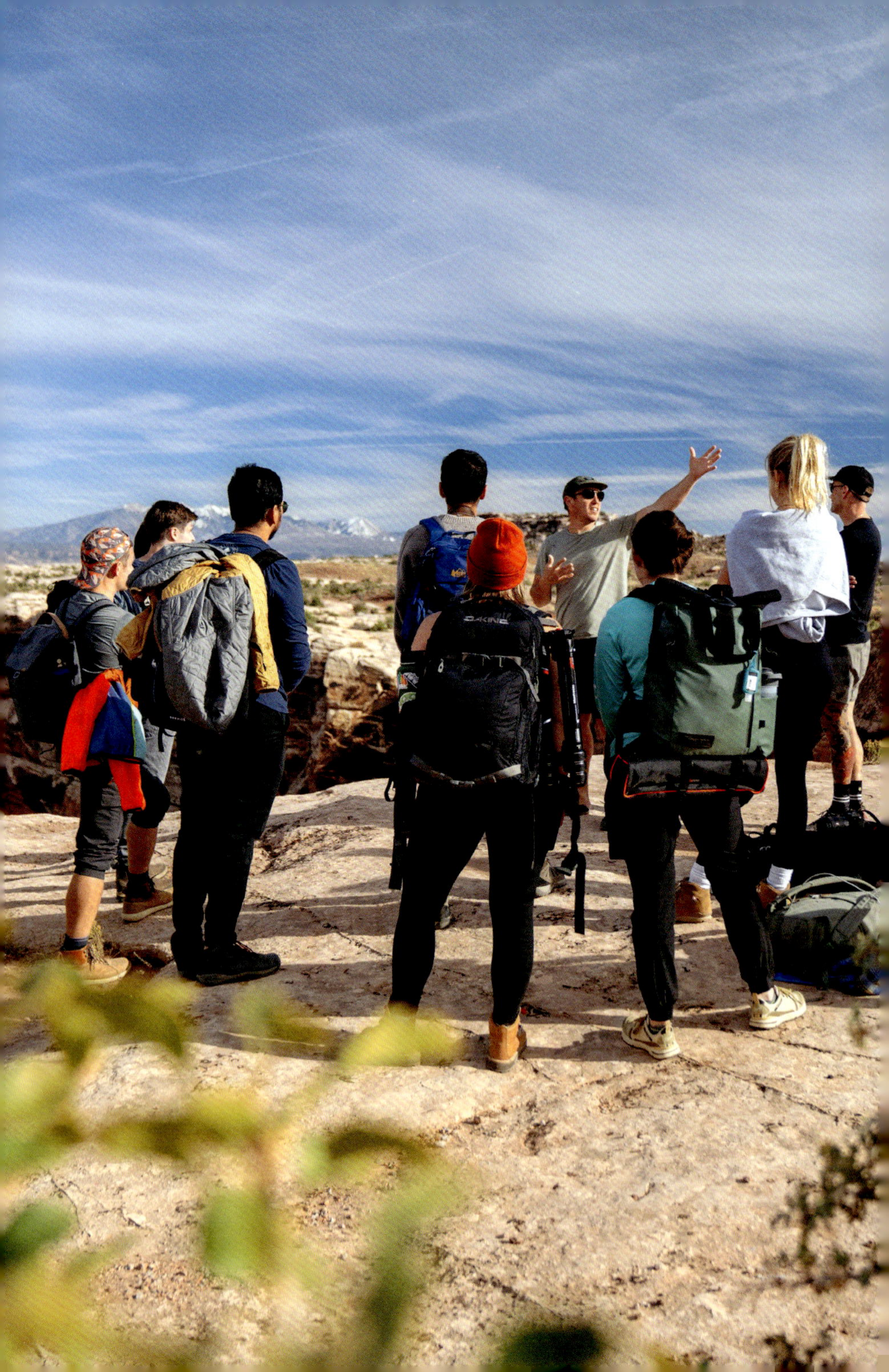
DAKINE

HOW TO MAKE FRIENDS IN REAL LIFE	HOW TO MAKE FRIENDS ON SOCIAL MEDIA
• ASK QUESTIONS	• ASK QUESTIONS
• CARE	• CARE
• BE A REAL PERSON	• BE A REAL PERSON
• BE KIND	• BE KIND
• SHARE A LITTLE BIT ABOUT YOURSELF	• SHARE A LITTLE BIT ABOUT YOURSELF
• DO THE RIGHT THING	• DO THE RIGHT THING

CHAPTER 15

Tell Your Story

Share yourself on social media

Social media is the space where you can freely tell your own story. Instead of rehashing a John Muir quote (e.g., "The mountains are calling and I must go"), you can tell people what you felt, what you saw, what you experienced *out there*. It's your story. To share your story, you can't use somebody else's words.

Social media is all about time. Time is the only currency social media operates on. It's not about some complicated algorithm forcing us to look at things we don't want to buy or things we don't want to read. It's about what we spend our time viewing. And sadly, often what gets our attention is the most vitriolic or the most shocking or jarring thing, right? That's what rises to the top.

When it comes to gaining traction on social media, I always tell people the best thing you can do is actually spend time getting to know other people—comment on their work and like their stuff and demonstrate interest. Be responsive. Be a real person. By doing that, you show that you care. That's how you gain a following.

Give your followers a piece of yourself. Be honest, be vulnerable. Vulnerability is key. I follow people because I am interested in and excited about what they have to say. They have a unique perspective. They give a piece of themselves. I know them as people. They aren't just random profiles that post pretty pictures or funny memes. They actually have original thoughts and ideas.

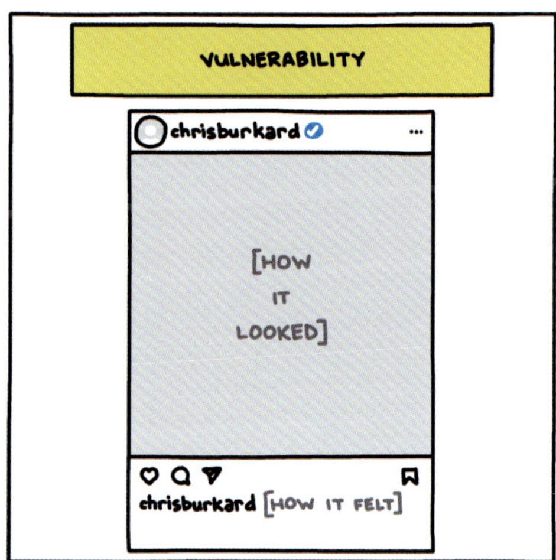

On social media, you're a brand, and you're making decisions like any brand would. Be consistent and use calls to action, which means asking questions and engaging with your community so that you get responses. At its core, social media is simply a glorified texting app, and if you aren't replying to the texts that are being sent to you, it's not really going to work out in your favor. You need to be responsive and use your voice to explain what you felt and saw or what you're feeling and seeing. You're the one who went out there and felt the wind change and the ice or snow crunch under your feet. Tell us about it!

Learning to use your voice is going to be one of your most valuable lessons and will take you from being a photographer to being somebody who can really expand upon a unique and vulnerable experience. You can start small; your posting doesn't have to be expansive. You don't have to talk about the most vulnerable thing you've ever felt. Just try to provide anecdotes or small pieces of what you saw out there. Tune in to more than just the photograph. Tune in to the senses.

Keep your gear simple

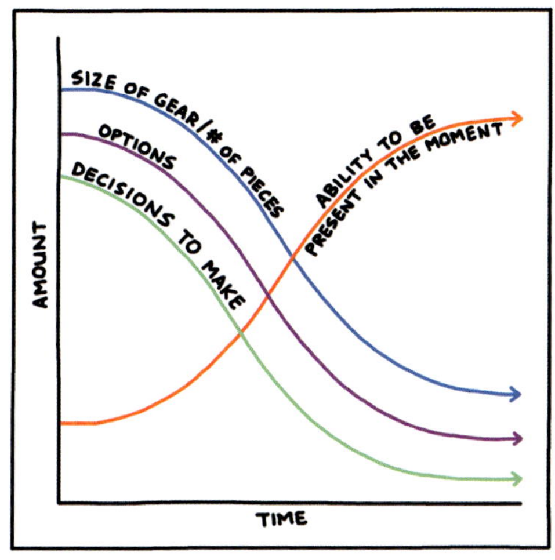

We often believe that having all the options (all the lenses, all the cameras) will give us more creativity. In fact, it overwhelms us. It allows for so many options that we often become *less* creative. Sometimes stripping away a lot of that stuff is one of the most important things you can do. "Dumb down" your gear for a more intimate experience. When I did the California Surf Project in 2008, I owned only two lenses (a 24mm and a 70–200mm), and I borrowed a 600mm. My camera was a Canon 20D. It was a minimalist kit. Nowadays, when I'm doing expeditions and bike trips and stuff like that, I'm looking for opportunities to *not* have all the gear. I want to have less. I want to go out and shoot with just a Sony Xperia smartphone or a point-and-shoot RX100 because those small kits allow me to quickly pull out a camera when a good opportunity arises.

Like I said in the last chapter, the best camera is the one you're willing to use. If that's a GoPro attached to your bike's handlebar, use that. When my only camera is a big DSLR with a big camera strap, I've often felt anxious to stick it in front of someone's face, and the subject tends to respond the same way. They feel more threatened and anxious by that experience. They feel less overwhelmed by a GoPro or a point-and-shoot or a phone. So starting with minimal gear is a great practice. Advance to that high-end camera with its full-frame qualities and high burst rate when you really need it, but don't start that way.

Another thing to keep in mind is that you're going to be more willing to *use* your gear when you aren't worried about what it cost you. (Think tools, not jewels!) You can allow yourself to beat it up a little and really push it. That's how it should be used. That's the goal and the way in which you should apply yourself day-to-day as a photographer.

I've shot so many of my favorite experiences—my favorite moments, my favorite portraits, my favorite action shots—with what the manufacturers classify as an amateur's camera, a "prosumer" APS-C camera. But these have their own advantages, and sometimes it's the one camera you're willing to pull out. Just because it might be less technical or lower quality does not mean you can't get a great shot. With today's highly advanced digital technology, most cameras can yield incredible results. The cameras we all have in our pockets today are much more powerful than the ones professional photographers were using twenty, thirty, or forty years ago.

Focus on the task at hand

Spend more time thinking about making a photograph and its composition than worrying about which camera you have. The more time you shoot, especially in remote places, the more you'll realize that big cameras can be threatening. But phones? Nobody's afraid of them. Everyone knows what a phone is. So when you pull one out, it's not this big scary thing. If you're pulling out a DSLR, something changes. People tend to act differently, or they might decide they want something from you. You need to find that balance between being a fly on the wall and preserving those intimate moments.

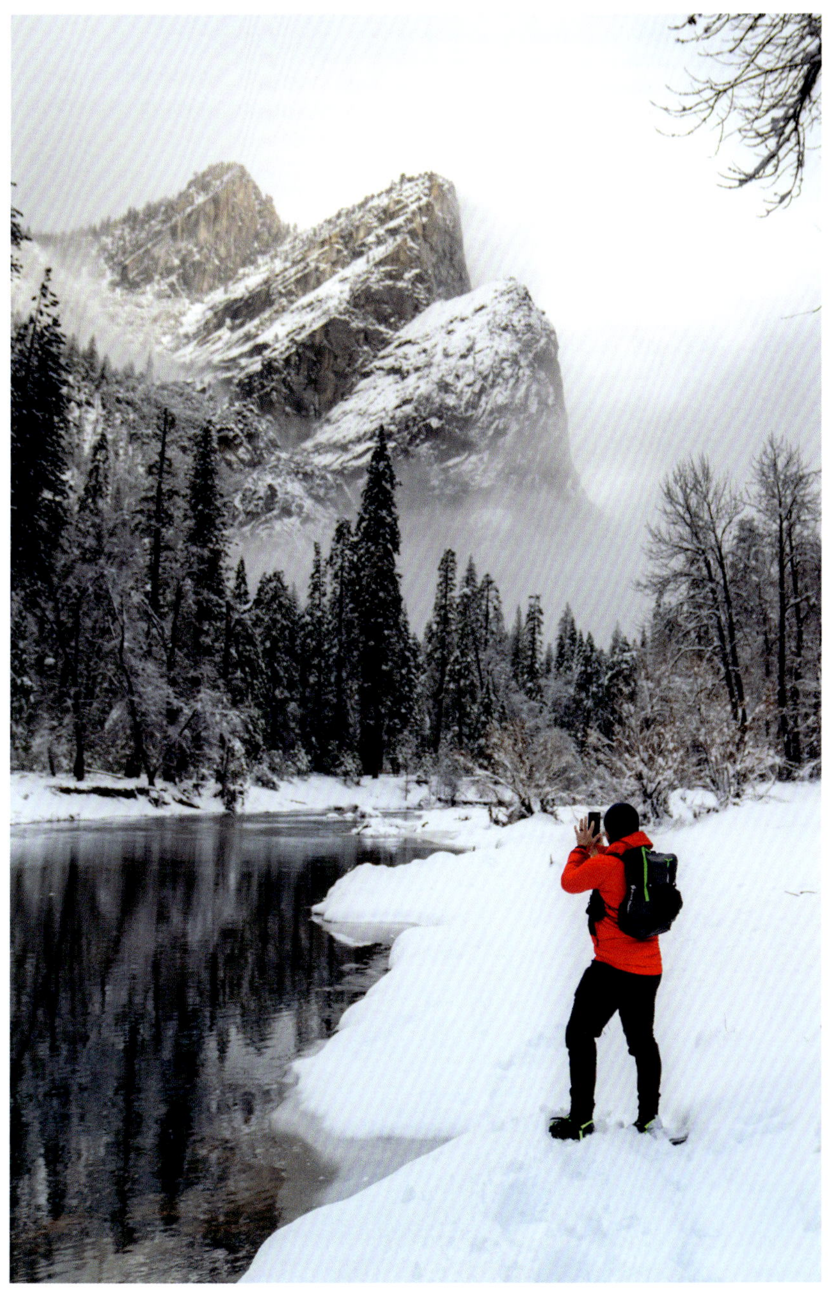

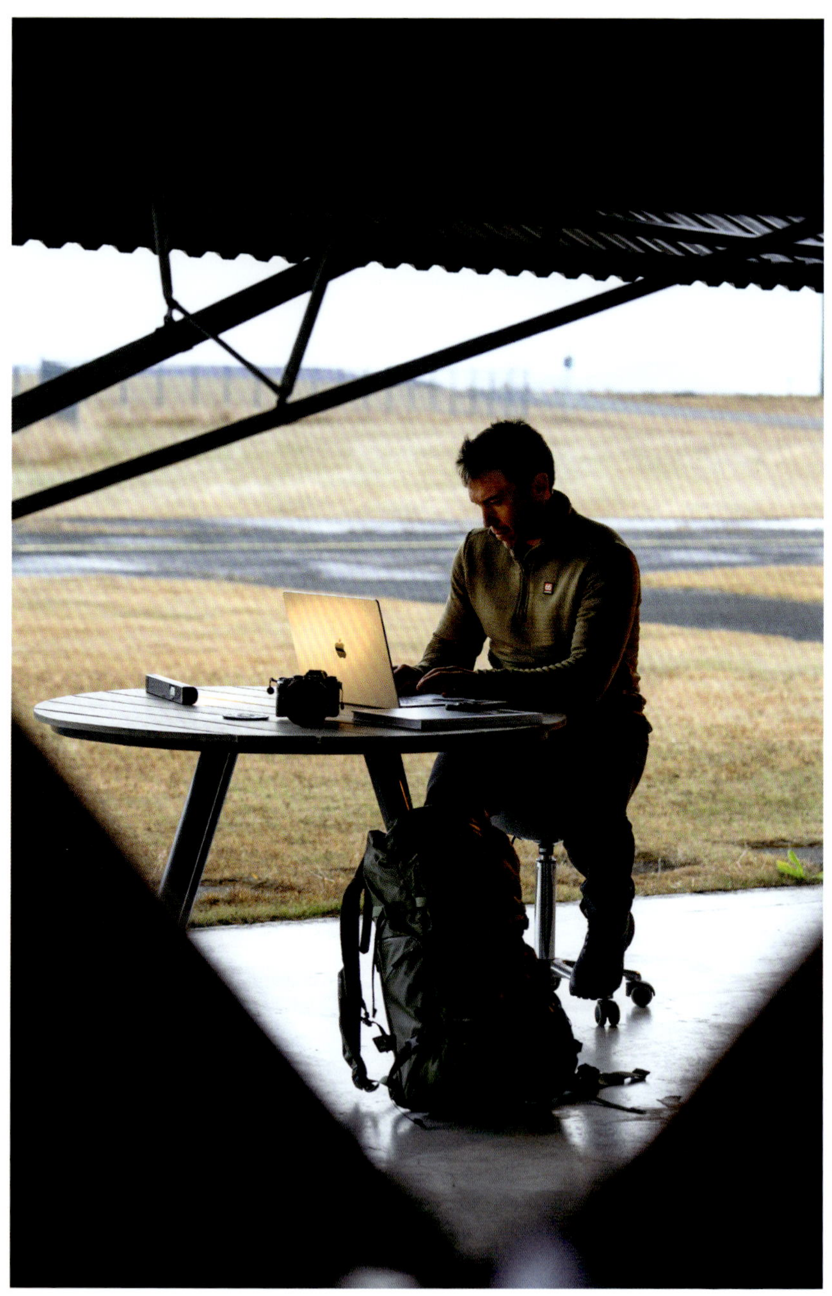

Take your time and write it down

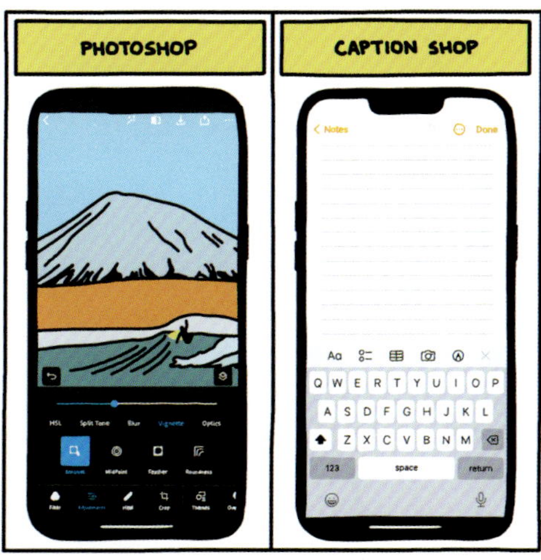

People ask me where I find the time to write long Instagram captions or to write about my experiences. When I'm flying home or I'm on a bus or a train, or I have a moment that I could be listening to an audiobook or whatever, I usually don headphones. I'll listen to some instrumental music and try to really home in on what I might write for the beginning of a caption. I felt *this* and *this* and *that*, and this experience gave me *this*. I usually make notes in a folder on my phone, and these are often the beginning of something bigger: a bigger thought, a bigger idea, a bigger caption.

Normally, during an experience, we don't really have the ability to expand on everything we see and feel. That takes time. This is why it's important that you give yourself a moment to articulate a little bit of what you felt and then revisit it later. It's the same as processing digital images. When I used to shoot film, it sometimes took two weeks before I got the film back and could finally see what I'd shot. But with digital, you see your photos immediately. This does not necessarily yield the time needed to really digest an experience, which is why I feel it's important to journal some thoughts, some reminders, some feelings, and then revisit them after you've had time to absorb and distill everything you experienced.

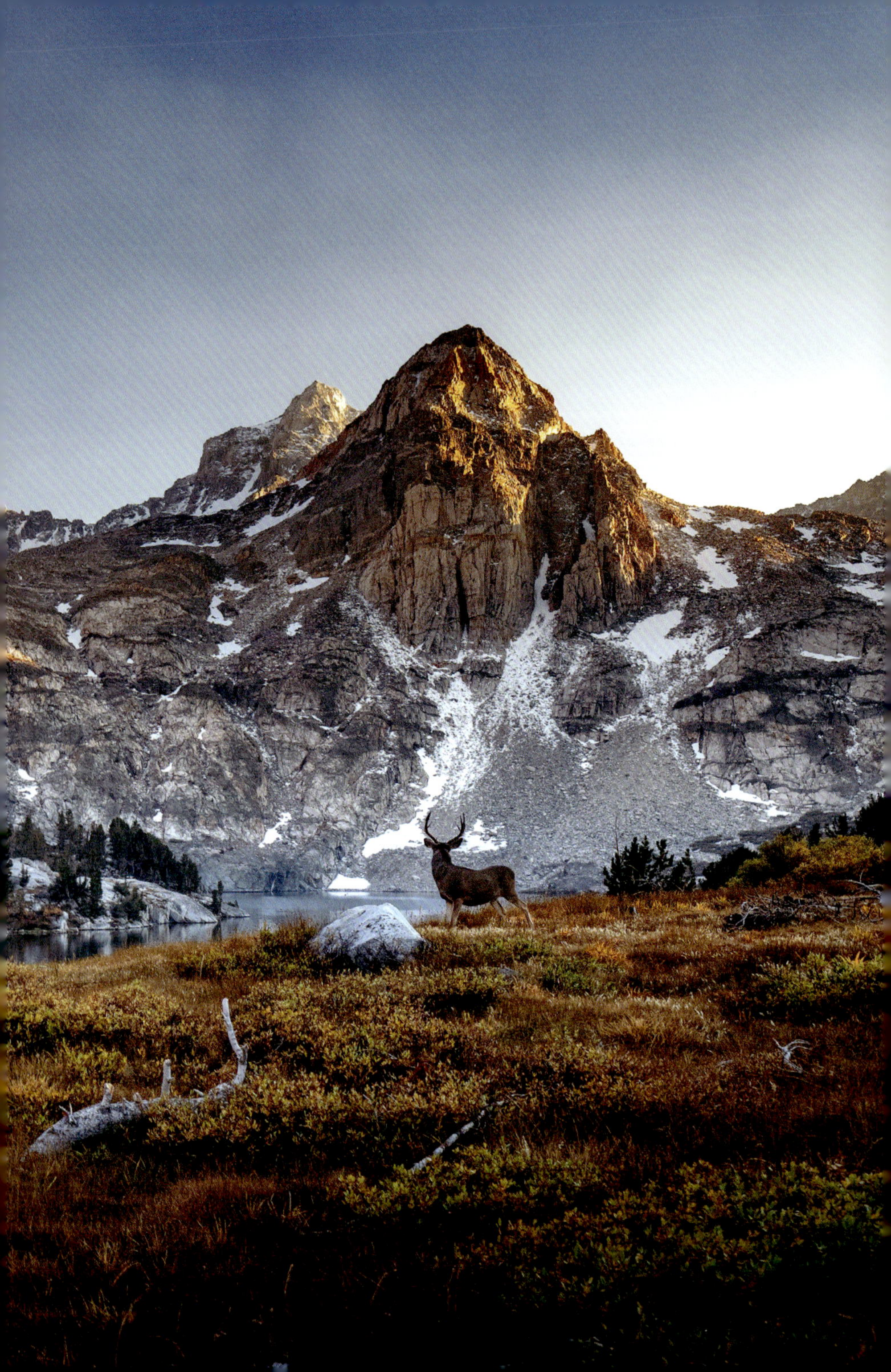

PERSONAL PHOTOGRAPHY	CLIENT WORK
☐ DON'T RUSH THE PROCESS ☐ SOAK IT ALL IN ☐ GO OUT WITHOUT YOUR BIG CAMERA OR WITHOUT A CAMERA ☐ EXPERIENCE THE PLACE SO YOU HAVE SOMETHING TO SAY ABOUT IT ☐ GET SOME GREAT SHOTS	☐ GET SOME GREAT SHOTS ☐ IF YOU HAVE TIME, EXPERIENCE THE PLACE AND ALL THAT OTHER FUN STUFF

CHAPTER 16

Marinate in the Moment

So how do you not allow the camera to compromise the experience? This is one of the most commonly asked questions I have gotten and, honestly, it is the hardest to answer. The goal of the camera should be to enhance the intimate experience of being in a place, with a person, or in a landscape. Here are my thoughts on how to protect some of the intimacy of these moments.

It's important to differentiate when you're shooting something for a job and when you're there for personal reasons. There are many times when I'm working and I don't really have the freedom to go out and just soak it all in. I'm there focusing on the client or the task at hand or the many looks I have to shoot. When you're shooting for personal reasons, you can take your time to experience places without the overhanging needs of a project or a job.

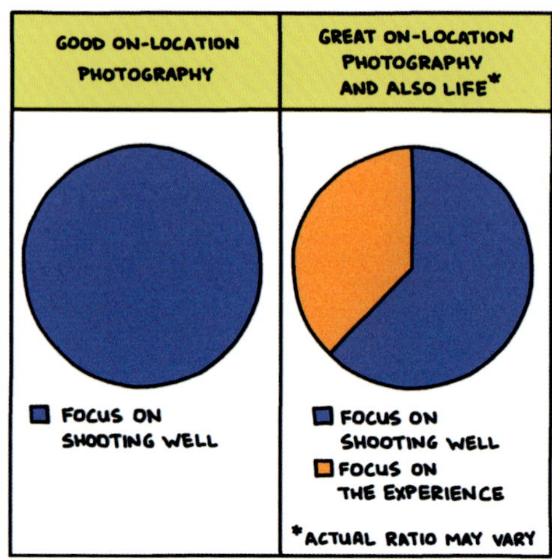

To get yourself into this thought pattern, don't rush the process. Allowing yourself time to actually create good images is important. So what does that mean? Well, when you're in a place like Cuba or India or wherever, put the camera away. Give yourself the time to go out without it.

When you do want to take a photo and you're maybe using a smaller camera that's more minimal, more mellow, more easy to use, less obtrusive, you're going to feel more intimate and connected to a physical setting. This is part of why an iPhone or an RX100 is so special—because you just pop it out and you're done. It's not about fumbling around changing lenses or deciding on a filter. It's about being more intimate and *in* the experience. Be present.

When I'm on location, I try to remember that simply being there and experiencing it and having something to say about it is a huge deal. If you've left an experience with nothing to say about it, that's a big challenge. If you have no memory, no fondness, no feelings, and no emotions, that's a sign that you were *too* focused on shooting and not on *experiencing*.

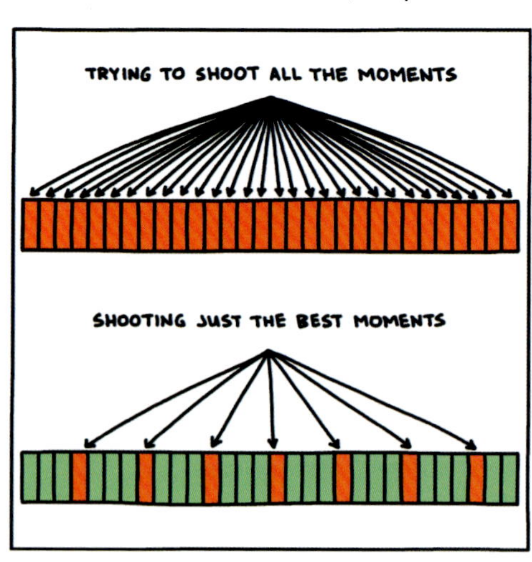

The more we think about the images we want to make, the more we'll soak it in. We'll be less reactionary and more intentional. Intentional photography is a big part of this. Like Ansel Adams said, sure, we can take a photograph, but it's more important we *make* a photograph. And *making* a photograph requires us to think about what we want to shoot.

As I've gotten older, I've realized that I'm not a great technical photographer. Many photographers are much more savvy. The only thing that I've improved on is recognizing when a moment is good and then homing in on that. The more I shoot, the more important it is to realize that if I can put my camera down 75 percent of the time and only pick it up when the moments are good, I'm going to be successful. But you have to be able to recognize when those moments are worth shooting. This takes time and effort. There's no quick tip or trick to do that. It's a personal thing. What's important to me and significant to me might not be important to you. I might be looking for a certain moment; you might be looking for something else. So, homing in on those important moments is crucial, as is learning to interpret the situation for yourself.

Defining who you're shooting for and why you're shooting will help you determine how much you should be shooting and where your attention should be directed.

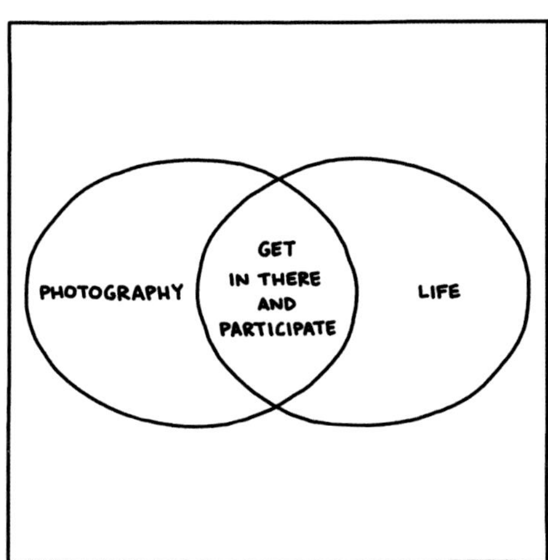

Sometimes we're in the moment, and it's hard to feel like a participant. A lot of photography makes you feel like you're on the sidelines. And the sidelines suck. As Galen Rowell said, photography is not a sideline sport. It's meant

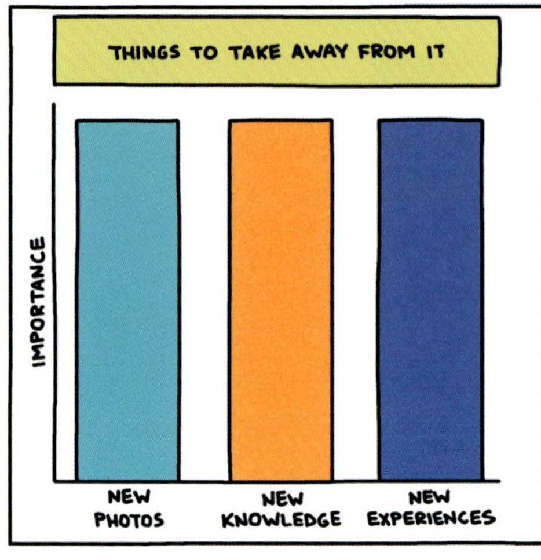

for the active participant. I've always loved that idea. This is part of the reason why I wanted to ride my bike and shoot photos, and climb and shoot photos, and surf and shoot photos. I wanted to be *in* the moment. I wanted to be part of the experience. I felt like that participation was important for my photography.

That being said, when you want to feel like you're participating, it's important to learn about what you're shooting. If you're shooting a certain sport, learn about it. You'll feel less like a mere observer. You'll feel like a participant and that your opinion matters. Of course, sometimes we shoot stuff we have no clue about. But, for example, if you're shooting a chef in action, learn about their process. Maybe try to cook something yourself. Get your hands greasy. Having your subject teach you something will often result in a more intimate setting and might yield a great photo. You must be an active participant to create lasting moments.

Being less of a quiet observer and more of an active participant requires learning—investing in the people, investing in the subject, giving attention to that one thing. All of these little factors play a huge role. The way I can be the very best version of myself is by giving my subjects my *interest* and giving the places that I love my *time*.

When I'm traveling to somewhere new, I want to research it. I want to talk with someone who knows its history. I want to be involved on all levels to understand and figure out how I can learn more about the places I'm shooting and feel more active once I'm in them.

Sometimes the experience of shooting is never going to be active. It's never going to be something where you are actually connected, but you'll have the ability to learn a bit more.

Walking away from a place, a person, a thing, or an activity and asking myself, *What did I learn?*—that's my barometer. What new piece of information did I gain? This is really what I'm after. But to each their own. Each person needs to determine for themselves how they want to walk away from an experience.

And yeah, maybe we're shooting stuff we don't know. That's OK. And it's acceptable to acknowledge that some jobs are purely for money and you don't really have much else to gain.

The best images—those that mean the most to you—are going to happen when you're spending a bit of time really investing in the process. Commit yourself to a place. Immerse yourself. Gain an intimacy with a place and build on it. This is important to me, and I highly suggest it for everybody.

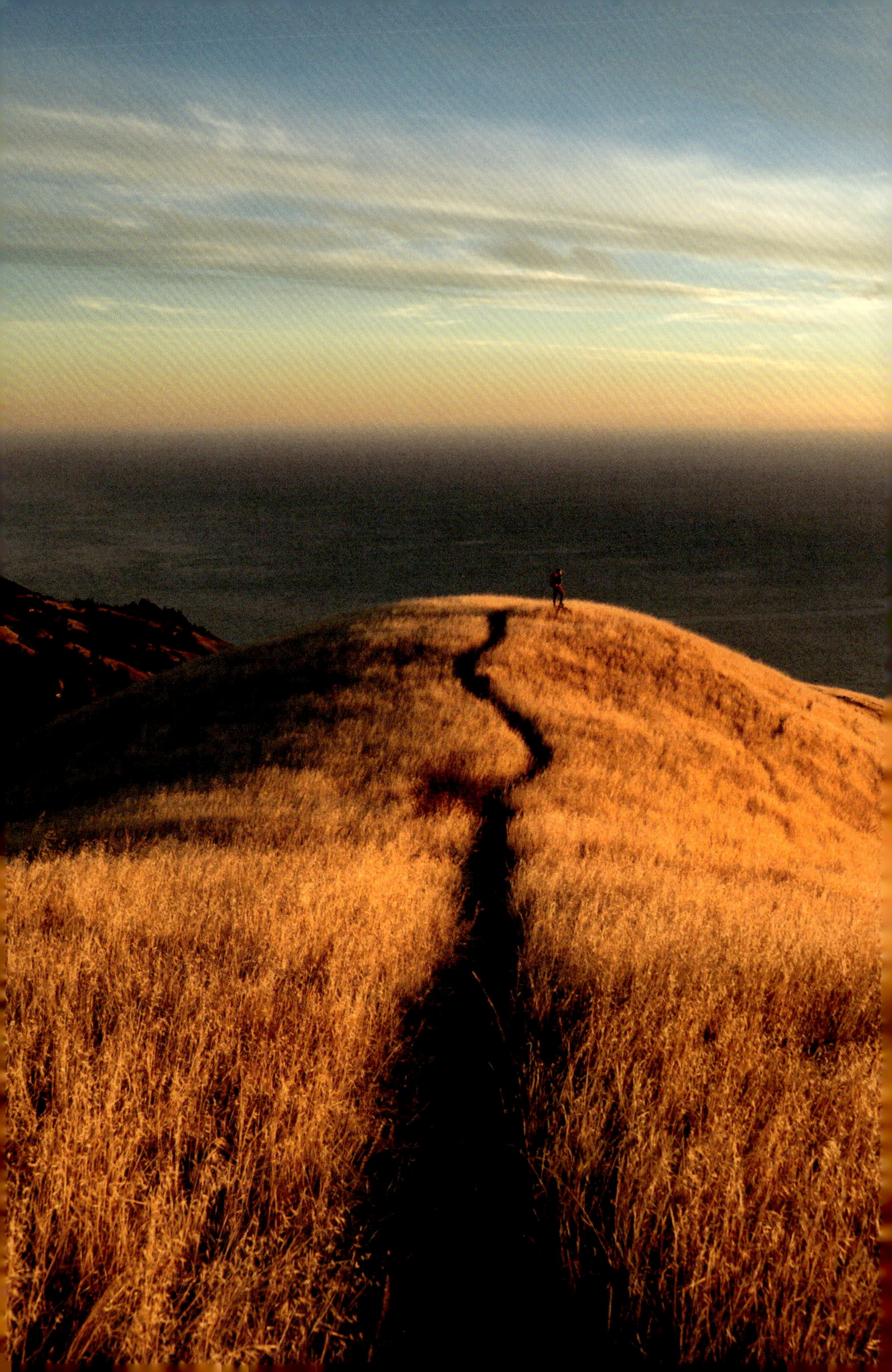

GET OUT THERE

Congratulations on making it this far! I hope it's been as fun for you as it has been for me.

Photography is a bit theoretical. In the simplest terms, we seek to capture a memory, to hold a piece of time still for a little bit. And that's truly a beautiful thing—something to celebrate. However, photography can detract from your core purpose of being in those places, of travel, of being able to meet new people.

Photography should never be more important than the simple act of being there, of being present. Of course, this can be difficult. It's easy to lift your camera to your eyes and create a level of separation from an experience. I want you to consider the moments when you can set your camera down and experience a place and develop something worth saying—something worth expressing from that place, from that experience.

What it really boils down to is this: These are your stories. You are making images of experiences, and if you leave those experiences having nothing to offer, nothing to share, then you've done yourself a disservice. Because most of these experiences have probably been really eye-opening or incredible or rewarding or whatever we want to call it, right?

My hope is to leave you with that feeling, with that message—this is just the beginning of finding your true expression. If photography is one avenue, imagine how many other epic ways there are to express yourself. That's what it really means to be an artist.

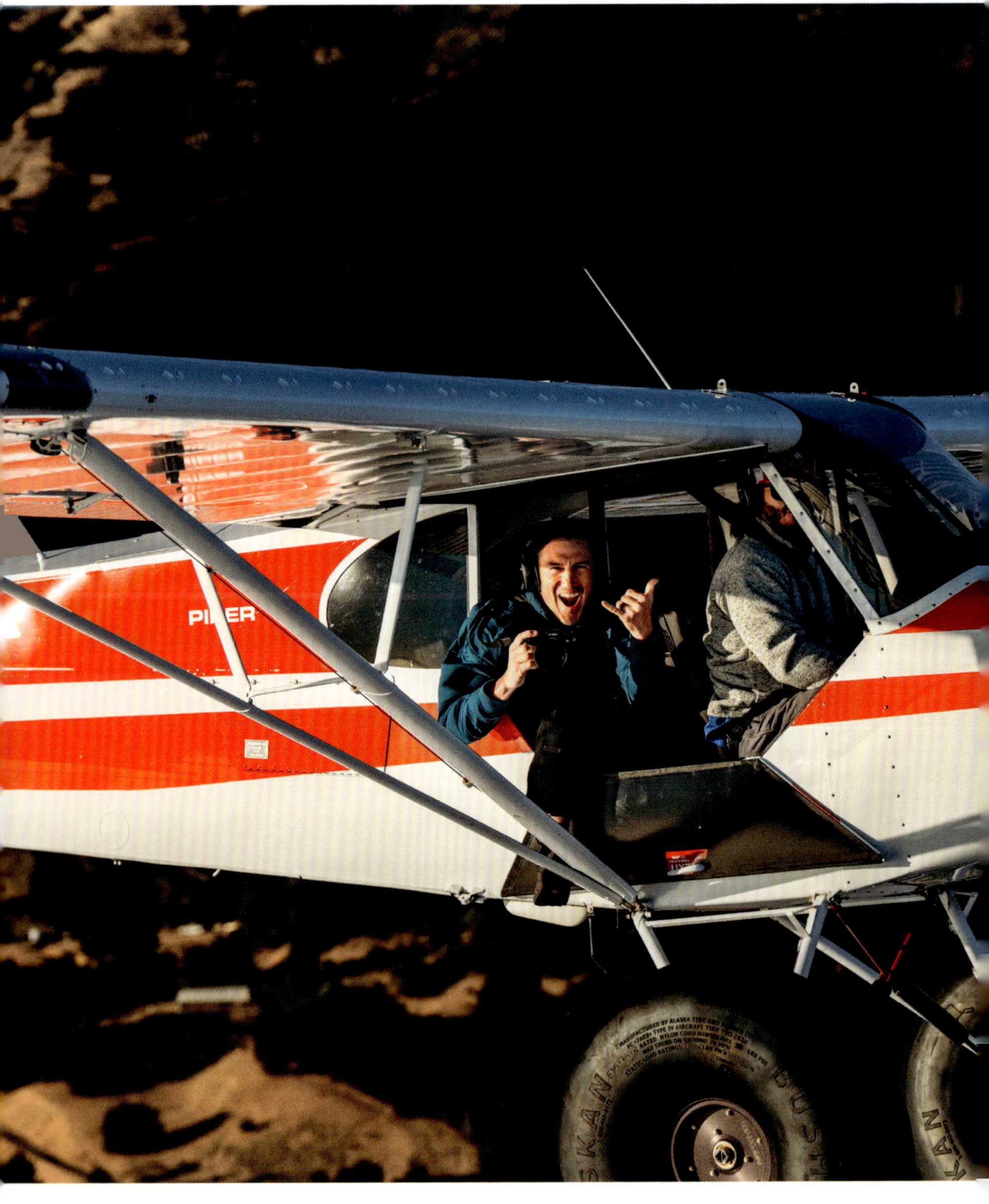

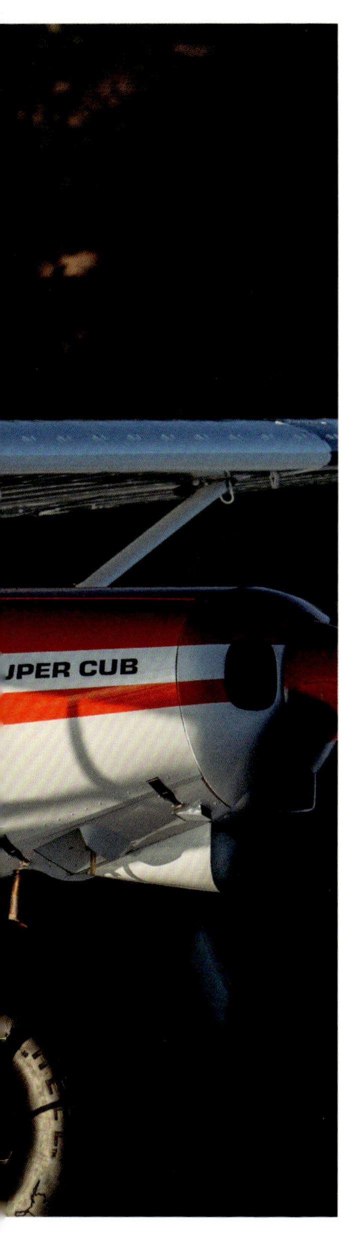

ACKNOWLEDGMENTS

First off, this book would not have come to life without the whimsical writing of Michael Kew, my longtime friend and one of the first journalists to ever take a chance on me as a young photographer interning at Transworld Surf. Secondly, thank you to Brendan Leonard, who graciously worked alongside us to keep this book fun and light with his illustrations and diagrams throughout. I owe you two a lot.

Most of all, this book is dedicated to all the assistants, interns, and epic humans who I have been lucky to call true friends, employees, and colleagues over the years. Your photos are strewn throughout this book as an homage to your time at "the Studio." Thank you for all the sleepless nights, long drives, heavy laden hikes, endless laughs, and incredible missions and projects we have been on over the years. It's been these relationships that has made it worth all the effort—some of my best memories and greatest lessons have been because of that time spent together. I could fill libraries with all the awesome moments, but for now this will have to do. Thanks for being there when it mattered most!

ABOUT THE AUTHOR

Chris Burkard is an accomplished explorer, photographer, creative director, speaker, and author. Traveling throughout the farthest expanses of Earth, Burkard promotes the preservation of wild places everywhere and works to capture stories that inspire humans to consider their relationship with nature. Known for his outdoor, travel, adventure, surf, and lifestyle photography, Burkard creates images punctuated by untamed, powerful landscapes. His visionary perspective has earned him opportunities to work on prominent global campaigns with Fortune 500 clients, speak on the TED stage, work as a Sony Artisan of Imagery, design product lines, educate, and publish a growing collection of books. When he isn't on assignment around the world, Burkard can be found on the Central Coast of California, where he grew up, or in Reykjavík, Iceland, with his wife and two sons. Chris strives to share his vision of wild places with millions of people and to encourage them to explore for themselves. Follow him on Instagram @chrisburkard.